REASON,
SOCIAL MYTHS,
AND
DEMOCRACY

REASON, SOCIAL MYTHS, *AND* DEMOCRACY

SIDNEY HOOK

GREAT BOOKS IN PHILOSOPHY

Prometheus Books
Buffalo, New York

Published 1991 by Prometheus Books
Copyright © 1940, 1991 by Ann Hook

Editorial offices located at 700 East Amherst Street, Buffalo,
New York 14215, and distribution facilities at 59 John Glenn
Drive, Amherst, New York 14228

Library of Congress Catalog Number: 90-63886
ISBN 0-87975-672-1

Printed on acid-free paper in the United States of America

Additional Volumes in Prometheus's Great Books in Philosophy Series

SIDNEY HOOK was one of America's leading philosophers and a man who had a profound impact on the thought and action of his times. He was born in New York City on December 20, 1902, and spent his formative years in the Williamsburg section of Brooklyn. He received his undergraduate training at the City College of New York, where he studied with Morris R. Cohen. Hook's graduate work was completed in the department of philosophy at Columbia University (M.A., 1926; Ph.D., 1927), where his philosophical orientation was challenged and redirected by John Dewey, who subsequently became his friend and mentor. Dewey wrote the Introduction to Hook's published dissertation, *The Metaphysics of Pragmatism* (1927).

In 1927 Hook joined the department of philosophy at New York University, where he remained (serving as chairman from 1934 to 1969), until retiring as emeritus professor in 1972. He then held the position of Senior Research Fellow at the Hoover Institution of War, Revolution and Peace at Stanford University.

Sidney Hook's untiring commitment to, and encouragement of, free inquiry and applied intelligence to human affairs inspired him to pen more than a thousand publications, and to actively engage on many fronts those who would undermine academic freedom and democratic society.

His more recent publications include: *John Dewey: His Philosophy of Education and Its Critics* (1959); *Political Power and Personal Freedom* (1959); *Reason, Social Myths, and Democracy* (1965); *The Essential Thomas Paine* (ed. 1969); *Academic Freedom and Academic Anarchy* (1970); *Revolution, Reform, and Social Justice—Studies in the Theory and Practice of Marxism* (1975); *The Hero in History: Myth, Power, or Moral Law?* (1978); *Philosophy and Public Policy*

(1980); *Marxism and Beyond* (1983); *Out of Step* (1987); and *Convictions* (1989).

In 1985 Sidney Hook was appointed the Jefferson Lecturer for the National Endowment for the Humanities, and in 1986 he was honored with the Medal of Freedom, the most distinguished award given to any citizen in civilian life. He also served as president of the American Philosophical Association (Eastern Division). Sidney Hook died on July 12, 1989.

PREFACE

The first chapter of this volume may serve by way of introduction to its contents. Together with Chapters II and XIII,
it states and develops the position which unifies these studies in
contemporary philosophical and social thought. Although most
of the material has appeared in previous form, in periodicals
not easily accessible to the reading public, some changes and
additions have been made in the interests of timeliness and accuracy.

The order of the chapters has been so arranged that the
discussion of technical philosophical issues, Part Two, follows
the evaluation of conflicting social philosophies. Depending
upon his interest, the reader may begin either with Part One
or Part Two.

SIDNEY HOOK

South Wardsboro, Vermont
September 1, 1940

CONTENTS

CONFLICTS IN SOCIAL DOCTRINE

CHAPTER ONE

CONFLICTS IN WAYS OF BELIEF

WE ARE LIVING in an age of troubles. All the commonplaces of dire prediction made during the last generation have come true, often to the surprise of those who uttered them. Literally hundreds of millions are under fire from shot and shell. Other millions are stumbling over highways and bypaths toward mirages of refuge and safety. With bated breath the rest of the world seems to be living from one news broadcast to another.

1. *Belief and Action*

At such a time it might appear that there is room in human consciousness only for questions of bare survival, not for questions of justification, direction, and value. To endure, to struggle, to survive—this seems to be the ultimate answer to all questions that may reasonably be asked. But human beings are peculiar animals who, even when they fight for survival, fight best when they know why or believe they know why. This is the testimony of all recorded history. There never was a mass movement that markedly changed the course of events whose individual members were not inspired by some belief. The belief may be part of an ethos—an integrated complex of social values which determines the station and duties of the individual. It may be a myth about this world or the next accompanied by a hope for greater felicity on earth or in heaven. Or it may be a sense of resentment against inequality rationalized as a demand for justice.

It is an interesting fact, however, that social action is the mother of inspiration and not, as is usually imagined, its offspring. The *causes* of a movement are rarely, if ever, to be found in its inspiring beliefs and doctrines. But the *results* of a movement cannot be explained without reference to them.

3

For they determine the ways of action, the human energies that are tapped in the course of it, and those ultimate decisions which often lead human beings to embrace death rather than survival. Indeed, it is hard to find a man who willingly fights only for survival. Else why should he risk death in the struggle for it? A man can almost always purchase his life if he is prepared to pay enough for it.

Even the fighting man, then, cannot be indifferent to why men fight and how they think. His emphasis upon morale is in part an acknowledgment of this. It was no less a military figure than Napoleon who said:

"Wars are won by those who think clearly and calmly and act vigorously and promptly."

It is therefore not merely wrong but senseless, even in the darkest hour, to call for a moratorium on thought and to cry out for action, or in ponderous solemnity to appeal for serious thought as if it were an alternative to action. Not only are thinking and acting natural to man, but to some degree they are both present wherever there is conscious behavior. If we bear in mind that to refrain from doing something, to stand and wait on any specific occasion, is just as much an action, *because it has consequences*, as to throw oneself into the thick of things—then we will realize that men always act. There is no wisdom in saying men *must* act. They always do. The point at issue is: *What* shall they enact and *how?* Similarly, thinking, in the broadest sense of the term, is a process which is always involved in conscious action and cannot be stopped at command. Here, too, the question is not whether we shall or shall not think but *what* to think and *how*—clearly or confusedly, with images or ideas, drawing conclusions from our fears and hopes or from evidence and argument.

Thinking is one of the instruments of survival. It is also an integral part of that form of self-justifying enjoyment which we may call understanding. The test of understanding is always control, but there are as many forms of control as there are generic types of things to be known. And not all of them are concerned with survival. There are many people who have an irrepressible urge to find out why things *have* happened even if it is doubtful whether they will ever have the occasion to use their knowledge to some purpose in the future. Strength permitting, even the dying are eager to know what they are dying of.

2. *Choice and Belief*

The ways of belief, then, are important. It is no exaggeration to maintain that there are few things in our time which are more important in their bearing upon questions of social survival. For in the field of social and political behavior, errors in belief are costlier than anywhere else. This is a lesson which has not yet been sufficiently learned in America despite the evidence for it piling up all over the world. Many are busy with politics but few are really serious about their political ideas. Social allegiances, even among self-designated intellectuals, wax and wane with fashion; they are functions of mood rather than considered argument. In an era of social stability, where the effects of differences in political and social ideas are negligible, they may be indulgently regarded as private conceits. But today, whether an individual is aware of it or not, he is staking his head—and the heads of others—on his ideas. They are loaded and can no longer be safely fooled with. In a world where everyone must be armed with ideas, it is well to look to our weapons.

But what shall we believe? The beginning of wisdom is to remember that we do not have to ask this question about everything at once. We are in possession of beliefs of varying degrees of reliability; and, when a specific problem of belief arises, we can take some initial steps in answering it by checking our tentative answers against what we already know or assume we know. This does not take us far. Unfamiliar situations are always cropping up. The cherished beliefs of yesterday may have to be revised. Everything now becomes subordinate to the question: What *method* shall we follow in developing new beliefs and testing the old? For it is clear that no matter what belief we come to regard as valid, the evidence of its validity will depend in part, at least, upon the method which has been followed in reaching it.

If the validity of beliefs depends upon the methods of reaching them, what does the validity of these methods depend upon? In some quarters it is argued that the choice of methods of reaching beliefs represents an arbitrary decision. It needs no justification because no justification can be given. Its validity cannot be established without begging the question, since, in testing it, we would have to appeal to the very method which was undergoing test. Fundamental decisions concerning the methods to be used in reaching conclusions, it is argued, are therefore on all fours with each other. One may be more popular, or simpler, or older than the others, but no one of them is more "valid" than any other.

Even if this were granted, it would not diminish the importance of understanding these various modes of reaching beliefs. Since we live in a world where different people make different choices, and since, whether we like it or not, these choices have consequences which affect us, elementary caution dictates that we give them some study.

The weakness of the view that our fundamental ways of deriving beliefs depend upon a basic decision is not in calling attention to the fact that some decision or resolution is involved. It is rather to be found in its suggestion that the decisions in the nature of the case must be arbitrary, and that the choices they express are never influenced by what we can observe about the specific beliefs and practices to which they give rise and for which they are *presumably* responsible. If we take as our point of departure the empirical occasions on which men discuss the question of the relative validity of different methods of deriving beliefs, we find that everyone defends his choice as in some sense "better" than others. An individual who asserts that one way of thinking is better than another does not mean merely that it is *his* way. For any other way, were he to adopt it, would be his way. Nor does he ever intend to be understood as saying, "I have no reasons for this decision or choice." No matter how he expresses the "reasons" for his choice of a method, *insofar as he urges its acceptance upon others*, they amount to a claim that the adoption of this method will enable us to control or anticipate the future more adequately than the competing methods. "Fundamental" decisions may be intelligent or unintelligent—they are not always, or merely, arbitrary.

Charles Peirce recognizes this in his assumption that the conflicting methods of iteration or tenacity, authority, apriorism or plausible intuition, and science, are all methods of fixing belief.[1] It is in the light, then, of their efficacy in fixing beliefs that they are evaluated. I believe that a more accurate designation of the aim of these methods, insofar as they are in *recognized* conflict with each other, is not the fixation of belief but the adjustment of beliefs, not so much the stability of beliefs but, as Peirce himself suggests, their reliability in settling doubt. But the sign of their reliability is the relative success with which they can predict the future.

Ways of belief are "fundamental" only in respect to the specific beliefs which they help come to birth. They are not fundamental if by that is meant that there is no getting around them, or that they need not or cannot be checked by something else. This conclusion is in line with what we observe when people tell us that they are making a "fundamental decision" whether it is a decision to take one's life, to abandon faith in democracy, to join a church or a political party, to take a wife or put one aside, or to think differently. Granted sanity, the decision never is made in the blue. There is always a controlling context, a specific problem, and a nucleus of difficulties. Rightly or wrongly, certain things are expected to follow from the decision. Some justifications are offered, or, at the least, reasons are advanced for rejecting alternatives.

The notion that there *must* be some fundamental belief from which all other beliefs, so to speak, hang, a belief which supports all others but itself needs no support, is a plausible error. Once we insist upon reducing the situation which evokes the "fundamental decision" to its concrete elements, the decision turns out to be a "conclusion," and like all conclusions depends upon something else. The bogey of an infinite regress is laid when we realize that although one problem always involves others, it does not involve all problems, and that it is possible to settle problems even when the answers suggest new problems.

All this may seem very abstract and far removed from the kind of decisions we have to make about democracy and totalitarianism, war and peace. If anyone is of this impression, let him ask himself how *he* justifies his belief or disbelief in democracy, or his acceptance or rejection of scientific method as contrasted with its alternatives. I venture to predict that he will discover his procedure to be something like this. He ap-

[1] *Collected Papers*, Vol. 5, p. 223.

proaches the problem of evaluation with a determinate store of knowledge, and a number of preferences or valuations. He knows, or more accurately, he unquestioningly assumes (i) that he is in possession of certain "truths" or "facts," (ii) that the problems to which these truths or facts are answers, have been solved in the past by employing certain methods, and (iii) that certain "goods" or "values" like health, wealth, friendship, loyalty, truth, honor, intelligence are desirable. These are immediately brought to the resolution of the problem. Insofar as he can envisage the consequences of carrying out the belief or beliefs in question, he evaluates them as "better" or "worse," more adequate or less adequate. At any point, what he assumed to be knowledge may be criticized as an unwarranted assertion, and what he took as a reasonable preference or value, dismissed as a prejudice. This sets another specific problem which is resolved *in the same way.* The process may be theoretically unending, but it is not viciously circular. Actually, however, it has its stopping points wherever sufficient evidence has accumulated to meet the specific difficulties which provoked the inquiry.

It is in the light of a procedure of this kind that the method of scientific inquiry shows itself to be more adequate than any formulated alternative in anticipating the future. We can use scientific method and be wrong about the future but not so often wrong as by using other methods. And no matter how wrong we are, since scientific method is self-corrective, we become less and less wrong as we continue its practice.

An examination of the counter-statements of those who deny that scientific method is the most effective method of deriving reliable beliefs about the future reveals flagrant inconsistencies, large but unsubstantiated claims, and gross misconceptions of the nature of science. They cannot indicate any definite connection between their generic way of belief and their *specific* beliefs in particular situations. They either assert an infallibility, which is conspicuously absent in practice, or when they acknowledge their fallibility cannot explain how, on their own premises, it is possible. In revising their specific beliefs, they often fall back upon crudely empirical scientific methods.

Take as an extreme illustration of a way of belief differing from that of science, one of Hitler's famous pronouncements, made after the military reoccupation of the Rhineland: "I go my way with the assurance of a somnambulist—the way which Providence has sent me." [2] There is no reason to doubt the subjective sincerity of this statement. It can be matched with similar expressions of this peculiar form of mysticism from his writings and those of his circle. But various things can be noted. Despite his somnambulistic assurance in the ways of Providence, Hitler finds it necessary to denounce the methods of science and reason as inadequate. He does not entertain for a moment the possible validity of conclusions reached by the somnambulistic assurances of others. He cannot show in any manner whatsoever how his specific statements and actions follow from his mystical way of "thought." On the contrary, once we grasp his objectives, disapprove of them as we may, we can explain his successes in achieving them as a result, in part, of a shrewd and scientific method of evaluation, preparation, and action. Whoever is responsible for Hitler's successes, does not act as a somnambulist. Even in a country whose rulers aim to prevent their subjects from thinking scientifically, there is always one group which must think scientifically in order to carry out this aim successfully.

3. Democracy and Scientific Method

There is common agreement that democracy as a way of life can flourish only when differences of opinion can be negotiated by free, critical discussion in which those who at any time, and on any question, are a minority, may become the majority, provided they abide by democratic processes. It is also acknowledged that the intelligence of decisions made by the majority depends upon the extent to which it considers alternatives of action and the available evidence for each. In brief, it depends upon whether those who participate in social and political affairs are guided by habits of scientific thought or are swayed by passion, blind tradition, and irrelevant "authorities." This is not to say that scientific methods and practices are not employed to implement the goals of totalitarian states. German military strategy is nothing if not highly scientific, and the Russian system of domestic espionage is the most scientific that

[2] Broadcast from Munich, March 14, 1936.

has ever been devised. But there is no room in a totalitarian culture for the scientific approach, with its critical probing of alternatives, when questions arise concerning the social ends and values which guide major national policies.

It is extremely difficult for the more notorious rivals and substitutes of intelligence to make headway in a democracy unless conditions have degenerated to a point where they have produced a psychosis of mass despair. The methods of somnambulistic intuition and personal authority have no plausibility in ordinary times. For in ordinary times, it is usually drift and improvisation, that is to say, no method at all, which rules.

Today we are not living in ordinary times. Nor, fortunately, have we in America as yet reached a state of mass despair. But time is short and a host of domestic and foreign problems press upon us which must be solved quickly and intelligently. We are now awake to the fact that more fundamental than armament, as essential as that is, is ideological rearmament—a rearmament of method rather than a doctrine. How are we to solve our problems and by what methods?

In all fields of inquiry, the recognition of a problem is tantamount to an invitation to use scientific method in its resolution. But this is far from being the case in the field of social and political action. Before scientific method can be successfully used, there must be the desire to use it. How to induce that desire is a tremendously complex problem of persuasion and education. The most convincing features to Americans of the educational process on this point are the consequences of following alternative methods—intuition and authority in Germany, Russia, and Italy; drift and improvisation in England and France.

But even the desire to follow scientific method is by itself not sufficient. If it is an intelligent desire, and if our actions are to realize its great promise, it must be based upon knowledge of what scientific method is and the ability to distinguish between its name and its substance.

Here we are confronted by a genuine difficulty to which most of the essays in this book are directed. There is an imposing variety of ways of thought, actually opposed to the ways of science, which nonetheless pretend to represent the last word in scientific reflection. Just as recent years have witnessed the emergence of totalitarian groups which profess an exaggerated allegiance to democracy, so we can observe ways of thinking, incompatible with scientific method, that piously invoke its name. No exact analogy or correlation is intended, of course, between these two phenomena. Confusion, not duplicity, accounts for identifying as scientific, ways of belief which are primarily metaphysical or religious. But "science" like "democracy" is often a catchword; and it is precisely because of honest confusion that the detection of spurious scientific methods of thinking is so difficult.

In subsequent chapters I have critically considered some ways of belief which seem to me to be incompatible with the ways of science. They fall into three groups—metaphysical, religious, and what, failing a better term, may be called "narrowly sociological." Whether there are *any* fields of genuine inquiry in which these ways of thought may lead to fruitful results is outside the purview of my present discussion. I content myself with expressing my opinion that, save for the third, and here only within carefully circumscribed limits indicated later on, there is none. I have selected for analysis illustrations of those ways of belief which declare themselves competent to deal intelligently with problems of science, society, and politics. And of these I have taken particular care to select doctrines which have recommended themselves to us as positively oriented toward democracy or socialism.

Although I have defined my task as primarily a critical analysis of these scientifically inadequate ways of belief, my hope is that by, and through, this analysis, some of the positive features of the genuinely scientific ways of belief will emerge more clearly.

CHAPTER TWO

ABSTRACTIONS IN SOCIAL INQUIRY

CONTROVERSY SOMETIMES rages in the physical sciences about what is true or false but rarely about what makes sense or what doesn't. By and large, the clarification of meaning in the physical sciences is forced upon scientists by their own laboratory practices, or by reflection upon their intellectual procedures whenever they make an analysis which wins general acceptance. In the social sciences this is conspicuously not the case. There is no more basic agreement among those who are concerned with social affairs today than there was in antiquity. Where agreement is found it is largely the result of a dogma imposed by indoctrination or force, and not by the acceptance of a common method. In the physical sciences the control of what people say is determined not only by laboratory procedures but by a common purpose—viz., to discover the truth. This is not the only purpose but a common one. It is often said that if one could assume that the same purpose is always present in social inquiry, it would only be a matter of time, despite the complexity of the subject matter, before a body of commonly accepted propositions was constructed. But it requires no extensive inquiry to establish the fact that not all who are engaged in social inquiry are interested in establishing the truth. Here more than in any other field, Bertrand Russell's dictum holds—the reason why so many people fail to find the truth is that they are not looking for it.

Why the quest for the truth is not so strong or widespread in social inquiry as it is in the physical sciences is an interesting question but one that is not relevant here. It is obviously bound up with the existence of conflicts, and the desire to influence people in order to secure an advantage that could not be so easily achieved if all claims were submitted to critical and public scrutiny. In passing, it should be noted that even in physics and biology in previous centuries definite obstacles to free inquiry existed wherever it was thought scientific findings imperiled traditional privileges.

Yet it is also unquestionable that many *are* interested in discovering the truth about social and political affairs. Indeed, hardly anyone would ever dare to admit publicly, in so many words, that in making a statement about what presumably is the case in any situation, or what will be the case, that he is not interested in the truth. Nonetheless, despite the fact that there are many who desire to discover the truth in the field, and despite the fact that it is so important to know the truth about ourselves and the society in which we live, it is only by a kind of courtesy that we can speak of the social sciences at all. What passes for knowledge of social affairs usually has currency only in a certain group; in other groups it is referred to as a prejudice. From this some have drawn the rash conclusion that it is impossible to discover "truths" in the social sciences, or at most only one "truth" or "law" which accounts for the relativity of truths.

The crying need for the improvement of social inquiry is the development of a common consciousness of the conditions which must be fulfilled before any statement that purports to convey knowledge, can be assigned meaning and be tested.

My thesis in this chapter is that the greatest intellectual obstacle to social inquiry, the most frequent cause of *intellectual* confusion, is the use of unanalyzed and unanalyzable abstractions in our speech. Note, I do not simply say the use of abstractions, i.e., the use of meaningful terms which do not directly refer to what may be seen, felt, touched or heard. For example, we say a man is "innocent," "reliable," "intelligent," etc., that "moral courage is a rare virtue," where all the important terms are abstractions that have no direct sensible reference. Yet we understand what we mean by them. Consequently, we must be absolutely clear about two things: (1) that abstractions are necessary for all developed speech, and (2) that the crucial difference between abstractions that may legitimately be used and those that may not is that the former can be analyzed in a certain way, and the latter cannot. This

difference, as we shall see, corresponds to the difference between scientific sense and nonsense.[1]

1. *Analyzable and Unanalyzable Abstractions*

We must be particularly on guard, in our desire to eliminate meaningless abstractions from our speech, not to speak as
if we wanted to get rid of all abstractions. That is the fundamental confusion of an entire popular school of writers who
have recently been trying to liberate us from the tyranny of
words. For example, here is a characteristic passage from the
work of one member of this school: [2]

"The promise of the semantic discipline lies in broadening the base
of agreement. Under the going canons of philosophy, theology, and
the rest, there is no possibility of wide agreement. Referents are too
few. There is little in these studies, which A can point to B and say:
'That is what I am talking about; go and touch it. Now do you see
what I mean?' Ideas and purposes lie behind the facts. B cannot touch
and see what A sees. One believes or does not believe, and between believer and non-believer lies bitterness, discord and sometimes death."

Now this clearly says that unless we can directly touch or see
that to which a term refers we literally do not know what we
are talking about. But this is absurd. The very words I have
just quoted would have no meaning whatsoever if we were to
apply the author's criterion to them. Whoever touched an
idea or a purpose or bitterness or discord? And although we
can touch a dead man, we cannot touch death.

What then is the difference between analyzable and unanalyzable abstractions? To begin with we must observe that
all meaningful terms are employed in sentences or propositions or statements. Indeed, it is only when a sentence or a
proposition or a statement (I shall use these terms interchangeably) taken as a whole is meaningful, that its terms can be
said to have meaning. When are sentences meaningful? Briefly,
a sentence is meaningful if we know how to go about testing it,

[1] The following bibliographical references are in line with, and in some
matters of detail the source of, the position developed here: Dewey, *Logic:
The Science of Inquiry* (1938) especially c. XXIV; Neurath, *Empirische Sozi-
ologie* (1931); Nagel, "The Fight for Clarity: Logical Empiricism," 8 *American Scholar* 1; Lundberg, *American Sociological Review* (Feb. 1939); Hook,
"The Social Use and Abuse of Semantics" (1938) *Partisan Review.*
[2] Chase, *The Tyranny of Words* (1938), 360.

and what would constitute evidence tending to confirm it or refute it. If we know what would be evidence one way or another
for our proposition, then we know what kind of situation to look
for or construct (as the case may be). We then would know
whether our proposition is probably true or probably false,
or, when judgment has to be suspended, what kind of possible
situation would be relevant to our inquiry. Every statement,
then, which purports to be a true account of what is so or
isn't, enables us by the use of certain rules of inference to
derive other statements that direct us to do certain things and
to make certain observations.

How, then, do we recognize that a sentence contains abstractions that are unanalyzable? Not by any special terms
employed but, roughly speaking, by the inability of the speaker
or writer to state at some point the conditions or situations in
which certain observations can be carried out to test it. Let us
consider a few illustrations:

(1) We often hear such expressions as "The will of the
people is sovereign in the United States." This seems to have
a meaning, for it is often affirmed or denied with some heat.
Now as soon as we inquire what evidence can be advanced for
this statement, perhaps someone will point to the fact that at
certain periodic intervals municipal, state and national elections are held; that the results are more or less carefully tabu-
lated; and that depending upon their outcome, one group of
men or another is invested with certain powers of office. But
now we observe an interesting and characteristic thing. If this
were the state of affairs which we would be prepared to accept
as indicating that the sentence "the will of the people is sovereign" is true, there could hardly be any dispute about it for
any protracted period of time. But the dispute continues even
when there is no question about the existence of elections. It
turns out that those who assert this proposition maintain that
they mean something *other* than this or *more* than this. What
is this other or additional meaning? Is it something of the
same kind as election procedures, i.e., something about which
by making experiments and observations we can come to a decision? Or is it something concerning which no statement of an
empirical kind will be accepted as adequately expressing its
meaning? In the first case, we are dealing with a legitimate

abstraction, i.e., one which promotes intelligent discourse and makes possible the acquisition of knowledge. In the second, we are dealing with an unanalyzable abstraction, with nothing except a sound that has certain causes and effects.

Now why is it that those who employ these unanalyzable abstractions are convinced that despite everything we have said their words have meaning? Because in some other contexts, the terms *will* and *sovereign* do have a clear meaning, and propositions concerning them can be verified. E.g., an absolute monarch or dictator or a group of individuals is "sovereign" in a political community in the sense that it is his or their decision which puts the machinery of government in action. And it is possible to speak intelligibly of the will of a monarch or a dictator, i.e., his written, spoken or communicated commands, in discussing the policies and decisions that control action. The confusion results from the transference of meaning from one type of situation to an altogether different type, and is facilitated by the use of the same symbols.

(2) Let us take as another illustration a statement which is made by people of the most diverse political allegiance: "Our party believes in the defense of individual liberty" (we might substitute equality, fraternity, security or any other politically potent noun). What does liberty mean here? What is it that our party wants to defend? And why, if everybody wants to defend it, should the Liberty League be denouncing others who want the same thing and be denounced by them? Each accuses the other of "betraying liberty." And so long as the term liberty is assumed to be immediately clear, so long as the sentences in which it appears, are assumed to be capable of being understood independently of application in a specific context of needs, interests and legislation—no clarification of the term is possible. The fact that people say they are willing to die for liberty may indicate, as we shall see later, some very interesting things about human behavior: it does not show that they are at all clear what they are willing to die for. We recognize that the term liberty is used as an unanalyzable abstraction whenever a speaker or writer is unable, or unwilling, to indicate the specific practices which he would accept as an answer to the question: liberty to do what? The term liberty is a legitimate abstraction if it is coupled with a schedule of

specific things an individual or a group of individuals wants to do or wants to be able to observe. When this is done, we understand the meaning of liberty, because we can readily see what set of observable practices is present or absent in a situation in which "liberty" is declared to be present or absent, and what any attempt to institute or abolish these practices would involve.

"Our party stands for liberty" does not mean anything unless it can be translated into a series of other propositions, like "Our party stands for liberty to invest capital wherever it can get the highest return," "Our party stands for the liberty to hire and fire, to organize holding corporations, water stock, etc.," or "Our party stands for the liberty of bargaining collectively, the liberty of the small investor to secure protection, the liberty of writing, speaking, meeting on everything that concerns us." It is clear that these different liberties are incompatible with each other; and that the controversy, if it is intelligent, is really being waged around them. Those who are in the controversy without knowing this, literally do not know what the fighting or shooting is about. Some of them have an image of a very beautiful woman whom they call Liberty. At the cry that Liberty is being violated, they rush headlong into the fray in somewhat the same manner as they would run to the rescue of any other beautiful woman. At such times naturally they are very impatient with anyone who asks questions about meaning, evidence and truth.

Substitute the term democracy for liberty today and you will find even greater intellectual confusion.

When we translate any proposition that contains the term liberty into a set of propositions that contain phrases like liberty to invest, liberty to spend, liberty to eat, liberty to do this or that, we notice the following: we can cancel the term "liberty" from every statement in the set of translated statements without in any way altering their meaning. In general, we can say that we are dealing with a legitimate abstraction if it is possible to interpret the sentence in which it occurs into another sentence in which that abstraction no longer appears as a term. If it is impossible to do this, then we are dealing with a metaphysical white elephant, an expression which cannot be true or false because it is scientifically meaningless.

(3) We consider now another illustration which indicates one of the practical reasons why people are encouraged in the use of unanalyzable abstractions. The reason is that if any empirical statement were accepted as equivalent to the one containing the abstraction, it would be demonstrably false. And in the situation, it is politically important that this be not understood by those who are chanting the abstractions. Of a host of examples that might be derived from Nazi Germany I take the following sentence which contains the fewest number of unanalyzable abstractions: "The Jew is commercial and unpatriotic." Normally, when a statement is made of the form "The lion is strong and fleet of foot," when no particular lion is referred to, what is meant is that all lions are strong and fleet of foot, or that most lions most of the time, have these qualities. But obviously, to say that "all Jews are commercial and unpatriotic" is false; and the proposition is just as false about most Jews or most Jews most of the time. To prevent the recognition of the falsity of such statements, Hitler is compelled to speak of the Jew as if he existed independently of any particular Jews, a kind of spook whose properties he can discern better than others. The Jew of whom he speaks is not this, that, or another particular Jew at a certain time or place, nor a group of them that can be distinguished from non-Jews by determinate characteristics. Rather, "the Jew" is an unanalyzable abstraction by the use of which Hitler stops thought, a verbal screen behind which he is able to hide discriminatory measures against Jews and non-Jews alike. When instead of using the term Jew as a noun, Hitler makes it an adjective and speaks of "the Jewish spirit," "the Jewish soul," "the Jewish race," he removes the statements which contain them further and further away from possibility of any control. It is hard enough to find a uniform meaning attached to the term Jew because of the great variety of contexts in which it is employed, but to speak of the Jewish Spirit without delimiting it to some kind of observable behavior capable of being described by certain true or false statements, is to cultivate purposeful nonsense.

The purpose as I have already suggested is this: It enables Hitler to characterize anything as Jewish or Aryan as he sees fit. For certain purposes the Japanese and Italians are Aryans. Even the Arabs, who are Semites, are good Aryans in Hitler's eyes when they fight the Jews. Were they to fall foul of Hitler's objective in any way, over-night they would find themselves included in the spooky abstraction "Jewish." In Germany today, in effect, "Jews," as members of a certain class of the population, are created or uncreated by a stroke of the pen. Whether the religious faith of two, or four, or six, or eight of one's ancestors in the last four generations is to be taken as the mark of differentiation between Jew or non-Jew, has nothing to do with biological, psychological, or personal properties characterizing any particular Jew. Like one of his Austrian anti-Semitic predecessors, a former Burgomeister of Vienna, Hitler is practically saying, *"Wer Jude ist, sage ich."* This is not only true in Germany but everywhere that anti-Semitism exists. The term Jew means so many different things to different people that it is no exaggeration to say that anyone is a Jew who is called one by those who have the power to enforce decrees against him. This should be borne in mind by everyone who thinks that anti-Semitism does not affect him.

(4) I take as a final illustration of an unanalyzable abstraction the statement often made by political partisans of the present Russian regime that "Russia is a democracy." As we have seen, there is no objection to the use of any term in any sense provided we have a clear and unambiguous notion of the conditions under which it is introduced in discussion, and what we should have to observe in order to confirm it or refute it. Where this is not the case, we have not a scientific term but a symbol which, because of its emotional connotations, can be applied to almost any situation where action of a certain sort is more important than understanding. Usually those who employ the term democracy in reference to Russia take great pains to indicate what they mean when they say it is present or absent in other contexts. For example, when they say that "the United States is a democracy" they mean that written and spoken criticism of all laws and policies are permitted, that opposition parties and press are legal, etc. When they say that "Germany is not a democracy" they mean that despite the formality of plebiscites, despite Hitler's statement that

Germany is a democracy in a higher sense, we cannot observe the set of practices which was taken as evidence that the United States was a democracy. But the very same people who speak of democracy or its lack in these situations, refuse to follow the same usage when they apply it to Russia. For obviously, to say that Russia is a democracy in the aforegoing sense would be utterly false—at best, a bloody jest. No matter what other criteria of democracy were used, if it enabled us to say that "Germany was not a democracy" and "the United States was a democracy," it could never under existing conditions justify us in calling Russia a democracy. Consequently, we find that in order to avoid uttering a demonstrably false statement, and in order not to be caught in flagrantly inconsistent usage, those who speak of Russia as a democracy use the term in the vaguest way. So vague that on other occasions when different symbols have to be used for political purposes, they themselves speak of Russia as a party dictatorship.

We can multiply illustrations of vicious abstractions indefinitely. Their exposure is a necessary task in social analysis, particularly in current political thinking. For an abstraction of the kind we have been examining prevents genuine issues from coming to light. What a difference it would make even in our day by day political attitudes if instead of saying "America" wants this or that, we say the leading politicians of America who are supported by such and such people, and such and such newspapers, want this or that. And the same for every other country in the world.

The psychological tendency of most people who use indefinable or irreducible abstractions is to personify them, and to endow them in their imagination with power to do things which only individual people of flesh and blood can do. They substitute a blurred image for a clear idea. When people speak of social forces without being able to specify the actual institutions and individuals intended in such reference, they imagine that there is an actual constraint exercised by something called, say, tradition, mode of production or legal system. When they speak of history or law determining events, they often forget, that history is nothing but the succession, and law nothing but the pattern of events, and that no law compels anything to happen.

2. *The Meaning behind Nonsense*

If we hold fast to the modest and simple demand that all doctrines which claim to be true indicate the procedures by which they are to be tested, most philosophical and social theories fail to meet the grade. Some of the most intense ideological conflicts, in religion, metaphysics, and ethics, turn out to be no genuine theoretical conflicts at all. That is to say, their central terms are unanalyzable abstractions. On the basis of the statements made, no verifiable issues of fact or policy are involved. But to conclude from this that therefore no genuine conflict of any kind is involved would be fantastic. For we would have to say that men are such queer animals that they have a positive tropismatic response to nonsense syllables, that they live, fight, and die for capitalized nouns which they cannot properly define to themselves or others. This is the position that a man like Thurman Arnold takes. According to him, "Most of the interesting and picturesque wars have been fought not over practical interests but over pure metaphysics." [3] His books have induced Mr. Chase to say that "the Supreme Court crisis of 1937 was due chiefly to the creation by judges and lawyers of verbal monsters in the interpretation of the constitution." [4] Mr. Arnold himself draws the very interesting conclusion from this that in the main the world is an ideological madhouse. According to him, political rulers must treat their subjects in the same way as psychiatrists or keepers of asylums treat their patients, i.e., take care of their material wants, provide them with comforts—and let them rave. Mr. Arnold soon after writing this went to Washington.

Despite the fact that during the Supreme Court "crisis" discussion revolved around verbal monsters, every intelligent person understood that there existed a genuine conflict over policy—that depending upon whether one set of verbal monsters or another was preserved in the speech of the Supreme Court Justices, different decisions would be made on cases presented to them for adjudication. And as for wars, there has hardly ever been a war fought under the banner of unanalyz-

[3] Arnold, *Folklore of Capitalism* (1935), 90.
[4] Chase, *op. cit. supra* note 2, at 22.

able abstractions which in perspective has not also been interpreted as a conflict between specifiable interests. At the moment of conflict many people, of course, do react to the immediate symbols, parades and other incantations under which they march into battle. But when we want to understand the causes of war, we discount heavily the influence of verbal monsters, for these are usually generated in the conflict or on its eve.

I am not saying that no wars, no conflicts, are ever fought over words. I am saying that where conflicts are intense, when populations are stirred up to action and especially to violent action, available evidence shows that the struggle is not over abstractions or nonsense but over concrete matters. By knowing these concrete matters we can even predict with some success the kind of nonsense that will be uttered.

This suggests a problem. Under certain circumstances an unanalyzable abstraction hides something—a purpose, a plan, a commitment. Of two varieties of syntactical nonsense, why do we distinguish between them on other grounds than that they sound different? Just as we sometimes say, "Though this be madness, there is method in it," so we often say, "Though this is nonsense, there is meaning behind it." What kind of meaning is this, and how do we check it? Does this invalidate any of the principles we have laid down earlier in our discussion? Briefly, my answer is that vicious abstractions are meaningful only in the sense that to the sociologist they may be a sign of probable behavior. They never tell us anything which is literally true or false of the world, as those who utter them presume they do, but they enable us, as students of social behavior, to make true or false propositions about the way those who utter them are probably going to act in certain situations. Just as a physician may on the basis of past knowledge use a man's cough as a sign of some respiratory ailment, so a sociologist, who has observed the historic contexts and antecedents of a man's verbal coughs—his unanalyzable abstractions—may predict his subsequent behavior. He may localize troubles and conflicts of which the individual may be unaware, or, when any kind of verbal coughing becomes epidemic, it may signify to him something of which a whole class of people is unaware.

However, it must be borne in mind that the statements we make about the meaning behind nonsense are subject to the same criteria of confirmation as scientific statements in any field. The moral of this excursion into the meaning behind non-sense should be clear. In social affairs it often is the case that when we have examined the utterances of statesmen and po-litical leaders, or the battle-cries and slogans of different groups, we discover that they are literally meaningless, because we can't tell what logically follows from them in the way of observable consequences. At this point, the logical analysis must be supplemented by social analysis. Our task is not com-plete until we have discovered, by exploring their historical context, what these logically meaningless statements signify about the behavior of those who claim to believe them. In poli-tics even more than in the circus, it is necessary to watch the performer's hands. We can make good guesses as to what the hands will do by studying the menageries of verbal monsters against the background of economic, national, and other social conflicts. The Marxist critique of ideology is an illustration of an empirical approach to verbal monsters, and one which can be fruitfully applied to the ideologies of many who call themselves Marxists.

If this analysis is justified, I think it can be shown that our approach to languages does not, as some critics have claimed, impoverish in any way the varieties of significant discourse. Rather does it enable us to distinguish between the content of words and their intent, between words as meaning-ful symbols and as causal signs. The intent of much speech is not to communicate content, as diplomats well know. Some-times the person who uses unanalyzable abstractions is not himself aware of the distinction between intent and content; sometimes he is. In this last case we say that a man is using words to conceal his thoughts.

3. *An Approach to Social Behavior*

We now must consider the claims of a fashionable tendency in social theory according to which it is a disastrous error to believe that the logic of inquiry, as it is exhibited in the physi-cal and natural sciences, can be used in the social sciences. The social sciences, or *Geisteswissenschaften*, on this view, are interested in understanding culture and human beings, not in describing or explaining them. The cultural, as distinct from the physical, they say, can be apprehended not by predictions about what can be observed but by an intuition of meaningful wholes. The essential nature of the art, the religion, the morals of a period, it is asserted, can only be understood by an imaginative grasp of pervasive meaning which runs through the whole. Investigation of the causal connection between one aspect of a culture and another is irrelevant and superficial, for the living unity between the parts—what is sometimes called the soul, or spirit, or style of the culture, escapes such causal analysis.

An analagous distinction between understanding, and explaining or describing, is sometimes made with reference to the nature of individuals. It is said that we can describe and predict everything about the behavior of an individual and still not "understand" him as a personality. We understand him when we have actively identified ourselves with his hopes, ideas, ambitions, and fears. The first approach is called external, unable to distinguish between the relevant and irrelevant, the significant and the trivial. The second approach boasts that it is able to penetrate to the inner experience of both individuals and cultures by perceiving "the identity or similarity of central meaning, idea or mental bias" (Sorokin) which relates apparently widely different things. This perception, it is alleged, is often immediate and direct, is not dependent upon experiment, statistical correlations, or even reasoning. It recommends itself by an immediate feeling of adequacy, vivacity, and certainty.

So much for the claims of this school among whose representatives are thinkers like Dilthey, Spengler and, in our own country, Sorokin.

Now to begin with, no social inquiry can recognize any sharp distinction between the method of understanding and the method of description. For no matter what the social facts are which are under investigation, a family system, an art form, a set of legal rules, a war, these always involve reference to some pattern of physical or biological behavior. As we have seen, any attempt to confirm or control any statement about the nature of the world, presupposes that we have been able to deduce from the original statement other statements in which some observation terms occur. What we observe always has a physical or a spatio-temporal context, and when men are the subject of investigation, a biological context. It is in this sense that we can say that the social sciences are also natural sciences. And it should be obvious that if human beings were not subject to physical and biological laws, we could not even begin to examine their social behavior. Thus, what is called our understanding of a social fact must at least include knowledge or explanation of the behavior of its physical and biological aspects. At first glance, then, it seems as if the understanding and explanatory modes of knowledge do not exclude each other in specific social inquiry.

To this the reply is made that although certain events in history and culture can be explained in terms of their physical and biological contexts, that which is distinctively social—indeed that which is distinctively human—can be understood only by an insight into human meanings and purposes, into certain ends and aspirations, *which are not confirmable by observation of any kind of overt, public behavior*. It is this last qualification, viz., that there are true statements about social life which are not confirmable by any kind of overt public behavior which really constitutes the basic challenge to the empirical approach to social inquiry.

The situation is briefly this. The empiricist aims to predict and control social events in the cultural world with the same set of methodological principles that he employs in the natural world. Recognizing all the differences that complexity in the subject matter and partisan bias make, he insists that the criteria of meaning and truth are one and the same whether we are discussing a man's weight on a scale (a physical question), his metabolism (a biological question), or his political allegiance (a social question). The empiricist is perfectly prepared to admit that where he is investigating the social relationships between men, he cannot predict what will occur merely on the basis of his knowledge of the facts of physics or biology. He must know something more—he must know the history, the traditions, the habits and language of the people whose behavior he is trying to predict. We can go still further and say that he must know, in many situations, their preferences, their emotions, their ideas. It is not true in the least that for those who want to predict human behavior, ideas, emotions and preferences do not exist. They are just as much a part of the world as atoms, stars, tables, and chairs.

The crucial question which divides the empirical school from the intuitional school, is over the conditions which have to be observed before terms like purposes, plans and ideas can be significantly introduced into inquiry. When shall we say that a group of people is "patriotic," or that a culture is "Faustian" or "Appolinian," to use an expression of Spengler? Terms like these are perfectly legitimate if some determinate context of behavior can be indicated, which will enable us to tell by some possible observation when an individual is patriotic and when not, when a culture has this or that quality and when not. Consequently, as distinct from the intuitionist, the empiricist denies that the "inner experience," whatever that may be, of an individual or a culture is inaccessible to scientific inquiry. He does not distinguish between "inner" and "outer" experience but between data of greater or lesser reliability.

Those who speak of a "self-enclosed" inner experience whose qualities can only be grasped by *Einfühlung* or empathy usually do one of two things. They either associate the term which designates the alleged quality of inner experience with publicly observable traits or they do not. In the first case, we can disregard the conjunction they make between the term and the alleged quality of inner experience, and identify the set of publicly observable traits with the objective reference of the term. In the second case, they are using an unanalyzable abstraction. For example, someone tells us that he knows that "X is a beautiful soul." He may even insist that only one beautiful soul can recognize another, and that that rules critics out. By definition we can't challenge this statement. But if we ask him to classify people, depending upon whether or not they possess this quality of beauty of soul, we may discover by observation that all of one class possess a certain property or trait possessed by no member of the other class. We may then predict how he will classify any given individual. Without claiming to possess a beautiful soul ourselves, and without reference to any intuition of anyone's immediate experience, we can become just as adept as the speaker in recognizing beautiful souls. We may even discover new properties about beautiful souls by studying the objective conjunction of the complex of traits observed in beautiful souls. The limit of prediction and control is also the limit of understanding.

The whole question of "inner experience" is a difficult one and it cannot be adequately discussed here. A few considerations, however, are in order. First, since social inquiry is primarily concerned with the behavior of groups, it is hard to take seriously the notion of their "inner consciousness" or "soul." Even Spengler is compelled to talk about, or refer to, political structures, art, currency, roads, buildings, when he speaks of the soul of culture—and these are all observable. A sentence in which a certain predicate is affirmed about the "soul of culture," may then be translated into a series of sentences about buildings, pictures, books, etc., in a determinate time and place. Secondly, when we reject the sharp distinction between "inner" and "outer" experience as scientifically valid, it is not meant to ignore or slight or call into question "consciousness," "imagination," "wishes," or "desires." There is no need to banish these terms from social inquiry if they serve a useful purpose. But they can only serve a useful purpose if we make clear to ourselves the character of the evidence which is accepted as indicating their presence or absence. And in science, all evidence is public evidence. What men think or feel is very important in predicting how they will behave but to say that men think this or feel that is to say that at some point we will observe this or observe that. An important part of the observable data of social behavior is that men use symbols and react to symbols. Speech itself can be accepted as evidence that a man is thinking or is in pain or is at prayer. But that evidence may have to be checked by other evidence, and given a certain weight in the light of its past reliability and so on.

Perhaps the whole problem may be made clearer if we imagine the following situation which is a variation of William James' famous illustration of the mechanical sweetheart. Suppose a man takes a trip or disappears. You know this man very intimately—know him by as intimate an understanding as any intuitionist could wish. Suppose he reappears after a few years, physically a little altered because of the intervening years. You accept his explanation of his absence. One day you receive an anonymous letter telling you that the man is an impostor. You can embroider the story as you wish. Now, how determine whether the statement made in the letter is true, if the appearance and behavior of the individual cannot in any important specifiable respect be shown to be different from what one would expect under the circumstances? You might have the strongest intuition that he is an impostor but if you cannot show that he walks differently, talks differently, remembers differently, etc., from what your friend did, then your statement that his personality, or soul or what not, is different from that of your friend, would be false, if you accepted these things as evidence—and meaningless, if you did not.

4. *Abstractions and Social Ideals*

We now come to another important problem—the place and validity of statements made about values and ideals in social theory. There are some writers who are sympathetic to the approach that has here been developed but who have come to the extreme conclusion that what are usually called "judgments of value," i.e., statements about the ends of human action, about what human beings should do or should not do, are all meaningless because there is no way by which we can test whether they are true or false. Those who assert this say that value-judgments are literally expressions of emotions. They show what we feel in the same way as a clenched fist or a cheer. There is therefore no more sense in calling them "true" or "false," "valid" or "invalid" than there is in applying these terms to other expressions of emotion. We can explain their causes, i.e., we can explain when, why, and where they arise. But taken by themselves, as expressions, they are not really meaningful sentences, for they say nothing, imply nothing, predict nothing.

Now obviously such a conclusion is unsatisfactory. One of our reasons for developing a science of society in the form of a set of reliable predictions is that we may more intelligently control the environment in order to build a world that is more desirable than the one in which we live. If judgments of value are meaningless then we cannot significantly say that one state of affairs is better than another. All preferences would be of the same order initially and finally. No one would be wrong because no one could be right. Further, every social philosophy, capitalism, liberalism, socialism, fascism, and the movements which are organized around them, stress various ends or ideals in behalf of which they urge us to do this or that. How are we to evaluate between them? We cannot in any case avoid making a choice, even if we choose the *status quo*. Are these choices purely arbitrary? Is there no evidence which is relevant to our choice? Can we seriously believe that to say in a given situation that peace is better than war or vice versa, is to say nothing significant? If empiricists are driven to such desperate extremities, no one will take them seriously or their approach to social affairs.

I wish to suggest that there is another approach possible to the question of judgments of value which conforms to the principle of empirical procedure, and yet does not involve dismissing such judgments as meaningless. Very briefly, it involves something like this. A judgment of value, or of better or worse, is an hypothesis that is formulated in the context of an existing situation in which there is a need or lack or interest. It asserts that if certain operations are performed, the consequences would be such that the original need or lack or interest would be fulfilled. Ideals or values, then, are hypotheses about the foreseen consequences of striving or acting in a certain way. They are true or false if the actual consequences which ensue agree or disagree with the foreseen consequences. But, someone is sure to ask, are the actual consequences themselves good? Must we not have some absolute standard by which we can judge in advance whether any particular consequence is good or bad? On this theory, the answer is no, for the goodness or badness of the actual consequences can only be understood in relation to the specific and concrete original situation in which the ideal arose. *New* problems and questions may arise about the goodness or badness of the actual consequences but they would be settled in the same way as the original question. No more than in science would we get final answers but we would get reliable ones from case to case.

What would this mean if applied to social ideals around which there wages such furious conflict today? This—all social ideals and all social philosophies would be considered as hypotheses, first, in relation to an existing set of social problems, wants and needs of an observable kind; second, as asserting that certain objective and observable means have to be employed, that certain institutional changes have to be introduced; and third, that the verifiable consequences of such means and changes will coincide with the foreseen consequences. More briefly put, this implies that we judge social ideals or ends in the light of their causes and consequences; and since actual consequences depend upon observable means, it follows that we judge ends by means. We judge ends by means, not by intentions or by foreseen consequences alone.

This apparent commonplace is of the utmost importance. For now we can distinguish between those ends and values which are unanalyzable abstractions and those which are not. Social values, ends, and goals are unanalyzable abstractions when they are untestable, and they are untestable whenever they do not point to the concrete instrumentalities by whose use the situation, to which they presumably refer, is to be met. Whenever, then, ends and means are not related, ends cannot be tested. Whenever anyone says, "My ends are good but my means are bad," we have every right to reply, "Your ends are never any better than your means," for we can only judge by what we observe, and we observe that it is not your words that have effects upon the world but your acts, i.e., your means. Here as elsewhere common sense is more empirical than sophisticated apologists when it says that we judge a person by his observable acts and not only by his words, by the consequences of his deeds and not by his good intentions— intentions that *he terms* good.

The cutting edge of this approach is sharp. For in politics, it judges the purposes of political rule by its techniques and the consequences of those techniques. What society will be fifteen years from now will depend upon what is done, the observable means and techniques used, during the next fourteen years, i.e., this year, next year, and the year thereafter, and not upon a *promise* of what will happen in the fifteenth year. If anyone says, then, that the next fourteen years will be a transitional period of cruelty, hunger and oppression, but that the fifteenth year will be a paradise (and he may say this sincerely) he is being victimized by a vicious abstraction. He either does not know what he wants or he does not admit what he wants. Here we have, with most of the details necessarily omitted, a method of testing social values and ideals which, as far as its logic is concerned, is continuous with the method of testing hypotheses in any field.

We do not have to regard ideals, certainly not all of them, as myths which rest upon fraud or force. We do not have to deny that they are important in controlling human conduct. But we do deny that there is any method of choosing intelligently between ideals except on scientific grounds. For various reasons only the beginnings of a scientific morality can be made today. Many prejudices, privileges, vested, as well as aspiring, interests, would not survive critical, empirical analysis. If a scientific morality is possible only when judgments of value have been subjected to critical analysis, then only a society whose institutions permit and encourage the widest possible use of free and critical intelligence can build up a common scientific social morality.

In conclusion, I wish to summarize the leading ideas of this discussion, restating them a little differently for the sake of emphasis.

a. Every significant sentence in social inquiry must be understood as asserting that, directly or indirectly, something about the behavior of men and women, or the behavior of the things that men and women control, can be observed.

b. Every statement which is a description or prediction is an hypothesis that can, in principle, be confirmed or invalidated by observations. As an hypothesis it may be more or less probable, never certain. No statement which contains expressions like "inevitable" or its synonyms can ever be scientifically tested.

c. Unless we can point out what *possible* evidence we are prepared to accept as an indication of the *falsity* of our theory, we are never in a position legitimately to assert its *truth*. For reflection will always show that we are employing unanalyzable abstractions.

d. Testing an hypothesis always involves, as Professor

Dewey has made abundantly clear, some directed transformation of things, some experiment.

e. No progress in social knowledge can be achieved by driving out one myth by another. If Nazi mathematics and Nazi physics are nonsense, just as much are proletarian mathematics or proletarian physics. If it is nonsense for Eddington to assert that the jump of an electron from orbit to orbit proves freedom of the will, it is just as nonsensical to say that such a jump proves that society develops by revolution or mutations. There may be a sense to the expression "freedom of the will" and there may be evidence of the evolution of societies at certain times by revolution, but the jumping electron has no more to do with either than the jumping Mexican bean.

f. The starting point of social theory as well as its terminus should be specific social problems, not the construction of systems. "Social laws" would be generalizations of what is revealed in the solution of past problems and would function as instruments in the solution of present problems.

g. Finally, all social ideals and philosophies which are not rhetorical devices to keep men in ignorance or subjection are to be understood as proposed ways of action, and judged like all other plans, by their consequences, their costs and their achievements.

CHAPTER THREE

KNOWLEDGE AND INTEREST

ONE OF THE great ironies of the history of ideas is the way in which absolutist philosophies either combine or give rise to doctrines that stress the relativity of truth. The result is a skepticism, in the large, of all knowledge which falls short of *the* Absolute Whole. This skepticism has nothing in common with scientific method which, when it is skeptical of anything, justifies its skepticism in the light of knowledge of something else. In no field of inquiry is the current mood of wholesale skepticism of "truths" so strong as in the social sciences. Because to some extent it buttresses itself by an empirical analysis of some factors that produce diversity of belief, it mistakenly imagines that its conclusions are the last word in scientific sophistication instead of the illegitimate offspring of the doctrine that truth can be found only in *the* Whole.

The empirical factors, cited in support of this view, are derived from a variety of sources. It was none other than Hegel himself who in his *Phänomenologie des Geistes* established the fact that a difference in historical perspective often makes a difference to (a) *what* one sees (b) *how* one sees it, and (c) how one *evaluates* what is seen. Marx accepted Hegel's view that all ideas are *Zeitgebunden* but added another determinant. He contended that within any given historical period, especially when it is dynamically conceived, differences in *social* and *class* status, likewise introduce differences in attention, evaluation, and patterns of action. In more careful and qualified fashion, avoiding large generalizations, Dewey and Veblen have offered some brilliant illustrations of the influence of *occupational* vocations upon world outlook, basic modes of satisfaction, and the criteria of excellence in non-vocational domains of experience.

Whether it is the historical period, or class allegiance, or vocational activity (or all three) which is stressed as the relativizing factor in thought, an obvious distinction must be recognized between those fields in which a body of knowledge has been developed that commands the assent of *all* qualified investigators, and fields in which such agreement has not been secured. The natural sciences fall within the first; most of the social sciences fall within the second. In the past, recognition of this distinction has often been preliminary to one or the other of two kinds of reduction. Either it has been maintained that *all* claims to knowledge are infected by an historical, class or vocational bias, and therefore fall short of "scientific objectivity," which is sometimes treated as a myth and sometimes as a legitimate but unachievable ideal; or it has been asserted that *qua* knowledge, none of them is so infected, and that social, philosophical, moral and aesthetic "truths" are on par with scientific truths, the appearance of diversity being explained by the comforting assurance, "truth (ours) is one, error (theirs) is many."

One of the most ambitious attempts to clarify the whole of this troubled question has been made by Karl Mannheim in his *Ideology and Utopia*, an influential book which brings together much of the material in the sociology of knowledge. Mannheim rejects both of the reductions mentioned above but formulates no intelligible third alternative. Although he leaves the subject in the same logical state as he found it, his discussion is suggestive.

Two distinct but related problems receive attention in Mannheim's treatment. The first is the definition of ideologies and utopias, their social contexts and consequences; the second is the influence of social processes upon the processes of knowledge where knowledge is carefully distinguished from ideologies and utopias.

The most original aspect of Mannheim's discussion of ideologies and utopias is to be found in his definitions. An ideology is a set of beliefs, naturally developed by ruling groups, which interprets and rationalizes the facts of mind, nature and society in such a way as to stabilize their rule and to obscure systematically the "real condition of society." It expresses the way in which a group in power surveys the world. "The concept 'ideology' reflects the discovery ... that ruling groups can in their thinking become so intensively interest-bound to a situation that they are simply no longer able to see certain facts which would undermine their sense of domination." Such a definition, it is clear, presupposes the existence of non-ideological scientific knowledge which does not obscure "the real conditions of society." Otherwise an ideology could not intelligibly be characterized as false, distorted, or obfuscating. Utopian thinking differs from ideology not so much in its nature as in its direction and class locus. "In the utopian mentality the collective unconscious, guided by wishful representation and the will to action, hides certain aspects of reality. It turns its back on everything which would shake its belief or paralyze its desire to change things." Ideologies are the conceptual constructions by which conservative groups preserve existing order; utopias are the instruments employed by revolutionary groups to transform the existing order.

Much can be said of the convenience of these definitions in classifying the pseudo-scientific doctrines which accompany the clash of interests in social life. Even so, certain difficulties are suggested by the unanalyzed notion of "a collective unconscious"—a notion whose validity is more dubious than that of the individual unconscious. These definitions also cut across the customary Marxist distinctions between utopian socialism and scientific socialism, for in Mannheim's view both are illustrations of utopian thinking. Nonetheless these are minor matters because, although Mannheim does not do so, the "collective unconscious" can be operationally interpreted to refer to the statistical distribution of unreflective behavior patterns of individuals where interests are involved; and even though, on his definitions, Mannheim would classify utopian and scientific socialism together, he would not deny their differences in other respects.

The real difficulty begins at the point where Mannheim recognizes that ideologies and utopias, expressing class standpoints as they do, lead to theories and discoveries about the nature of things which are held to be "true" in a scientific sense. He then shifts the question to whether these "truths" are dependent upon the class standpoint and interest which led to their search and discovery. Since class standpoints and interests change with historical periods, the question becomes one, for Mannheim, of the sociology of knowledge. Each class has its own "truth" just as each age has its own "truth." And this not only in the fields of art and politics but in every field. Assuming now that scientific treatment is synonymous with objectivity, the problem which arises to plague Mannheim is: How is any kind of scientific knowledge possible? Mannheim gives different answers on different pages of his book and leaves the reader completely in the dark as to what he really believes.

I shall take as a basis for critical discussion one of the answers which he gives, and then show, once certain important distinctions are introduced, that a consistent answer can be given to the problems he raises which recognizes both the objectivity of science and the relativity of class points of view.

"It has become incontrovertibly clear today," writes Mannheim, "that all knowledge which is either political or which involves a world-view is inevitably partisan. The fragmentary character of all knowledge is clearly recognizable. But this implies the possibility of an integration of many mutually complementary points of view into a comprehensive whole." (p. 132) To begin with, it is not clear in what relevant sense knowledge *qua* knowledge, and *a fortiori* political knowledge, must be partisan. Knowledge as such is either true or false (probably true or probably false). The same bit of knowledge may be put to different class uses just as it may be put to different personal uses but the character of the use cannot be inferred from the nature of the knowledge. And what is meant when it is said that knowledge which "involves" a world-view is partisan? If by a world-view is intended the logical presuppositions of any piece of knowledge, then since all knowledge has some logical presuppositions all knowledge would "involve" a world-view, and the original distinction between the kinds of knowledge, recognized by Mannheim, becomes pointless.

Further, what is meant here by a "world-view"? Does it consist of a set of propositions which describe the world or a set of resolutions which indicate how we are going to evaluate or act upon the world. If the first, then it is a claim to be knowledge; if the second, it may be partisan but the partisanship flows from the fact of purpose, use, or interest but not from its claim to be knowledge. When Mannheim adds, "The fragmentary character of all knowledge is clearly recognizable," he makes the matter even more obscure by injecting a distinction not at all germane to the sentence which precedes it. That all knowledge is fragmentary implies either that there is always something more to be known or that the knowledge we have can be made more accurate. But what has this to do with partisanship? If true, it must be recognized by partisans of the same color to hold for whatever *they* claim to know as well as for what partisans of different colors claim to know. To proceed to talk about "the integration of many mutually complementary points of view into a comprehensive whole," where "points of view" presumably represent the partisan bias, is to make a flying leap from the position of the first sentence which makes all matter-of-fact knowledge partisan, to a new position according to which resolutions, bias, axioms of evaluation and preference are illustrations of knowledge. Think of the many mutually complementary points of view expressed in the political scene. What can it possibly mean to say that they are "integrated"? And integrated into "a comprehensive whole"? Does this mean there are many comprehensive wholes or that there is one whole which like the Hegelian Absolute does not depend upon any point of view but presupposes them all? Mannheim leaves the problem in a muddle.

The fundamental source of Mannheim's difficulty is that he discusses "truth" in the large without specifying the type of problem or question concerning which we want the truth. When I ask: Is the medical hypothesis of a twelfth century physician truer than the hypothesis of a twentieth century physician?, I am asking a question in which "true" has not the same meaning as when I ask: Is the world-view of a medieval philosopher truer than the world view of a modern philosopher? In the first the hypothesis concerns some matter of fact capable of being partially verified or falsified by actual inquiry. In the light of the data at hand, the twelfth century physician may have even been justified in asserting that his proposition was probably true. And we may grant that even though we assert today in relation to the much more extensive data at hand that the hypothesis in question is probably false, the physician had a scientific right to entertain it as a valid hypothesis at the time. The history of science does not establish the relativity of truth as much as the shifting probability relationships between propositions and the data in reference to which they are probable. In the second case the medieval philosopher is not asserting mere propositions of fact but expressing resolutions, preferences, or commands. Here history and social status enter constitutively into the meaning of the statements made but they are not statements concerning which we can literally say they are true or false. We can utter true (or false) propositions of the circumstances and occasions under which these statements are made but *per se* they are not truths.

Now let us grant that the twelfth century physician and medieval philosopher are one and the same person. Let us even grant that "the reason" he was led to formulate his medical hypothesis was the world-view he held. Matters are not in any way altered. Only if it could be shown that the hypothesis in question was entailed by the "world-view"—that "the reason" which led him to his hypothesis was logical and not psychological or historical—would the necessary connection between scientific knowledge and the world-view, of which Mannheim speaks, be established. And if that were so, the world-view, which served as the presumable premise of the hypothesis, could be shown to be either a proposition of fact or a compound statement of propositions of fact and assertions of value; but only the propositions would be logically relevant to the hypothesis.

Many reasons can be offered for the validity of the distinction. Two will suffice in this connection. First, Mannheim himself recognizes it in distinguishing between the ideological and utopian on the one hand, and the scientific on the other, but unfortunately he does not abide by the implications of the distinction. Secondly, to deny this distinction is to be compelled to assert that all judgments of value can be *simply* reduced to judgments of fact or all judgments of fact to judgments of value—positions that are open to grave difficulties.

One might even grant that before we inquire into the truth, before we engage in science, an antecedent judgment of the value of the truth or the value of science is made. What of it? This judgment of value determines our interests and guides our activities but it does not determine whether the outcome

of these interests or activities is true. One might even grant
that every proposition which asserts "this is logically true"
or "this is scientifically true" presupposes, in the first case, an
acceptance of certain conventional rules of syntax, in the second, certain convenient criteria of simplicity, predictability,
etc. This constitutes no problem once we insist upon making
questions concrete. Is it the case that you are denying my
assertion "this is logically true" because you are operating
with a different set of syntactical formulae? In that event
either the problem of which set of syntactical formulae to
use may be settled in the light of the consequences of their
use, or the formulae will merely express decisions determined
by our own sweet will and fancies. On the first alternative,
there will presumably be agreement about the truth or falsity
of the consequences: on the second, "truth" will always have an
intrasystemic meaning so that the question of whether this set
of language rules is truer than that becomes meaningless.
Science, insofar as it attempts to describe the nature of the
world, continually restricts the occasions in which free value-
determined criteria of what constitutes valid scientific experience can operate. In science, convenience is subordinated to
fruitfulness.

The vagueness and generality of Mannheim's discussion is
focalized in remarks like "people in different social positions
think differently." About what do they think differently?
Everything? Of course not. Everybody who thinks at all thinks
the same way about many fields of science and mathematics;
and where they differ, social position has nothing to do with
it. Do people, then, in different social positions think differently of *social* matters? All social matters? Hardly. It is quite
often true that people in different social positions think similarly about social questions; and where they do not, it is not
uniformly true that differences in thought can be correlated
with differences in social position. If Mannheim were to say,
"People with different interests, when aware of them and of
the fact that they conflict, are likely to think differently concerning policies and programs which involve these interests,"
he would be more nearly correct. Here is a proposition which
is verifiable, whose truth does not depend upon anyone's interest, although the promulgation of it may, and which avoids

the popular error that because propositions *about* interests are true, therefore interests themselves are true or false.

The advantages of a sociological analysis of ideas are two-fold. It enables us to answer questions about the career of ideas, and sometimes, about their reference or meaning where logical analysis can make no headway in the face of syntactical peculiarities. The dangers of its uncritical use are many. It tends to wipe out the difference between scientific truth and falsity as both equally the expressions of historical taste or class bias. It interprets *all* social ideals as meaningless or illusory. These dangers are particularly in evidence when this method is applied to specific doctrines. In the following two chapters, I shall consider two illustrations of the results of an uncritical sociology of knowledge.

CHAPTER FOUR

THE FOLKLORE OF CAPITALISM *

1. *The Politician's Handbook*

ANYONE WHO has read Thurman Arnold's *The Folklore of Capitalism* will understand that no disparagement is intended in characterizing it as the politician's handbook. It is not a handbook of specific practices but of general ideas and principles. Whoever has a firm grasp of them and is capable of sober analysis of concrete situations can write his own shrewd recipes. These ideas and principles are fascinatingly illustrated with a wealth of data. But insight into their relevance and validity depends upon an appreciation of the author's basic attitude or point of view.

"The point of view which we are attempting to sketch here is one which allows a place to the folklore necessary for social organization, which does not mislead us with respect to its function in society. It is the point of view of modern psychiatry without its classifications. This attitude has not attained the dignity of a formulated philosophy. It is one which the realistic politician has taken all along. The task of the philosopher is to make it respectable so that respectable people can use it" [p. 142].

It is a book, then, *about* politicians *for* those who want to be politicians or to understand them, *by* one whose politics includes, among other things, a desire that respectable people become politicians. Let us note in passing that the author regards it as peculiarly important that *respectable* people (however they are defined) should become realistic politicians. Later on we shall examine the basic assumption in the light of which this preference becomes intelligible.

Insofar as it is a book *about* politicians and their ways, Ar-

* This critical article, together with Mr. Thurman Arnold's reply and the author's rejoinder, appeared in the *University of Chicago Law Review*, April 1938, and is here reproduced, without change, by permission of the editors.

nold's *The Folklore of Capitalism* is a little masterpiece of insight, expository skill and suggestiveness. For him politics is as broad as social life. He demonstrates that if we take political behavior as the subject matter of our inquiry, little of our customary academic political theory touches it at any point. Where it does play a role, it merges into popular social theory which is little more than a kind of "ceremonial literature that reconciles conflicts by concealing them." Organizations are the *dramatis personae* of conflicts. To be effective, organizations must say one thing and do another. Those who judge organizations by what they say are confusing incantation with rational analysis. Those who would do the business which organizations must do, without these incantations, will find that their organizations will melt away. For it is "tears and parades . . . which are the moving forces of the world in which we happen to live." Whoever understands that will understand both why it is necessary to have a folklore, a set of myths, ideologies, and isms, and why this folklore must be irrational. "For the purpose of binding organizations together nothing makes as much sense as nonsense, and hence nonsense always wins." Here, too, we must stick a pin to which we shall return. Nonsense, by definition, always wins. Why, then, one kind of nonsense rather than another, the nonsense of the New Deal rather than the nonsense of rugged individualism? In places the author suggests that the victory of one organization and its hallowed nonsense over another depends upon some standard or ideal by whose light individuals judge the fruits of public tub-thumping and *sub rosa* practices. But it is clear that on the author's own view all standards and ideals are nonsense—high and profound nonsense to be sure—but nonsense all the same.

On the descriptive level of political behavior, creedal and practical, Arnold's book is a noteworthy achievement. Particularly for America whose intellectual life has been comparatively unaffected by the writings of Pareto, Michels, and the Marxian critique of ideology. Even if he has rediscovered truths that were already known, to have rediscovered them in the context he did—American folkways in economics, law and politics—is a genuine contribution to realistic stocktaking. No summary can communicate the freshness and incisiveness with which the illustrative material is handled. For example, I know of no clearer presentation of the discrepancy between institutional myth and practice than is revealed in Arnold's analysis of the mechanism of control in bankruptcies, in holding companies, and in taxation policies. We laugh when we read De-Man's account of the Constantinople date vendor who did a brisk trade to the cry of: "Hassan's dates are larger than they are! Hassan's dates are larger than they are!" But few are aware of the extent to which the American public reacts to generically similar slogans, symbols and "fundamental principles" in political life. Whatever the science of politics is, it must recognize how easy it is for people to live by inconsistencies; and it is obvious that those for whom politics is an art must make knowing use of this.

The limitations of Arnold's book begin to emerge just as soon as we leave the level of bare description. The author has two unco-ordinated theories of *why* social philosophies which have no significance nonetheless have effects. At times he writes as if allegiance to ideologies arises out of an original tropismatic reaction to words. People go counter to their own selfish interests and that of the community "out of pure mystical idealism." Indeed, Arnold does not hesitate to attribute the most overt forms of struggle to excessive metaphysical enthusiasm, thereby suggesting another causal explanation for the World War. "Most of the interesting and picturesque wars have been fought not over practical interests but over pure metaphysics." At other times he admits that social philosophies have no significance at all "except with reference to the conflicts out of which they arise." But what are the basic conflicts out of which social philosophies arise? Arnold does not so much as state an hypothesis concerning them.

His failure to do so has a peculiar effect upon his own intellectual procedure. Most of his book, and decidedly the best part of it, consists in exposing the inspirational and non-descriptive character of the bulk of old-style capitalistic folklore, which is popularly called "hokum." But his strictures are very severe against the Utopians and rationalists and academic purists who think that a society can solve its bread and butter problem without hokum. Vital lies and illusions, he asserts, are even more necessary to sustain organizations than they are to sustain men. And in his criticisms, Arnold concentrates exclusively upon the hokum of the old style (Hooverian) folklore leaving untouched the hokum of the new style (Rooseveltian) folklore or, more accurately, mythology, since it has not yet been institutionalized. His contempt for liberals and radicals who are critical of both kinds of folklore is nonetheless apparent despite its restraint. In the absence of a theory concerning the interests which motivate ideologies, Arnold has no answer to the simple questions: Well, then, what's all the verbal shooting about? On the basis of what data can you predict that one myth or another will be accepted? What set of considerations determines the type of ideology an organization will embrace?

The consequences of the failure to relate interests to social ideals lead to an ambiguous account of the nature of creeds and mythologies. We read that "institutional creeds, such as law, economics or theology, must be false in order to function effectively." Yet we are also told that ritualistic beliefs sooner or later affect behavior, that institutions like personalities "become very much like the little pictures which men have of them." Mr. Arnold is not clear in his own mind (i) whether or not social doctrines are strictly meaningless, incapable of being confirmed or invalidated by relevant evidence, or (ii) whether they are all demonstrably false, or finally (iii) whether some are true and some are false. If he holds to the first, he must regard them as expressive statements. To differentiate them properly for scientific purposes, he must analyze the interests they express and translate them into *specific programs of action* as preparatory to intelligent evaluation. This he rarely does. If he holds to the second, then he must recognize that we are already in possession of a sufficient store of true information about the social process—sufficient to enable us to declare ideologies to be false—which justifies the hope that some scientifically valid social doctrines may be developed. Yet if I understand Mr. Arnold aright all social science is part of folklore. If he holds to the third, he owes the reader an account of the methods by which he determines the truth or falsity of social doctrines.

As a book *about* politicians, then, Mr. Arnold's discussion suffers from the failure to present some hypothesis which will account for the varieties of political verbal behavior which his own descriptive survey has uncovered. But as Mr. Arnold makes abundantly plain, his book is written *for* those who would be successful politicians (statesmen, publicists, professional revolutionists, etc.) and it must be considered from this point of view, too. In fact, it is a safe bet that Arnold's views here will have a practical impact upon American political life —right, center and left. The nub of Arnold's advice, based upon his study of the ways of man as a political animal, is this: fundamental loyalties must be given not to principles but to organizations (p. 384). Creeds and doctrines are the invisible but potent agglutinative forces of organizational solidarity and effectiveness. They must be judged only in relation to the techniques of political control. He addresses himself particularly to "respectable people with humanitarian motives" and tells them, almost in so many words, "instead of cussing out the politicians, imitate them." Organizational myths must not be criticized, or weakened by logical analysis; nor, if practical results are desired, are they to be believed in. The populace loves large talk and circus play: it cannot be kept content with a mere diet of bread and cheese. Again Arnold's argument takes an ambiguous form. When he appeals to "respectable people with humanitarian motives" to take politics away from the "selfish" (p. 37) professional politician, the implied assumption is that the organization is to serve the *community* interest, whatever that may be. When he describes and defends the life career of the effective organization, he shows that its primary concern is to further the *organizational* interest and to take note of and appease conflicting interests only to the point where organizational security demands it. This curious reluctance to explore the relationship between concrete interests and organizational structure makes it possible for Arnold to insinuate that the respectable politician represents the interest of everybody.

It is in conjunction with this theme that Arnold realizes he is skating on very dangerous ground. After all, the most successful political organizations of our time are those headed by Hitler, Mussolini and Stalin. They have developed the most elaborate forms of hokum and have won complete freedom to carry out organizational policies. We must not be too superior to learn from them. Yet at the same time Arnold is obviously

bothered by the fear that critics will point to these totalitarian
regimes as constituting the *reductio ad absurdum* and, if I
may be permitted the phrase, the *reductio ad nauseam* of his
position. He is, therefore, compelled to be "choosy" in evaluating their accomplishments. On other occasions, however, he is
impatient with unrealistic philosophers who, starting from
certain principles, try to separate the good from the bad in
situations where they mutually involve each other. He writes:

> "The strength of Hitler lay in the fact that he put everyone to work
> and managed to develop national pride. His weakness lay in his per-
> secutions. Such persecutions are not, I believe, *necessary* to the exer-
> cise of national power or the development of rational morale. The
> reason why they are apt to occur in times of change is that respectable
> people in such times are too devoted to principles to solve immediate
> problems or to build up morale by the objective use of ceremony" (pp.
> 41-42).

It has been said that when a great mind commits a blunder,
it does not content itself with an ordinary one. And when a
hard-boiled realist goes soft, we get an uncommon variety of
naïve mush. How does Mr. Arnold know that the persecutions
were not necessary to put everyone to work and to develop
national pride? To put everyone to work in Germany meant
the establishment of labor and concentration camps and the
abolition of the right to strike. Is this possible without persecution? To build up morale by the objective use of ceremony
meant the suppression of all those who argued that the racial
myth and the legend that Germany had been stabbed in the
back by the liberals and socialists was not justified by the evidence. What method does Arnold know of keeping critics of
fraud and nonsense silent different from those employed by
Hitler? And to put the responsibility for persecution upon
those who are too devoted to principle is tantamount to blam-
ing them for not doing what Hitler did before Hitler did it.
From a narrow organizational point of view, and only from
that point of view, the criticism is just. If an organization is
to survive, it must beat the other organizations to the gun.
But from the same point of view, it is the sickliest sentimentalism to bewail or question the necessity of the means employed to achieve the end. Insofar as Arnold touches the

means-ends problem, his thinking is in the pre-reflective pupa stage.

Even more grotesquely naïve is his treatment of Stalin's regime. He quotes a piece of apologetic writing by Walter Duranty according to which Stalin is "making men out of mice" (including the mice who made the revolution of 1917) by encouraging games, publicity stunts, and celebrations of the power of the Communist Party. This is good as far as it goes. As Duranty says it makes the Russians "men, not mice or slaves." The pity of it on Arnold's view, is that Stalin spoiled matters by "abandoning this technique for a great purge." What Arnold does not see is that Stalin has not abandoned this technique but accompanied it by a purge, that one reinforces the other, and that with greater or lesser intensity, Stalin's regime, like all minority dictatorships, has been one continuous purge. And whom has he purged? The critical, the courageous and independent—the mice that were already men.

There is a reason for this glaring blind spot in Arnold's normally acute political perception. It is to be found in a revealing analogy which runs through this book as well as his *Symbols of Government.* The ideal politician is cast in the role of a trained psychiatrist. His function as head of the state organization is to make the patients (citizens) comfortable and "as little of a nuisance" to themselves as possible. They can even be permitted their rantings (ideologies). The latter have only diagnostic value. They indicate the types of insanity by which the patients are afflicted. No psychiatrist who knows his profession would dream of refuting them as part of his curative technique. The world may be regarded as one vast madhouse whose needs are ministered to by trained psychiatrists in the guise of patient politicians. This interesting analogy explains why Arnold is so indifferent to the kinds of ideologies which flourish in the political world and lumps them indiscriminately together. That is why he resents normative judgments as meddling intrusion by preachers and moralists who really constitute just another class of patients. That is why the methods of Hitler and Stalin seem to him unnecessarily crude.

Now there may be some justification for Arnold's lack of first hand knowledge about Germany and Russia, particularly if he relies upon journalists who write like government officials. But his unfamiliarity with the procedures of insane asylums is difficult to explain for one who thinks in psychiatrical metaphors. The regime which provides material comfort and freedom from the most luxuriant fantasy can only operate if it has at its disposal padded-cells, straitjackets, and, in extreme emergencies, the black bottle. On Arnold's own analogy, there is no more sense in *approving what* Hitler and Stalin have done and *disapproving how* they did it than in praising the cures asylums effect and, in the present stage of knowledge, condemning their methods.

That Mr. Arnold appreciates, despite his flirtation with the metaphors of psychiatry, the danger of making a fetish of organizations as such, is clearly expressed in the purpose of this book. We will recall that the author's declared objective indicates it is a book *by* one whose politics includes the desire that respectable people become politicians. It is in developing the implications of this objective that Arnold's actual, even if unformulated, theory of social causation appears. And in developing the implications of Arnold's theory of social causation, we shall make the startling discovery that he is committed to a point of view which, on *his* own analysis of the nature of folklore, is mythology.

Loyalty to organization rather than loyalty to principle is the first lesson which Arnold would have the realist in politics learn. Once this is granted the author makes no pretense that organizations by themselves are sufficient for good government. He is aware that a political machine can become corrupt and tyrannical. Its mythology may have such cohesive force that the corruptions and tyrannies may not even be risky for its own survival. How, then, safeguard against them? Arnold's answer expresses the only theory of social causation to which he clings consistently—and unconsciously—in his book. Our safeguard is the character of the men, the personality of the leaders, who dominate organizations. In discussing the rise of new organizations, he writes:

"All he [the observer] needs to worry about is the character of the people who are gradually coming into power. Does he think they are good organizers and at the same time tolerant and humanitarian?" (p. 342).

If he does, there is no reason to worry about programs, principles and institutional abuses. He has just got through showing that good organizers cannot be tolerant and that their humanitarianism extends only to those who are acquiescent and tractable, but we pass this minor inconsistency by. The significant thing here is the decisive role which Arnold assigns to the individual, to the good man in government. And not only in government! Even in economics different types of men will give rise to different types of mercantile organization. Specifically, the reason why the "ten-cent store chains" have contributed so tremendously in reducing the cost of living whereas the "grocery chains" have conspicuously failed is attributed to the different types of men who have come to the top in these organizations (p. 351). Naturally, there is the inevitable reference to Henry Ford. The author feels that if Henry Ford had gone into the grocery business (perhaps any business), "he would have accomplished the same kind of results as he did in the automobile business."

I am not interested in criticizing the author's theory at this point. My concern is to show that he holds it. It makes intelligible his purposes, his criticism of existing politicians whose techniques he approves, and his explicit identification *of organizational structure with personality structure* (*passim*).

We now rapidly approach the *dénouement* of the author's argument. Organization is the instrument of political action. Men determine the quality of organization. Therefore we need *good men*—the respectable, the humanitarian, the sensitive— in order to have good government and good society. These men will presumably still remain good even though they employ the techniques of politicians from Machiavelli to Stalin. But this is not the main point. The main point is that Arnold is committed to ethical judgments—ethical judgments, which he began by declaring to be the bane of intelligent political analysis, to be part of the meaningless mythology of principle. There is no place for a theory of the good in Arnold's analysis but its upshot makes the existence of the good man central. How the good man is to be distinguished from the bad, what schedule of ends and theory of means characterize his thinking and action, what *kind* of organization he wishes to build, what specific *program* of institutional reform he must espouse here and now—all these remain unillumined. Failing to realize that politics is a branch of ethics, the author is forced into a left handed acknowledgment of the central place of ethical judgment in his own analysis. Unaware of the implications of his own analysis, he does not feel called upon to develop a theory of the good or even to qualify his original position according to which ethical judgments, strictly speaking, are nonsense statements. His brilliant treatment of illustrative material suggests a plausible theory of the good as intelligently evaluated interest, but he passes it by.

Surprising as it may seem, once the author abandons the purely descriptive level his thought is astonishingly naïve. His methodology is naïve. His theory of social causation is naïve. His unexamined commonsense ethical assumptions are naïve. And in places where he is aware of a difficulty but not of a solution his logic is naïve.

This combination of realism concerning techniques and naïveté about principles is nothing new in the history of social thought. It is generally allied to a social interest. In our own day the social interest which gives a philosophy such as Arnold's driving force is the vocational need of the intellectual worker and professional who make a career in public service or the business of government—a group which regards itself as independent of other classes, in fact as a special class whose function is to mediate between others. It constitutes the permanent staff of officials who observe with amused cynicism or resentful irritation that the more things change (in ideology) the more they remain the same (in practice). In periods of relative stability, it is content to identify its interests with those of the dominant group in the economy. In *effect*, as Arnold himself observes, that is the function of all government, in ordinary times, despite its mythology of universalism. In periods of transition, however, where social tension becomes so great that it threatens the prestige and security of the dominant group in the economy, and with it the tenure, power and privileged routines of the masterful servants who always *imagine* that they rule behind the scenes, a dissociation of interests takes place. If the dominant group adopts an intransigence which bids fair to carry the public servant (bureaucrats or political engineers or technicians—you may take your choice) down to a common ruin, the latter look around for a "leader" who can save what can be saved. In the last resort this means a kind of Bonapartism. But if the leader can serve as the symbol of the vague aspirations of the dissatisfied multitude, as a symbol of distrust of the old myths and acceptance of the new, he can more easily do the practical things which must be done to save the existing economy. Roosevelt is Arnold's leader. Although the theme and implications of his book involve enduring problems, its present impact must be considered in the light of the present clashes of interest in America. But this is a large subject and these pages are not the place for it.

2. *The Folklore of Mr. Hook—A Reply*

Thurman Arnold

The editors have requested a comment on Sidney Hook's review of my book, *The Folklore of Capitalism.* I comply because perhaps a brief statement of my position will serve to clarify the differences between our respective points of view. At the outset, I wish to say that Mr. Hook's very generous praise of parts of the book is particularly gratifying since it comes from a scholar for whom I have the greatest admiration and respect.

If I were to describe the differences in our attitudes, I would say that Mr. Hook is an inspirational philosopher attempting to discover and analyze ethical formulas while I am an unphilosophical observer attempting to write of what I have actually seen and felt in my contact with governmental institutions. That latter type of writing is not essentially different from the creative work involved in writing a novel. A novelist in his best books usually writes of his own early life. His second best books take in the odds and ends which he left out of the first. His inferior books are historical novels in which life is seen through the eyes and theories of other people and other books, and here ends his creative career. The same is true about the kind of observations of social institutions which I am trying to make. My book began as a description of the reorganizations on which I had sat as trial examiner for the Protective Committee Study of the Securities and Exchange Commission. When it was finished, it was found that the detailed account of these reorganizations made the book too long and unwieldy. They were, therefore, omitted, except as illustrations of general statements. However, in so far as I was able to describe them, the book is an account of the actions and thoughts of people whom I have seen and observed.

For such an undertaking Mr. Hook's recommendation that I consider politics as a branch of ethics and define the "good life" seems to me to be the wrong technique. To be vital and accurate this kind of description should be expressed in the best rhetoric of which the writer is capable rather than logical dialectic. I can illustrate this only by analogy: Professor Yerkes of Yale has made some interesting and valuable observations of monkeys. Suppose he were interrupted by Mr. Hook during his observations with the following which I paraphrase from Mr. Hook's review: "Failing to realize that the habits of monkeys is a branch of ethics, you are forced into a left handed acknowledgment of the central place of ethical judgment in your own analysis. Unaware of the implications of your own analysis, you do not feel called upon to develop a theory of the good or even to qualify your own original position according to which ethical judgments, strictly speaking, are nonsense statements."

I suspect that Professor Yerkes reaction to this would be to say, "Please go away, Mr. Hook. If I listen to you I won't be able to put down in simple English what these monkeys are doing."

Of course, Mr. Hook would not make this remark to one studying monkeys. However, I suspect him of thinking that more careful analysis of the concept of the good life in Germany would have prevented the excesses of Hitler, and more thought on revolutionary principles on the part of the Russian people would have saved Trotsky. Certainly he thinks that my own observations of the conduct of political bodies would have been more accurate if I had first analyzed the good life. This is a necessary position for a philosopher to take. However, I think its chief utility is to give force and morale to good preaching, and that it is not an accurate tool for describing moving social phenomena.

I hasten to say that I would be the last to do away with the philosopher who first defines the good life, and then writes about how far human institutions have erred and strayed from the notions in his own head about how they ought to behave. There is comfort and amusement in such literature. There is also the inspirational statement of ideals in such a way as to give them moving force. I do not think, however, that this point of view gives an accurate description of the effects of ideals any more than ethical philosophies give rise to psychiatric techniques.

Take one example from Mr. Hook's review. He states that certain of my observations about Russia in particular and history in general are naïve. Starting from Mr. Hook's notion that politics are a branch of ethics which the political observer must first define before he can describe or act, I can see how that conclusion follows. According to Mr. Hook's definition of the political "good life" recent Russian history involves a moral crime against Trotsky. This point of view led Mr. Hook to lend his name and prestige to a trial of Trotsky before a volunteer court in Mexico. I admire his courage, in this enterprise, but think this point of view obscures political observation and judgment. Such gallant and romantic ceremonies seem to be one of the predictable results of looking at politics as a branch of ethics. Such, it seems to me, are the adventures of one who first defines the "good life" for a nation, and then looks at its conduct through the lenses of that theory. It is, I think, this habit of the philosophical mind of first determining what they want to look for, before they actually look, which makes them inept in actual organization. It is on account of this that when the smoke clears away we always find politicians rather than intellectuals running the actual day to day government while the intellectuals are writing its songs and poetry.

Philosophies, legal, ethical, and economic appear very different from the outside looking in than from the inside looking out. The "inside" point of view assumes that if reasoning men get their heads together, they can make the concept of a good life a workable tool. From the outside it is obvious that reasoning men never agree. Their conflicts only create more literature. On the attacking side that literature is courageous and romantic like the communist manifesto of Karl Marx. On the defensive side it is dull and complicated like the writings of our conservative economic philosophers and lawyers. On the defensive even Marx becomes dull and complicated. Taken as a whole, the parade of philosophers resembles a ballet. The sound theorists, lawyers and philosophers are in the center of the stage repelling the attacks of the unsound ones. Mr. Hook is a brilliant expositor of Marx and is today, at least, in the attacking party. His function is to provide the opposition without which there would be no ballet at all just as there would be no Harvard-Yale football game if the two teams reached an agreement beforehand on the score. Tomorrow Mr. Hook may be a conservative with others attacking him. At least, this often happens. Sound theories have no meaning in the absence of unsound theories. Both are essential parts of the whole spectacle.

This philosophical ballet at any given time will represent all the conflicting ideals uppermost in the minds of the articulate people of the times. Failure of the judicial institutions to function creates an outpouring of legal literature in which the realists and fundamentalists clash. Gaps left by industrial institutions create an outpouring of definitions of contradictory economic and political ideals. Accepted institutions like the Post Office create no philosophical literature. Therefore, if you are looking at philosophers from the outside rather than from the inside, you reach the conclusion that socialism has no meaning except as a dissent from an order of things to which the term capitalistic is applied. When that dissent is most articulate, it means that two types of organizations are struggling for supremacy.

If you are observing these phenomena the most effective platform is one which does not put moral values on the types of organizations. A naturalist who said that butterflies led a better life than tumble bugs or that lambs were superior to lions because lions were so cruel would be introducing an irrelevant and disturbing note into his study.

It is for this reason that I cannot follow Mr. Hook's advice and define my ethical standards when writing about institutions from an objective point of view.

It is important, however, for me to point out that the point of view of the objective observer of social institutions is not one which serves every purpose. It has a narrow and a special utility. It is not adequate for the leader or for the preacher. One cannot get beautiful portraits out of pure dissection and beautiful portraits have their place in our life. The point of view of the dissector is one which is useful only to explain how institutions work.

An analogy is useful here. Certainly a dissecting room is not a pleasant place. Nor does one hang an anatomical chart of one's grandfather in the place of a portrait because it is a more accurate portrayal of the internal workings of the old gentleman. Nor does the psychiatrist, when he falls in love, take the same point of view towards that highly ethical emotion as he does when examining a maladjusted patient. There is, however, no real contradiction here. All that is necessary to say is that when you desire an inspirational portrait of your wife, you call an artist, but when she is ill you call a surgeon. These two individuals look at the lady from different angles, but each of their very different techniques is essential to orderly living.

It has been pointed out by many that the platform on which I stand in dissecting human institutions does not furnish inspirational philosophy. In a dissecting room there is no place for an altar. This does not mean that I am quarreling with the intellectuals or philosophers or the believers in fundamental principles of the law and economics and ethics. For they sit in the seats of the mighty. I did not put them there, but I would not remove them if I could. I only ask the privilege of taking them apart, partly from sheer curiosity and partly from the hope that by doing so, some sort of political techniques may be evolved.

Of course, I realize that when I speak of developing political techniques and diagnoses of social maladjustments, I imply a set of values which are not defined. I think, however, that definition of such values only confuses. These values are not derived from definitions; the persons moved by such values do not have their ideas clarified by such definitions. The actual result of dialectic definitions of social values is only to create a group of words like fascism, communism, regimentation, bureaucracy, etc., which impede practical methods of distributing goods.

I leave to the philosophers the task of providing an inspirational philosophy which will give us confidence to distribute goods more effectively. I do not think, however, they will arrive at that philosophy through logical processes. My own observation leads me to believe that philosophies have no meaning apart from organizations, and that the philosophy of tomorrow will grow in connection with the organizations of tomorrow. I do not wish to enter into an argument as to whether the philosophy or the organization comes first. That is like the old argument about the chicken and the egg. I prefer to say that they grow up together and each molds the other.

And finally, it is my belief that the realistic or debunking attitude is not a bridge between the dissecting room and the inspirational philosopher's chamber. It is only a ceremony in celebration of one of our current myths commonly called intellectual integrity. To illustrate the futility of debunking I have used in one of my books the motto which runs across the façade of the New York Post Office. It reads: "Neither snow nor rain nor heat nor gloom of night stays these couriers from the swift completion of their appointed rounds." Debunked, this phrase is changed to "mail will be delivered even in bad weather." Yet one who so changed it would understand neither the functions of architecture nor the emotional factors which bind organizations together.

Neither Myth nor Power—A Rejoinder

SIDNEY HOOK

Mr. Arnold's reply to my review has the qualities of charm and debonair irrelevance which characterize all his writings. But it fails to join issue with me on any of the basic points I have raised. Certainly, to describe my attitude as "inspirational" is not only polite name-calling, it is demonstrably inaccurate. Nor is he justified in contrasting it with his own "observational" attitude. After all, it is *he* who tells us that he is writing for "respectable people with humanitarian motives"; it is *he* who refers to politicians as "selfish"; it is *he* who explicitly affirms, "All (the observer) needs to worry about is the *character* of the people who are gradually coming into power. Does he think that they are good organizers and at the same time tolerant and humanitarian? If he reaches this conclusion, he need not worry about 'failure to balance the budget' " (my italics).

When I ask Mr. Arnold what he means by these ethical terms and how he squares his use of them with the contention that all ethical statements are meaningless, he replies that I am trying to substitute inspirational exhortations for description and analysis, and that his book is merely "an account of the actions and thoughts of people whom I have seen and observed." If this be so, I should like to ask Mr. Arnold who wrote Chapters XIII and XIV, as well as many other pages of his book. In the very first paragraph of Chapter XIII introducing "The Social Philosophy of Tomorrow," we read: "Something must be said to point out what men *should* believe in order to make them better, more co-operative, more just and more comfortable" (p. 332, italics in the original). I do not assert that this is inspirational but it is something more than descriptive. That Mr. Arnold should be compelled to repudiate a large portion of his book in order to escape from the impasse into which his own inadequate analysis has led him is highly significant.

But unfortunately, even in his retreat to mere description, Mr. Arnold does not stop to meet the difficulties I raised about the adequacy of his report of political behavior. He does not explain why, if all political behavior is mythology, one theory is accepted rather than another; why one organization triumphs over another when both use the same techniques of hokum and the circus. He speaks casually of "interests" but does not indicate what they are or how they enter into political life. He does not clearly distinguish between mythologies which are "false" and mythologies which are "meaningless"; and of the latter between those that are meaningless because they are "uninterpreted" and those that are meaningless because they are "self-contradictory." Nor does he ever make it clear whether it is only the politicians who run the government "while intellectuals write its songs and poetry" or whether it is the intellectuals "who sit in the seats of the mighty." In his book and in his reply, he says both.

In view of Mr. Arnold's difficulty in understanding his own position, I am not at all surprised that he should so completely misunderstand mine. It is not the case that I believe that one must have a theory of the good life before one can describe the political scene. What I assert is that a competent survey of the political scene must take note of the fact that men sometimes act intelligently, i.e., in the light of consequences. There is nothing unnatural in such behavior and nothing inspirational in calling attention to its importance. Whether we will or no human acts have consequences. The ability to perceive these consequences, and to organize preferences for some consequences over others into regulating norms to control subsequent action is natural to men and not to Yerkes' apes. Scientific study will show that this form of behavior is found among the first and not the second. One does not need to have a code of morals to discover that there are codes of morals. All one needs, in this as in every other intelligent inquiry, is an hypothesis. What Mr. Arnold refers to as the ineptitude of the philosophical mind, viz., the habit "of first determining what it wants to look for before it actually looks" is the *sine qua non* of scientific investigation. One wonders how Mr. Arnold can ever find anything, if he doesn't know what he is looking for.

But when we leave the plane of political description and urge that a *policy* of some sort should be adopted (as does Mr. Arnold in that part of his book which he has disowned), or when we assert that the character of this leader is *preferable* to the character of another (as does Mr. Arnold when he supports Roosevelt)—then we are explicitly making value judgments of a sort. Intelligence demands that we be clear about the nature of these judgments, and their grounds and their consequences. Now, Mr. Arnold himself, admits that when he speaks of techniques to remove social maladjustments he is implying "a set of values which are not defined." But he immediately adds, "I think however that definition of such values only confuses." His reasons I shall examine in a moment. The concession, however, that every policy presupposes value judgments is all that I need to substantiate my criticism that he is inconsistent in his descriptions of the nature of political policy and unclear about his own value judgments. No wonder he glosses over the brutal tyrannies of Stalin and Hitler while he pleads for politicians to be tolerant and humanitarian!

But why does Mr. Arnold believe that the definition of values only confuses us? Because "these values are not derived from definitions: the persons moved by such values do not have their ideas clarified by such definitions." Of course values are not derived from definitions any more than a disease is derived from a definition of a disease. His observation has no pertinence whatsoever. Mr. Arnold is using "definition" here loosely as a synonym for analysis. Does he really believe that people understand the values they accept without analyzing the contexts in which values emerge, and the causes and consequences of their acceptance? If Mr. Arnold maintains that such knowledge can be achieved without analysis, he is literally committed to an inspirational theory of value. To be sure, many persons moved by values are unable or unwilling to clarify them by analysis. This is a fact and every scientific theory of history must take note of it. It still remains true, however, that there is no other way of clarifying them. Does this mean, as Mr. Arnold suggests, that I believe "a more careful analysis of the concept of the good life in Germany would have prevented the excesses of Hitler?" Not at all. On my theory of history, there are other factors which have much more influence in shaping events than proper semantic analysis. But a more complete analysis would indicate the moral quality of Hitler's (or Stalin's) excesses, prevent us from making a fetish of organizational power and success, and within certain narrow but important limits strengthen our opposition to attempts at extending them elsewhere.

The real issue, as I see it, between Mr. Arnold and myself is whether politics as a science and art can dispense with normative judgments, and whether normative judgments can be analyzed into statements about objects of intelligent interest, i.e., objects desired after reflection. I answer no to the first question and yes to the second, while Mr. Arnold seems to give inconsistent answers to both. As a concrete illustration of how hard it is to find his meaning and of the inconsistencies it runs into on any interpretation, we may take his reference to the Trotsky case. No more than John Dewey am I a political partisan of Trotsky or the other Moscow defendants. But it seemed sufficiently important to me to establish the truth about the Moscow trials to support the Dewey Commission of Inquiry. Concerning this, Mr. Arnold writes:

"According to Mr. Hook's definition of the political 'good life' recent Russian history involves a moral crime against Trotsky. This point of view led Mr. Hook to lend his name and prestige to a trial of Trotsky before a volunteer court in Mexico. I admire his courage, in this enterprise, but think his point of view obscures political observation and judgment."

Now what is Mr. Arnold trying to say? That there is no such thing as "a moral crime" in politics and that therefore governments cannot be guilty of them? Or does he mean that it is unimportant whether or not "moral crimes" are committed in politics, or perhaps only that this particular crime is unimportant? Or, as his last sentence suggests, that no political crime has been committed at all and that Trotsky, despite the findings of the Dewey Commission, is guilty as charged? If he means the first, then I think the conscience of mankind is against him, and his own verbal habits play strange tricks on him. For he uses the language of moral judgment in his book, and when not in the mood of hard-boiled romanticism would probably admit that a "frame-up" is a moral crime. (If I am not mistaken, he has even protested against some, e.g., Sacco-Vanzetti.) If he means the second, then the judgment that it is unimportant whether moral crimes are committed by governments is certainly a moral judgment. This would mean that Mr. Arnold himself has a point of view concerning the political "good life"—one which is tolerant of frame-ups— but is unaware of what it is. And for some strange reason he thinks it is a virtue not to be aware of this point of view, thus depriving himself of the opportunity of checking or criticizing it. If, however, he believes that only this particular frame-up is unimportant, on the ground that it does not affect America, he is clearly wrong and would be a bad political scientist. For the Russian system is being urged upon the American people as an alternative to our own and the methods of frame-up have already been attempted in America by certain interested parties in order to further Russian interests. Finally, if he believes that the Moscow trials were not frame-ups, on what possible grounds can he imagine that the desire to discover the truth about them necessarily obscures our judgment and observation? Indeed, on this last view he should have been among the first to support the Dewey Commission of Inquiry. What Mr. Arnold really believes is his own secret, but the *objective* effect of his verbal confusion is to support the position that whatever is, is right.

Mr. Arnold is perfectly justified in assuming that organizations are necessary to implement social philosophies. But they are not sufficient. One must also have a social philosophy. Absolute loyalty to a social philosophy, in independence of the conditions and circumstances which make it applicable, is unintelligent Utopianism. Absolute loyalty to organizations independently of the qualities of life they generate is degrading to discriminating intelligence. Mr. Arnold gives us a choice between the insanity of uncontrolled myth and the inhumanity of uncontrolled power. We reject both.

CHAPTER FIVE

ON IDEAS AS WEAPONS

1. *Interpretations of Ideas*

IDEAS MAY BE approached in various ways. We may inquire concerning their validity. We may investigate their origins either as events in a man's biography or as forces in social history. We may lay bare their internal articulation, neatly ordering them so that the pattern of logic or illogic is apparent beneath the rhetoric. We may investigate the causes of their acceptance or rejection, correlate them with other phases of personality and culture, interpret them as expressions of need and interest.

All of these approaches to ideas are legitimate. But they are not equally relevant to all fields and to all problems in any one field. The history of physical theories does not seem to be as germane to the problems of the natural scientist as the history of economic or legal doctrines to the social scientist. Relevance, of course, is a matter of degree. But the degree can be evaluated only when we have a relatively clear conception of *the problem* to which we want to find an answer. It is this failure to set down the problem which is to be, let us not say solved, but further clarified—that is responsible for so much loose thinking about the nature of ideas in current sociology of knowledge.

These reflections may be tested by a reading of Max Lerner's *Ideas as Weapons*. In many ways it is a curious book. Curious in organization, curious in its textual meaning, curious even in the author's intent. What seems to hold these miscellaneous essays and reviews together, composed over a period of eight years and ranging from the Supreme Court to the novels of Dos Passos, is Mr. Lerner's declaration that they exhibit "the inner unity of a cohesive point of view." This point of view is described by the title and amplified in the first chapter: "Ideas Are Weapons."

A considered approach to Mr. Lerner's book must at the very least pay some attention to what the author insists is its unifying feature, even if it turns out that his point of view, as in the case of some thinkers he discusses, is neither clear nor consistent, and his purposes different from what he imagines them to be. The more natural approach to these essays, had not Mr. Lerner stressed the importance of the point of view which allegedly unifies them, would be to consider them as occasional pieces, some good, some not, some indifferent, and to make a general appraisal of Mr. Lerner's qualities as a writer rather than as a political thinker.

2. *Ideas and Intuitions*

I should like to begin by taking this more natural approach, for Mr. Lerner's gifts as a writer are not inconsiderable. These consist primarily of a certain freshness of style which enables him to make even commonplaces crisp and palatable, and a power of sympathetic interpretation, especially valuable in presenting the doctrines of writers who are themselves obscure. Lerner's piece on "What Is Usable in Veblen?" is a good illustration of these capacities. He carries the reader to the very heart of the perspectives from which all of Veblen's main ideas radiate. In this way he induces an imaginative comprehension of the whole body of Veblen's thought without which, to the ordinary reader, Veblen makes dreary reading.

The essay on "Hitler as Thinker" is perhaps a more masterly illustration of interpretative power. The rationale of Hitler's obsessions takes form as the intertwined compulsions of his personality, his background and post-war German misery are described. We understand why "the very quality of not making sense is exactly what gives effectiveness" to *Mein Kampf*. Criticism is not spared but its point lies not so much in demonstrating that Hitler's ideas are unintelligent, an easy task, but in making his emotional tensions and thought construction intelligible. He emerges not as a monster but as a case understood. Our understanding includes the social and cultural traditions in which such a case can establish the norms of apparent sanity. "Hitler is, in a sense, the Edward Lear of political thinking. He has taught us that, just as a limerick drives Shakespeare out of our minds, so by a similar Gresham's law illogical political ideas drive out the logical." [1]

This represents Lerner's interpretive approach at its best. It also yields some insights whenever he restates the position of thinkers whose writings are fragmentary, like Holmes, or when he discusses literary figures like Dos Passos, who develop ideas by indirection. On the other hand, the defects of Lerner as a writer are glaring whenever he is confronted by a position which is clearly stated. He can do nothing with an argument which depends upon explicit assumptions, whose logical implications are developed, and whose validity rests on alleged evidence. In this sense there is no analysis of ideas whatsoever in Lerner's book. He seems equipped to explore almost every aspect of a man's ideas except that which is of the greatest importance for purposes of scientific understanding and action. By approaching ideas intuitively and poetically, where they challenge scientific inquiry and analysis, Lerner misstates even the obvious and obfuscates what is already clear. He emotionalizes other people's ideas to a point where their outlines are lost. What might be forgiven in a poet, is a serious lapse in one who would be regarded as a political scientist.

How misleading Lerner's intuitive interpretation of ideas can be is illustrated in his essay on Lenin's *State and Revolution.* Whatever else may be said about this book the argument is clear. This has been recognized by all critics even when they have regarded the argument as clearly wrong. It remained for Max Lerner to discover, what no one ever had the temerity to suggest during the balmiest days of the Popular Front, that Lenin's *State and Revolution* can also be interpreted as an argument in behalf of a class collaborative variant of the Popular Front. Valid or not, Lenin's argument from first page

---

[1] It matters little that in communicating the quality of Hitler's thought, Lerner makes an extraordinary blunder of fact. He portrays Hitler sitting in the cheap, pre-war restaurants of Vienna "holding them [customers] spellbound with his attacks on the Jews and the Weimar [!] governments." It matters little because it is not a question here of evidence for an hypothesis about Hitler's ideas but of some appropriate incident to suggest the calculating and resentful hysteria of a frustrated egomaniac. We no more hold Lerner's error of fact against him than we would the liberties taken by a poet with some fact of history or geography in order to insure the proper assonance of a line.

to last is directed precisely *against* such a view. But according to Lerner, Lenin's book

"contains two divergent lines of direction. . . . One of these strains [!] is the inevitability of a violent revolution. The other is the uniqueness of each national experience, and of the economic development, the political forms, and the revolutionary temper of each. . . . The first leads to austere anti-reformism. . . . The second leads to an emphasis on 'the national question,' on national traditions and temper, and, in Engel's works, on the theme that 'the working-class can only come to power under the forms of the democratic republic.' . . . By Lenin's own reasoning . . . revolutions of the majority, such as the Jeffersonian, Jacksonian, and the New Deal revolutions, must in the end, if conducted with courage and skill, make an anti-democratic capitalist coup merely suicidal adventurism."

Again it is not a question here of the truth of Lenin's ideas but their meaning. And it is their meaning which Lerner distorts beyond recognition. *Nowhere* does Lenin counterpose his theory of how state power must be won to the uniqueness of each national experience. He emphasizes distinctions of national experience only to argue that they do not affect the essential validity of the laws of capitalist development, the class struggle, the theory of the state, and in the era of finance capital, the conquest of power. It is not only Lenin's meaning which escapes Lerner but Engels'. The sentence he quotes from Engels is immediately followed by this remark: "This is indeed the specific form for the dictatorship of the proletariat, as has already been shown by the French Revolution." And had he consulted Engels' own writings instead of contenting himself with Lenin's quotations from Engels, he would have seen that Engels is here criticizing the failure of the German Social-Democrats to strive for a democratic republic, and their belief that such a republic could be achieved in Germany peacefully, not to speak of the further belief that a democratic republic could grow peacefully into socialism.[2]

2 "Man redet sich und der Partei vor, 'die heutige Gesellschaft wachse in den Sozialismus hinein,' ohne sich zu fragen, ob sie nicht damit ebenso notwendig aus ihrer alten Gesellschaftsverfassung hinauswachse, diese alte Hülle ebenso gewalstsam sprengen müssen wie die Krebs die seine, als ob sie in Deutschland nicht ausserdem die Fesseln den nocht halb absolutischen und obendrein namenlos verworrenen politischen Ordnung zu sprengen habe." *Die Neue Zeit*, Jhrg. 20, Bd. I (1901-1902), p. 10. Engels goes on, like Marx before him, to make possible exceptions of countries like England. Lenin takes issue with them on this point with arguments of dubious validity, but his position is unambiguous.

Because he is not concerned with the structure of ideas, but with imaginative reconstruction unchecked by easily available data, Lerner runs together questions which although related must be carefully distinguished. It becomes difficult in consequence to tell exactly what problem it is that he is discussing. In his essay on Lenin there are at least four problems that he handles as if they were one: whether the transition to socialism can be achieved peacefully, whether it should be carried out by a mandate of the absolute majority of the population, whether the form of majority rule should be the dictatorship of one class; whether this last involves the dictatorship of one party. On every one of these questions Lenin's views may be wrong; but it is also true that on every one of these questions his views are clear, even when they differ, as in some respect they do, from those of Marx and Engels.

3. *Ideas and Action*

The point of view which unifies these essays, Mr. Lerner tells us, is that "ideas are weapons." A simple sentence which seems clear until Mr. Lerner begins to explain what he means by it. It then turns out, as we shall see, that the terms "ideas" and "weapons," as used by the author, are bewilderingly ambiguous, that his own characterization of the career of ideas is not consistent, and that the point of view, which he modestly refers to as "a Copernican revolution" in ideas, is so confused that it even infects the author's purposes.

Of his approach to ideas, he says: "I saw in short that my approach was an instrumental one; that I have increasingly sought to view them as weapons in the personal struggles that every individual has for the resolution of his tensions, and in the struggles for power and order that every age has and every culture." And in his first chapter: "It [this approach] sees that the idea has meaning only in a dynamic context of a struggle over power and values."

This is straightforward enough, except for the unfortunate "only" in the last sentence. All ideas are weapons in the struggle for power—social or personal. But note: although "the shape that ideas take is relative to the culture and era in which they develop and are used; yet there are internal standards of validity in ideas themselves. The sum of these internal standards is what, for lack of a better term, we call 'science,' although the philosophers may prefer to call it 'truth.' " Scientific ideas, then, are also weapons to achieve power in personal and social struggle. As weapons how do they differ from, or compare with, non-scientific weapons? It is important to know because, according to Lerner, "more than anything else, what will ultimately defeat fascism is its anti-scientific bias." Apparently, then, when the instruments (ideas) by which power is won are unscientific (false), the chances of power enduring are not as high as when it is achieved by ideas that are scientific (true). But this cannot be Lerner's meaning because it contradicts the whole burden of discussion, which runs: whether or not ideas are accepted has nothing to do with their truth or falsity; if anything, the more an idea appeals to the "irrational" the more likely it is to make headway.

What does Lerner mean? It is hard to tell because at this point there is a double confusion in his discussion. He sometimes speaks of ideas as "valid" or "true" because they are effective; and sometimes ideas are "valid" independently of their effectiveness. He seems to slip from the statement: *it is true that the use of certain weapons (ideas) is effective to achieve purposes of power;* to the statement: *weapons (ideas) which are effective in achieving purposes of power are true.* But from the true statement that some purposes can be achieved by a lie, a half-truth, a verbal incantation, it does not follow in the least that these ideas (weapons) are true.

Again, from his thesis that ideas are weapons in the fight for power, it follows that *all* social theories and doctrines are ideologies, i.e., instruments of power politics. But Lerner seems to shrink back from this conclusion and condemns *Realpolitik* for its cynicism in using ideas as weapons, despite his express statement that "ideas are necessarily weapons." Speaking of the Stalin-Nazi Pact, which he admits caught him short, he says: "What we are dealing with is the cynicism of *Realpolitik* that still cuts across ideological considerations as it has always done, not because they are irrelevant but *because it uses and discards ideas as one might use and discard weapons.*" (My italics.)

Is this not passing strange? Lerner has just got through telling us that all ideas are necesarily weapons but now he is in full flight from his own thesis and protests that *Realpolitik* uses even ideologies—which have no scientific warrant—as weapons. This is just what he should expect and applaud were he consistent.

Lerner now shifts to another distinction in order to save his thesis that ideas are weapons, and at the same time distinguish between *Realpolitik* and other forms of politics. He distinguishes between the *purposes* for which ideas are used. What, he asks, is the "real difference between the totalitarianisms and the democracies in their attitude toward the use of ideas"? Both use ideas as weapons in the struggle for power but "the important difference is the difference between the instrumental approach to ideas and the manipulative approach. The *instrumental* approach recognizes that ideas are used in behalf of a way of life and in the struggles for its achievement. But it is also humanist. . . . The *manipulative* approach sees the common people only as so much material to be used. . . . If you view ideas instrumentally your primary regard is for their validity,[3] and for the social cohesion that will result. If you view them manipulatively, your only regard is for the use you can make of them."

I defy anyone to make sense of this passage if it is taken in conjunction with the other things Lerner has said. "Instrumental" previously meant a way of analyzing ideas; now it characterizes a way of *using* ideas. What makes ideas, used instrumentally, valid or true? Their purposes or their effectiveness in achieving purposes? If it is their purposes, then what Lerner is saying is that good purposes make ideas true, and bad purposes false, which is absurd. If it is not the character of the purposes which makes ideas as weapons true, but the *effectiveness* of these ideas in achieving purposes, no matter what they are, then the distinction between "the instrumental" and "manipulative" approach loses all point. And why the correlation of these different approaches to ideas with democratic and totalitarian states? Do not totalitarians, who "manipulate" ideas, effect creative actions and social cohesion —sometimes too much so? Are not ideas in a democracy re-

---

[3] Yet in the foreword Lerner, characterizing his instrumental approach to ideas, says precisely the opposite: "What interested me mainly was *not* their symmetry or logical structure or even their validity." (My italics.)

garded for the use that can be made of them? And if, according to Lerner, ideas are necessarily weapons, how can anyone be reproached for regarding them from the standpoint of the use that can be made of them? Besides, Lerner himself has insisted that democratic states are just as willing to betray ideologies as totalitarian states, that the "basic difference" between them is that in the second "the military, economic, and propaganda skill groups are openly part of the government," whereas in the first, "great subtlety is still required in order to conform with the rhetoric of democracy." Perhaps so. Why, then, are their purposes suddenly depicted as essentially different?

It is not the lack of consistency in Lerner's writing which is so puzzling but the difficulty of assigning coherent meaning to his words. It is quite doubtful whether the author of the sentences quoted knew what he wanted to say. It is a pity that Lerner speaks of his approach to ideas as "instrumental," for it may mislead people into thinking that it has anything to do with Dewey's instrumental approach to ideas. For Dewey an idea is an instrument for the resolution of a difficulty or problem only in this sense: that the operations and experiments to which it directs us on symbols and things results in observations confirming or refuting the predictions that logically follow from its assertion. This enables us to determine first, whether we have an idea; and second, its degree of truth or falsity in the light of the relevant consequences of acting upon it. Lerner has no idea of what an idea is nor an adequate conception of the method by which ideas are validated.

4. *Ideas in Action*

Sometimes a man's intellectual procedure is better than his doctrinal formulations, particularly if he lacks methodological sophistication. Let us therefore examine what Lerner does with his "instrumental approach" to ideas. How much actual light does his approach shed on ideas "as weapons in the personal struggles that every individual has for the resolution of his tensions, and in the struggles for power and order that every age has and every culture"?

A careful reading of these essays discloses that where Lerner is at his interpretive best in uncovering patterns of feeling and intellectual bias, he provides very doubtful confirmation of his thesis. On the other hand, where he does treat ideas explicitly as weapons in the struggle for power, his interpretations shift with his own moods and political allegiance. Sometimes his interpretations are so wide of the mark that they suggest he is writing more with an eye to what his audience is likely to accept than with scrupulous regard for the evidence. On the few occasions when he discusses the validity of ideas, he abandons his "instrumental approach" without achieving a greater degree of accuracy in expounding their meaning. I offer illustrations of each point.

Of the set of ideas and institutional practices which comprise the New Deal, Mr. Lerner says late in 1933 that they represent "an approach to the corporate state," indeed, that in effect, they constitute a "semi-dictatorship." By 1936, Lerner recognizes the New Deal as one of the crisis-democracies, almost the American equivalent of the Popular Front. And by 1939 (but before the Stalin-Nazi Pact) he refers to that "something called the 'New Deal' that has put America today in the forefront of progressive governments." Mr. Lerner does not admit that his views of 1933 were wrong but merely that his phrases were "overstrong." But wrong he was either in 1933 or in the spring of 1939 (or at both times). An instrumental approach to the New Deal that can give us such incompatible readings within such a short span of time is not of very great help in showing how ideas are weapons in the struggle for power.

How Mr. Lerner's "instrumental approach" to ideas can get into the way of understanding them is evident in his patronizing discussion of Pareto, and in his remarks on the social process theory of American thinkers. He admits that Pareto has brilliant intuitions but when he states them they all reduce to the commonplace that human behavior is irrational. He fails to grasp the significance of Pareto's method, even though it is more of a program than an achievement, as well as its chief weakness, the neglect of the role of hypothesis. He is blithely unaware of the whole cluster of problems which center around the doctrine of the circulation of the élite. It is dismissed as an expression of Pareto's contempt for democracy even though many lovers of democracy regard it as a valid historical truth (not psychological as Pareto did) which challenges democrats to discover specific mechanisms to control bureaucratic abuse of power. As for Lerner's contention, which crowns his interpretation, that "Pareto's republic is now a reality—it is Hitler's totalitarian state"—one can only say "Poppycock!" or more descriptively, that it is on a level of criticism which Malcolm Cowley has made famous.

American sociologists will be surprised to learn that the social process theory and its pendant, the belief in multiple factor causation, "through its function of rationalizing the adherence to the *status quo* and the fear of revolutionary action . . . has in the movement of events carried implications of a definitely anti-liberal character." Limitations of space prevent an adequate analysis of this statement and its assumption that the only alternative to revolutionary action, as Lerner conceives it, is defense of the *status quo*. Suffice it to say that Lerner misstates both the theory of the social process and the multiple factor theory of causation: the first, by attributing a doctrine of unbroken and gradual continuity to its proponents, to be found, perhaps, in Savigny but not in Hegel, Marx, Simmel, Cooley, Dewey, and others who did most to develop the idea; the second, by attributing to it a belief that all factors are equally relevant and of equal weight in explaining specific problems—a truly fantastic notion. Further, even in the mistaken form in which Lerner states these theories, it can easily be shown that they do not entail an acceptance or glorification of the *status quo*. They are logically compatible with more than one attitude towards a given social order.[4]

Lerner's exposition of the theory of historical materialism is an illustration of a non-instrumental approach to ideas. Here is no interpretation of a weapon to be used in the personal or social struggle for power but an account of a doctrine, as Lerner understands it, and a plea for its acceptance on the ground that it is true. And what does Lerner understand by truth in this context? The theory of historical materialism is true because "it gives a basis for predictions which, while never

---

[4] Unfortunately a good deal of Mr. Lerner's knowledge of writers of this school is derived second hand. When he speaks of their reliance upon "Eichhorn's theory of the complexity of society and the multiplicity of factors," it is evident that he has read Albion Small not Eichhorn.

infallible or exact, nevertheless furnishes a starting point for action." Note that the purposes for which the action is to be undertaken are not indicated. The validity of the theory, we gather, is independent of whether or not action is "creative" or results in "social cohesion." If valid it can be used by a thinker of any political persuasion who wants to understand society, i.e., to predict events and act on the prediction.

If this is the way to approach the question of the validity of historical materialism, why should not the validity of every other theory be tested in the same way? The question of validity can be clearly distinguished, if not separated, from the questions: how did X come to believe or discover this theory?; what factors in the cultural soil and climate made for its acceptance or rejection?; what political uses and purposes did it serve? Where a doctrine is not sufficiently clear in its meaning to enable us to tell what evidence would bear upon its validity, then questions of the kind asked in the previous sentence may throw some light on its meaning. But under no circumstances is knowledge of the historical, social, class, vocational, or psychological conditions in which ideas have emerged, flourished, and disappeared *sufficient* to decide the question of their validity.

Unfortunately, even the non-instrumental approach which Lerner takes to the theory of historical materialism is vitiated by a fundamental error. "In Marxian terminology," he writes, "the conditions of production determine the relation of production." The result of this error is something closer to the technological interpretation than to the Marxian, despite Lerner's attempt to avoid this conclusion. When he adds that "they [the conditions of production] determine the class structure of a society—in short, its social order—not in the sense of a rigorous and mechanical determinism but in the sense that they represent a tough and unyielding compulsive in a society *with which the social order has to reckon and on which it must be based*," [5] he has reduced them merely to the status of a necessary condition. His proposition would be equally true or false if we substituted for his "conditions of production," physical factors or biological needs, for these, too, are elements with which the social order "must reckon and on which it must be based."

[5] My italics.

By the time Lerner gets through expounding the theory of historical materialism, he has admitted the importance of human effort, choice between alternatives of action, the operation of chance and contingency, tradition and social lag, and the influence of ideological elements, including science, on the economic structure of society. Ironically enough, he is committed to a theory of multiple factor causation in which the economic factor, about whose character he offers no clear account, is given the greatest weight, without any indication of how that weight is to be established.

5. *Ideas and Purposes*

Mr. Lerner tells us that "the instrumental approach" to ideas differs from "the manipulatory approach" in the purposes which it serves. We owe it, therefore, to Mr. Lerner to consider his purposes. Perhaps they will throw some light on his instrumental approach. Alas! his purposes are as baffling as his account of his method. For if we construe them from the methods by which he proposes to implement them, and the action in which he engages to further them, they hardly square with his avowed purposes.

Lerner declares himself to be a democratic socialist, a humanist, and a liberal, if that word is detached from its connotations of economic laissez-faire. For a man of such purposes, his proposals in the essay "Freedom in the Opinion Industries" are truly astonishing. He would apply to the market of opinion a procedure analagous to that followed by the S.E.C. in the marketing of securities. His Truth in Opinion Act provides for the organizing of a government board (this despite Lerner's acceptance of the Marxian theory of state), consisting, of course, of good and wise men, whose function would be, among other things, to regulate "anti-social propaganda" and "to ban material that is poisonous and spurious." The late Ernest Sutherland Bates in an otherwise kindly review of Lerner's book said of this proposal, "Anything more addlepated than this Stalinesque suggestion would be hard to imagine."

Precisely what is Stalinesque about it? Addlepated it is not. The suggestion itself is not new. Neo-Thomists have argued

that we do not permit people to disseminate or even to adver-
tise disease germs and poisons that hurt our bodies; why
should we permit the peddling of lies and inflammatory half-
truths that corrupt the mind? Lerner has rediscovered this
argument but he is not a Thomist and certainly would not
entrust the Church with the administration of the Act. What
is Stalinesque about the proposal—and here we have the central key to Lerner's line in thought and practice—is this: the
willingness to use or condone any method of achieving and
holding power for avowedly good causes like "socialism," without reflecting upon the consequences of those methods on the
character and direction of power so achieved. This explains his
"shock" at the Nazi-Soviet Pact and his belief that whereas
only power-politics was the guiding imperative for Hitler, for
Stalin "the survival of socialism [*sic!*] in Russia seems to have
been the imperative." This also accounts for his systematic
blurring over of the similarities between German and Russian
patterns of dictatorship, and his faith that despite these similarities "there is a deep and unbridgeable chasm" between the
purposes of these dictatorships. It accounts, too, for his refusal to make *legitimate* distinctions in dealing with groups
who although opposed to each other are both opposed *for
different reasons* to a third group with which Lerner is at the
moment sympathetic. In a savage and unfair attack on Oswald
Garrison Villard, he forges the crude amalgam: "While he
[Villard] approaches the anti-Roosevelt encampment by a different entrance from the anti-New Deal and isolationist re-
actionaries, he comes out at the same door." By the same logic
this could have been said of Lerner in 1933.[6]

Perhaps only a fine interpretive psychological study, which
Lerner himself does so well, can reveal the true sources of his
thought and feeling. I choose to believe that his ideas are a consequence of intellectual confusion rather than of opportunism.
I trace this confusion to the fact that although he declares

---

[6] It is this belief that holy purposes can be served by any means which provides the most charitable explanation of some of Lerner's public actions: his
participation in the attempt organized by the Communist Party to disrupt
the Commission of Inquiry into the truth of the Moscow trials; and—most
shameful of all—his approval of another Communist Party document in which
John Dewey, Ferdinand Lundberg and other outstanding progressives are
denounced as "Fascists and allies of Fascists" for characterizing Stalinist
Russia as a totalitarian culture. Cf. *Daily Worker,* August 14, 1939.

himself a socialist, he fails to see: (1) that socialism must be marked not only by a more efficient economy than capitalism but by a greater extension of democracy and cultural freedom than is already found in the most democratic of democratic capitalisms; (2) that the weight of historic evidence indicates that methods which Lerner has countenanced to further good causes set up attitudes, and prepare the way for practices, which are incompatible with *both* a democratic culture and an efficient economy, evaluated from the standpoint of the consumer; and (3) that it is possible without violating the spirit of the democratic process energetically to combat organized attempts to subvert programs authorized by a majority mandate.

Lerner professes fear lest concern with methods and means lead to "the fetishism of principles." Fetishism of any kind is unintelligent, including fetishism of goals that justify the use of *any* means. It is true that experience often compels us to qualify principles. But it is precisely because all principles are subject to qualification that the particular principle with which we approach any specific situation is of supreme importance. What holds for scientific truths, holds at this point for social and ethical principles: from the fact that they are all subject to correction, it does not follow that they are all equally valid. Qualifications of ethical principles must themselves be justified in part, at least, by other values which are involved in the concrete situation. Each situation may have its unique good to be achieved by action here and now but situations are continuous with each other. Today's action in some respect determines what we are prepared to do tomorrow. This is not a counsel to refrain from action but to act with consciousness of the wider consequences as well as of those near at hand. Machiavelli was a patriot not a cynic. The trouble with Machiavellianism is not that it is cynical or even unintelligent but that it is not intelligent enough.

The uncontrolled relativism associated with the sociology of knowledge, and its inadequate analysis of ethical ideals, naturally fortifies the position of metaphysical idealists and ethical absolutists. We turn, therefore, to a consideration of an influential representative of a school of thought which seeks to reconstruct society in the light of "eternal principles."

CHAPTER SIX

INTEGRAL HUMANISM

CATHOLICISM IS THE oldest and greatest totalitarian movement in history. Other totalitarian movements have borrowed from it even when they have fulminated against it. Its essential totalitarian character is at times obscured, particularly when it finds itself in conflict with the newer movements which must consolidate their power at its expense. Compare it with Fascism, Nazism, Stalinism. In every case the *mystique* is different; but in every case we find present not merely dogmas, sacred and profane, rituals of canonization and excommunication, but the desire to revolutionize "the soul" of man through the directing force of a highly organized minority, using those three great instruments described by Dostoevski's Grand Inquisitor— *miracle, mystery,* and *authority*—to order a society in behalf of the interests of a bureaucratic hierarchy. *Miracle* in the form of bread in return for absolute submission; *mystery* in the form of doctrine to conceal the true source of the bread and the exploitation of those who make it; *authority* in the form of sacred script, a leader and the secular arm to make doctrinal mysteries acceptable.

The greatness of Catholicism as a movement, leaving aside the historical reasons for its varying fortunes, consists in its theoretical adaptability and practical resourcefulness. The extent of its theoretical adaptability may be gauged by the fact that in its struggles against other forms of totalitarianism, it sometimes assumes the vestment of ideological liberalism even though its authoritative spokesmen have on occasions held that the logical consequence of doctrinal liberalism is Bolshevism. Despite Jefferson's outspoken Deism, Catholic writers insist that his inspiration was Thomist. And if we are to judge by the writings of the outspoken apologists of Catholicism in

Europe and America, they are just as ready, if necessity arise, to baptize Marx as they once baptized Aristotle.

The practical resourcefulness of Catholicism is exhibited, to mention one of many things, in the skillful use it can make of everyone. It has a place and function for all who accept the Catholic dispensation—for every type of mind and personality, for every interest and talent. Soldier or social worker, scholar or man of action, poet or astronomer, converted Jew or converted Protestant—the virtues of each individual's excellence can be made to serve the purposes of the Church. Its base of common dogmas is sufficiently broad to permit of a wide and *controlled* variation. It has countenanced a modernist and fundamentalist wing in politics, a realistic and nominalist tendency in philosophy, a rationalist and mystic emphasis in theology. In the past it has found use for a St. Francis Assisi and a Torquemada just as today it can find uses for a Maritain and a Coughlin.

1. *The New Christendom*

M. Jacques Maritain has been aptly described [1] as the general commanding "the ordered offensive of Thomism" in the Western world. His appeal is therefore not demagogic but intellectual; his audience not the masses which follow slogans more easily than fine distinctions but the intellectuals who lead them. More particularly, his writings are addressed to those intellectuals who, dissatisfied with the cheap dogmas of current political ideologies, are seeking a way of life which can integrate the values of personal experience into a significant pattern and at the same time provide a dynamic perspective for social action—and this without intellectual stultification. Normally, Catholicism would be the last faith to which intellectuals of social conscience, historic knowledge and some intellectual training would look for such a new basis. But M. Maritain's books while breathing a simple piety and convincing personal integrity display such formal sophistication that, despite the *nihil obstats* of the *censor librorum*, they can circulate to the unconverted as illustrations of how one can be Catholic even though intelligent, yes, even though radical and intelligent. Such distinguished preaching to the unregenerate

[1] By Mr. Montgomery Belgion.

is not without its profound influence upon the faithful themselves, especially those errant sons of the Church who have grown critical of its institutional practices. Their doubts are appeased and the role of the Church in supporting the regimes of Dollfuss, Mussolini and Franco, its "neutrality" to Coughlin, appear as accidents in its temporal career, in no way related to its essential nature.

To say that M. Maritain's ideas are dangerous is no argument against them. M. Maritain would be the first to admit it. For every idea that bears on social action is dangerous—whether it be true or false. The danger of M. Maritain's ideas is greater today than they could have been at any time previously. For the demoralization of the radical and socialist movements throughout the world, the one indisputable consequence of Stalinism, gives M. Maritain his great opportunity. Already many of the literati and professionals have flocked back to their ivory towers from which the depression drove them, intellectually defenseless, into the doctrinal storms. A few of greater intelligence and moral integrity, have devoted themselves to the cultivation of a spirituality whose logical consequence, whether in Tolstoy or in Aldous Huxley, is a withdrawal not only from politics but from the world. To those whom Hitler and Stalin have not frightened into making their peace with capitalism, M. Maritain's "integral humanism" presents itself more and more as the only apparent alternative to democratic socialism in any of its reformulated variants.

M. Maritain broaches his philosophy of "integral humanism" in a subtle and persuasive way. According to him the socialist movement is a Christian heresy, doctrinally in error, but moved by the same spiritual dynamism as historical Christianity. Indeed, when M. Maritain speaks of the aims of Catholic "integral humanism," which seeks to found on a secure basis the modern and yet age-old desire for a better life, his words would not be out of place in a socialist tract.

"This new humanism, which has in it nothing in common with bourgeois humanism, and is all the more human since it does not worship man, but has a real and effective respect for human dignity, and for the rights of human personality, I see as directed towards a socio-temporal realisation of that evangelical concern for humanity which ought not to exist only in the spiritual order, but to become incarnate;

and towards the ideal of a true brotherhood among men. It is not to the dynamism or the imperialism of a race, or of a class, or of a nation, that it asks men to sacrifice themselves: it is for the sake of a better life for their fellows and for the concrete good of the community of human individuals. . . ." (*True Humanism*, p. xvii.) [2]

Nor is M. Maritain frightened by the revolutionary elements in Marxist thought, if only the revolution, harsh as may be its means, will uproot the "bourgeois man" whom M. Maritain loathes with an almost unchristian contempt. For M. Maritain, the social ideals of Marxism are not objectionable. The Marxian critique of capitalist economy and of the consequences of the operation of that economy upon human freedom and culture is described as a "great lightning-flash of truth." It is only the "metaphysical" basis of Marxism, its atheism, which M. Maritain deplores because it results in the apotheosis of collective man, in the conception of the absolute sovereignty of the collectivity, and negation of true personality whose ends are not all historical, social, or natural. That "Marxism" has a dogmatic metaphysics, false though it is, makes it superior to bourgeois nominalism which has no metaphysics.[3] Substitute the true metaphysics for the false, the religion of Catholicism for the "religion" of Socialism, then the social revolution of the Marxists, without abating one jot of its fiery opposition to capitalism and bourgeois humanism, can more surely move towards its legitimate objectives—without of course ever achieving the Kingdom of Heaven upon earth. M. Maritain is profoundly indifferent to the fate of bourgeois property. Nor does the church's real estate seem to concern him overmuch, for once the Marxist heresy is supplanted by the true doctrine, there will be no reason to be suspicious of the corporate property of God's shepherds which, after all, is held in trust for the flock.

The assumption that Marxism is a Christian heresy seems

---

[2] New York: Chas. Scribner's Sons, 1938. I have centered the argument around this book because it is the latest available to me.

[3] This is also the judgment of the eminent Catholic historian, E. Gilson. "Against the crude, yet fundamentally sound craving of Marxism [Stalinism] for positive and dogmatic truth, the skepticism of our decadent philosophy [all non-Thomistic philosophy] has not a chance. It deserves to be destroyed as it actually is in the minds of many of our contemporaries who embrace Marxism because it is the only dogmatism they know." *The Unity of Philosophical Experience*, p. 294.

to draw it into an orbit of common tradition and discourse within which a humanist solution is possible—until we remember how Christian heresies were treated by the Church. M. Maritain does not approve of physical extermination of heretics today; but neither does he approve of an earthly city (state) which is *neutral* towards heresy. "It is necessary that Christ should be made known; that is the work of the Church, not of the State. But, be its type sacred or secular, a temporal Christian city knows that it is its duty to assist the Church in the free accomplishment of this mission."

The Christian city, not to be confused with the City of God which is outside of time, is of two types—consecrational and secular. In the former, the assistance which the State renders the Church "is of an instrumental order: the secular arm puts its sword at the disposition of spirituality. It is then normal that the coercive force of the State should come into play to protect the faith and the community against disintegrating influence. . . ." In the secular city, the State integrates "Christian activities in its own temporal work." The Church is assisted by the State "in the fulfillment of its rightful mission" without the use of the sword.

Which mode of collaboration should exist between Church and State, says M. Maritain, depends upon historical conditions. He does not approve of the consecrational state today on historical grounds; and historical grounds, as M. Maritain himself never tires of reiterating, are variable. Clear it is that he does not *in principle*, as an integral humanist, disapprove of the secular arm putting its sword at the disposition of spirituality. He states the circumstances under which such practices may be extenuated, i.e., where heretics offend "the consciousness of the community (which) is vitally impregnated with the same unanimous certitude. It may even happen that the intervention of the State in such matters will moderate and curb the excesses of spontaneous popular reaction; what more natural impulse to the crowd than to lynch the heretic?"

In order to save the heretic from lynching in a consecrational community, the State steps in to put him to the sword according to whatever due process of law obtains at the time. Such practices are not incompatible with the *principle* of integral humanism. They are incompatible with the principles of that "bourgeois" free thought and humanism to which, according to Marx, the socialists fell heir, and of which M. Maritain says, departing from his customary urbanity, that it is "the stupidest thing the world has ever known."

I hasten to repeat, however, that M. Maritain does not under present historic conditions, and with an eye on France and the Anglo-American world, advocate the consecrational form of the Christian city but the secular form. But I must confess to a deep dissatisfaction with M. Maritain's failure to explicate more fully under what set of *historic* conditions he would justify one or the other form of Christian state. He does not call for a return to the Middle Ages but for a new Christendom. It will incarnate the *same* (analogical) principles as the medieval world but will belong to an essentially (specifically) distinct type. About M. Maritain's use of the analogical argument I shall have more to say. But insofar as he attempts to state the empirical conditions, and on his own view they must be primarily empirical at this point, for departing from the medieval way of treating the heretic, he flatly fails. His failure is very disturbing even when, perhaps it would be more accurate to say just because, we recognize that the problem lies within the field of "prudence" which does not admit as high an order of certitude as of caution.

M. Maritain frankly avows that he has no desire to condemn the theory according to which the temporal power is justified in putting heretics to the sword for the good of their souls and for the spiritual unity of the community. "I have no desire to condemn such a system in theory. In one sense an earthly order capable of putting to death for the crime of heresy showed a greater care for men's souls and held a higher ideal of the dignity of the human community centered in this way on truth than one which only looks to punish crimes against the body" (p. 144).

Why, then, does M. Maritain in delineating the respects in which the new Christendom differs from the old, make provision for what he calls "the extra-territoriality" of the person, which would preserve the life of the heretic even though his heresy, as a threat to men's souls, is declared an abomination? His answer deserves careful consideration. Because putting to death for crime of heresy "is the point where human nature must most fatally lead to abuses; abuses which became [note the change of tense!] more and more intolerable ... when, *after* the ruin of medieval Christendom, the State, ceasing to act as the instrument of a higher and legitimate spiritual authority, arrogated to itself and in its own name rights of spiritual interference." (*Ibid.*, my italics.)

The gravamen of M. Maritain's disclaimer is not that the method leads to abuses, for all coercive means of implementing a good end, since they are employed by creatures of limited wisdom, lead to abuse. Rather is it that it leads to intolerable abuse. And why intolerable? Because when the consecrated Christian city loses its authority, the practice may be—and has been—adopted by those who have usurped that authority. But so long as the *consecrated* city retains its authority, abuses there may be; but intolerable abuses—never. And suppose there were a way of retaining authority in the consecrational state, so that there would be no danger that Protestants, absolute monarchs, and Jacobins would borrow a leaf from the pages of church history with which to light the fires of Catholic martyrs? On what ground could M. Maritain condemn a practice—temporal suppression—which flows from a theory—the right to save souls from heresy—of which he approves? The intolerable abuses of which M. Maritain speaks occurred *after* the ruin of medieval Christendom. Is he prepared to argue that the ruin of medieval Christendom is the result of its treatment of heretics? Hardly, for he has previously argued that as a means of achieving a good end, this treatment of heretics was justified by the historic context and conditions. But if the ruin of medieval Christendom is not the result of its treatment of heretics, he is still owing us an explanation of why he disapproves the practice but not the theory; at the very least, an indication of the historic conditions under which in the future the practice may be as unexceptionable as the theory.

Before we conclude this section of our study, we must look a little more closely at the type of collaboration between Church and State which M. Maritain proposes for his *secular* Christian city. The spiritual (Catholic) principle is to have a commanding influence on the life and morals of the community but it must not command the state to enforce these principles on those—pagans and heretics—who do not or will not see the truth. Here the familiar scheme of pluralism operates. But this pluralism, M. Maritain expressly warns, must not be confused with "theological liberalism." Theological liberalism is the belief that the commonwealth "should be obliged to recognize as licet for each spiritual group the law worked out for that group according to its own principles." This is impermissible to those who are concerned with men's souls and who know that they know *the* truth about the only path by which these souls may be saved. The pluralist form of political organization "Signifies that in order to avoid greater evil ... the commonwealth could and should tolerate (to tolerate is not approve) ways of worship more or less distant from the truth. . . ." These greater evils are civil strife and the insecurities it breeds. Tolerance of non-Catholics and heretical Catholics in M. Maritain's secular Christian state is an evil, a *lesser* evil but an evil nevertheless. It is a lesser evil which is suffered by the true believers until they become strong enough to save the false believers from themselves without danger of provoking widespread civil strife. The measure of the strength of the integral humanists, we must therefore conclude, is the limit of the tolerance of integral humanism. Salvation is always a greater good than tolerance. Civil war is always a greater evil than tolerance. If repression could stop short of civil war, it would be a lesser evil than tolerance.

How faithfully M. Maritain follows official Church doctrine on this point, despite his gracious prose and terminological liberalism, may be gathered from the following passage in the Papal Encyclical, *Libertas,* of Leo XIII. "Although in the extraordinary conditions of these times the Church usually acquiesces in certain modern liberties, she does so not as preferring them in themselves, but as judging it expedient to allow them until in happier times she can exercise her own liberty." Among the liberties of the church are not merely the right to teach her doctrines as alone true but the right to judge and punish.

The basic feature of M. Maritain's secular Christian state is that it cannot be neutral in religion. Insofar as public education is concerned, not only must provision be made for religious instruction, with due regard for the extra-territorial rights of heretical religions, but any teaching that falls within

the very broad category of atheism must be proscribed in order to save the souls of the young from corruption. M. Maritain is much too civilized a person to join in a man-hunt
against atheistic professors of philosophy like Bertrand Russell. But he has formulated the theoretical premises which can
be used to justify the tightest restrictions against a critical and
experimental approach to the fundamental questions of religion, morality, and *a fortiori*, politics.[4]

That M. Maritain's views are dangerous, then, we may consider as having established. Reasonable they may also be, but
there is at least as much gall and blood mixed up with the
reasoning as sweetness and light. For M. Maritain, religious
freedom is a contradiction in terms, intellectual independence
on matters of faith and morals a form of arrogant impiety,
urbane skepticism of metaphysical assertions, spiritual de-
cadence, and simple courage in the face of death defiance of
God. The position he represents may be found congenial by
those who, having surrendered one or another specific variety
of totalitarianism, have not yet repudiated its generic form.
It deserves attentive consideration from those who refuse to
acknowledge that the good life, personal or social, can be built
on the pillars of myth, mystery and authority. We turn now
to an examination of M. Maritain's reasoning.

2. Theology and Politics

M. Maritain is a subtle and persuasive writer. But this is not
to say that he is a rigorous thinker. Despite the reputation for

---

[4] The real secret of M. Maritain's ideas is their organizationally orthodox
character. How orthodox his conception of the New Christendom is may be
gathered by comparing his position with that of Max Scheler, in his Catholic
phase, (*Vom Ewigen im Menschen*). Scheler sought to bring Catholicism and
Socialism together in the interests of a new European culture by assigning
to the first an educational and spiritualizing function in a socialist society,
and not by giving the Church a place at the political controls. As an Augus-
tinian, he was more interested in the direct relationship between the individual
soul and God than in the mediating role of the Church. He, therefore, could
embrace a Catholicism which falls short of totalitarianism. But it is necessarily an heretical Catholicism. Aquinas leaves no doubt as to the central
place of the Church, as an organization, in Catholic theory and practice. "The
practice of the Church possesses the highest authority, and we must be directed
by it in all things. Even the doctrine of the Catholic teachers has its authority
from the Church. Hence we must hold the custom of the church in higher
esteem than the authority of an Augustine or a Jerome." (Quodlib. 11, A. 7,
cited by Grabmann, *Aquinas*, p. 50.)

cogent argument which he enjoys among literary men and his Catholic brethren, there is hardly a conclusion he reaches that is not begged at the outset. He considers few of the possible alternatives to his controlling assumptions, and of these, only the crudest. *The whole bent of his intellectual procedure is to make distinctions that enable him to withdraw the issues with which he is most concerned, from the possibility of scientific or empirical determination.* The result is that to the unwary he seems to extend a vast area which includes almost all of the domains of scientific knowledge, art, and social action, within which conclusions may be freely reached by competent methods, without reference to Catholic dogma. Provided an individual is prepared to abandon his naturalism or his religious heresy (atheism, Protestantism, Greek orthodoxy, etc.), M. Maritain is willing to extend a friendly hand to him. It matters not at all whether the individual is a Darwinian, a Freudian, a logical empiricist, a Marxian socialist, yes, even a Stalinist! But the interests of the Catholic church must be served, and so we find that M. Maritain at crucial points steps into the realm of time and social struggle to settle issues concerning the nature of mind, the state, political and moral hygiene (which includes questions like the relation of church and state, education, divorce, birth control, etc.) by reference to Catholic-Christian principles whose validity is declared to be timeless.

The mysteries of Catholic dogma, which can best be stated in negative terms, and cannot be justified on rational grounds, give M. Maritain a strategic vantage point. They enable him to criticize any basic belief concerning man, which is not centered in the Church, as inadequate, even when he admits a certain measure of truth in its claims. In this way the Church appears as the repository of all "truths" without being compelled to show how they can all be rationally held. The unity which embraces all "truths," pruned of exaggeration, is a supernatural mystery. In practice, i.e., in judgments applied to temporal institutions, this unity dissolves into the barest kind of eclecticism. For example, of the pessimism of the Reformation, M. Maritain can say that it "unduly exaggerates the Christian concept of original sin." Of the optimism of the Renaissance that it unduly exaggerates the equally Christian but opposite concept "of the value of the human being." Man is naturally evil but not only evil. Man is naturally good but not merely good. The same may be said of human ignorance and knowledge, ugliness and beauty, weakness and strength. M. Maritain is helpless, however, before a position which denies that men are "naturally" either good or evil, and that the qualities of good or evil are acquired by them in the course of time in relation to each other. He lumps together *all* positions different from his own as relatively unimportant variations of the same essential heresy.

How like the procedure of the totalitarians! The integral humanism of Catholicism offers men a choice between two alternatives: either pure Christianity (i.e., the Church) or some form of atheism, implicit or overt. Just as the Stalinists were wont to regard all intermediate groupings between Fascism and Stalinism as forms of Fascism, so Catholics in a frank mood, and M. Maritain in a less explicit one, lump Luther, Kant, Hegel, Croce, Dewey, Marx and Stalin together as phases of an inevitable transition of decline from the true faith. In these days when the mystical law of the unity of opposites seems to be translated into the practical co-operation between totalitarians with opposite ideologies, we must not take too seriously M. Maritain's sharp disjunction between Catholicism and Stalinism. As will be shown subsequently, he has built more than one bridge for possible use between the two. After all, the political liaison between Fascism and Catholicism in some countries is a fact; and a Concordat between the Pope and Stalin is no more improbable today than the Hitler-Stalin Pact was some years ago.

This may sound shocking to those readers who recall M. Maritain's passages in criticism of Stalinism. But what does he criticize? Not so much Stalin's cultural *terror* but its spiritual *error*—the same spiritual error which presumably is found in democratic countries that are free from cultural terror. He does not criticize in any fundamental way, the structure of the Communist Party hierarchy; the absence of political democracy in Russia; the censorship of the mind; the thousand and one evils which flow from a minority party dictatorship. He does criticize the principles by which these practices are regulated, not in the light of their empirical effects but in the light of Catholic principles which are equally exempt from check by any empirical effects. The Stalinist stewards are unworthy of their leadership! Insofar as their practices are sinful, it flows from their false religion—their atheism which is nothing else, according to M. Maritain, than the *ne plus ultra* of bourgeois humanism. He voices his distrust of this religion even as he accepts—gingerly to be sure—the outstretched hand of the Communist Party in its Popular Front disguise. "It is in the logic of things that one day or another a hatred, a religious vindictiveness will be awakened against the faithful of other religions, as generally happens in the case of all political non-conformists, if only in the least degree they refuse to conform" (p. 32).

That M. Maritain should hurl this reproach at the Stalinists is puzzling because were it true—and it is—it would seem as if he were accusing them of recapitulating the history of the Church itself. But it is at this point that M. Maritain rears himself to his full height as a Catholic apologist. In order to evade responsibility for the acts of the Church, he invokes a distinction between "authentic Christianity" (*the Church*) and the historic career of the Church. From the standpoint of "authentic Christianity" (Catholicism) there are many things which historic Catholicism has done from which we might well shrink in horror. But nothing it has done can affect the essence of *the Church*, its sacred and holy validity which it has received from the source of all validity. None of the deplorable acts and programs to which the historic Church has committed itself can be deduced from the principles of the authentic Church. But if it is impossible to deduce from authentic and revealed Christianity the particular programs which M. Maritain condemns, it is just as impossible to deduce their contraries of which he approves. *If* authentic Christianity comprises a set of general, eternal and immutable truths beyond history and time, they cannot serve as a guide to *specific* problems of history and time. M. Maritain's dilemma therefore is either to admit that no positive political program, (which must of course consist of more than vague and unqualified injunctions to love one's neighbor), is deducible from Authentic Christianity, or *that the political programs of Catholicism, including his own proposals, are to be explained by the concrete interests of the Church as an historic organization in time.*

He cannot do the first without cutting himself off from a prin-
cipled basis on which to criticize political formations in time;
he cannot do the second without running the risk of being
compelled to condemn Church and Pope and of suffering eternal damnation.

M. Maritain attempts to slip between the horns of this dilemma with another distinction. *The Church* itself must not be
identified with the Kingdom of God; it is only the chrysalis of
the Kingdom of God which can never be achieved in time. "It
is in time but not of time." Insofar as it is "in time" it must
strive to realize the Kingdom of God although it can never
completely succeed; insofar as it is "not of time" it is the Kingdom of God already realized. But this distinction, which is
based on a religious mystery disguised as a metaphysical necessity, avails nothing. For even *the Church* in time is distinguished from the Church as an organization of men
hierarchically organized to exercise power in the political and
social struggles of the day. When the Pope issues an Encyclical (not to mention his prayers for Franco) it may be that
he is not proclaiming the truths of the Kingdom of God. But
does he speak for *the Church in time* or for the Church as a
corporation whose seat is in Rome and whose representatives
bargain for the extension of its corporate rights in almost
every court and chancellory of the world? [5]

The importance of M. Maritain's intellectual procedure justifies restating this in another way. On the one hand, Catholicism is neutral to things in time including politics. On the
other hand, it is essentially concerned with them and especially
with politics, for politics falls within the domain of morals,
and moral values "imply a reference to the supernatural order
and to revelation." This revelation is granted to the Catholic
church and *only* to the Catholic church. Consequently, no
right order of society is achievable, no science or philosophy

---

[5] No one really knows when the Pope is speaking *ex cathedra* except the
Pope himself. For all practical purposes, however, the Papal Encyclicals have
a binding force not only on the behavior of the faithful but on their religious
assent. "Encyclicals are not necessarily *ex cathedra* pronouncements, though
the Pope could, if he so willed, issue definitions in that way. The faithful are
bound to give them a religious assent, *interior as well as exterior, and obedience and respect.*" Addis and Arnold, *Catholic Dictionary*, p. 298 (my italics).
Cf. Poynter, "Catholicism and Sociology" (*XIXth Century and After*), Jan.
1940.

of politics can be true or even wholly useful, which does not judge and evaluate its objects "by the light of revealed principles." The objects judged are secular and temporal. The principles by which they are judged are supernatural, substantially of the Kingdom of God. The Kingdom of God can never be realized in this world but it can be prepared for by the Catholic church.

Now the *extent* of the temporal power which the Church should claim in order to effect this preparation, is not a matter for sacred Catholic theology to decide but for Catholic politics informed by supernatural truths. In principle it is unlimited: in practice, a function of expediency—a high expediency. Empirically, however, it varies with the power (wealth, numbers, influence) of the Church communicants in specific historical contexts, and with the shrewd estimates by the hierarchy of the danger that its own principle of intolerance, used to further the Kingdom of God, might be applied by other religions against Catholics, to further the Kingdom of the Devil. M. Maritain cannot in *principle* condemn the aspiration of the Catholic Church to monopoly of temporal power without falling into heresy; he cannot condone all its practices without lapsing into spiritual sadism which would be very shocking to bourgeois liberals whom he accuses of lacking "both erotic feeling and ontological sensibility." It is to escape from this and similar difficulties that he introduces his double mystery about time.

To what pitiable straits M. Maritain is reduced as a Church apologist is indicated by the following. Attempting to explain away the assumption of vast temporal power by the Church during the Middle Ages, the Counter-Reformation, and the *ancien régime*, he writes: "The Church, as such, was not involved in these excesses but they were produced within the Church" (p. 99). If this is not another divine mystery, how can an organization not be involved in that which is produced within it? Perhaps the excesses were the work of outsiders—pagans dressed in the vestments of clerics? Such things have been often alleged. For example, the Nazi excesses of 1933 were all explained as the work of Communists in the uniform of Storm Troopers. But if these excesses were the work of outsiders, surely M. Maritain might tell us when the Church as such disavowed these excesses. Unfortunately, he does not. Even on the assumption that M. Maritain's distinction between what is "involved in" and what is "produced within" makes sense, were he discussing the good works of the Church during this period, instead of its *auto-de-fe's*, he would not be likely to say: "The Church, as such, was not involved in these beneficent measures but they were produced within the Church." Yet there is as much warrant for one piece of verbal legerdermain as for the other. It is not a question of whether the distinction between the temporal activity of the Church-as-such and the temporal activity of the Church-not-as-such is tenable or untenable, since it involves the mysteries of sacred theology. The empirical question is: To what forms of behavior, intellectual and practical, is the use of such words an index?

Although M. Maritain allows a formal autonomy to questions of empirical fact, he shows absolutely no respect for empirical facts where they conflict with his ideological mission. In justifying his mission he writes as if he has come to recall the Church to a sense of its obligations to the secular world. He would have us believe that the Church has confined its ministrations to the religious sphere and that "matters of social, of political and economic life it has abandoned to their own secular law." Nothing could be further from the truth. The Church has played a very active role in the social and political history of Europe and the Americas, particularly in those centers where its communicants are numerous. To speak only of our own hemisphere, the history of Mexico in the last hundred years, and of Chicago, Boston and New York City in the last fifty, is incomprehensible without reference to the open and sometimes decisive participation of the Catholic hierarchy— with or without benefit of the light of authentic Christianity.

The advantages which the community is to derive, if the Church will only heed M. Maritain's injunction to spiritualize temporal political life, are illustrated, according to our author, by the activity of the Catholic Church in Fascist Italy. Here in its very cradle, totalitarianism has been checked, if not tamed, by papal intervention. "It is highly remarkable," he writes, "that in the very country where the totalitarian State first had that name, *the totalitarian principle has been, in the sequel, half broken by the resistance of the Catholic Church, with which historical circumstances obliged it to come to terms."* (p. 278, my italics.)

A masterpiece of misstatement! Were it not composed by M. Maritain we would consider it a devastating piece of irony from an anti-Catholic pen. The simple fact is that in coming to terms with Mussolini the Catholic Church strengthened totalitarianism in Italy. 1931, the date of the papal agreement, marks the stabilization of Italian Fascism in the eyes of the world. It was the Catholic Church that affixed the certified seal of stabilization. Clericalist sentiment which was at a low ebb in democratic Italy has grown tremendously in Fascist Italy, aided and abetted by Mussolini for value received. Did the Church lift up its voice against the Ethiopian campaign or did it rather improve the opportunity to convert heretics? Is there any doubt that Mussolini's invasion of Spain was carried out with the active collaboration of the Papacy? True, the Church took exception to Mussolini's ideological adventure into "racism," not on scientific but organizational grounds. The ideology of Catholicism after all is indispensable for its proselytizing efforts outside of Italy. But it did not succeed in deflecting the course of Mussolini's policy one iota.[6] Most eloquent of all, however, is the implication of the admission that it was with the Italian Fascist State and not the Italian democratic state that the Pope succeeded in coming to terms.

3. Integral Humanism and War

M. Maritain is a faithful son of the Church not only in doctrine but in the accurate way in which he reflects the inconsequentiality of doctrine when confronted by momentous social and political issues. *In any crucial situation the behavior of the Catholic Church may be more reliably predicted by reference to its concrete interests as a political organization than by reference to its timeless dogmas.* Analogously for M. Maritain. His attitude toward the Second World War is not what

---

[6] The only concrete evidence M. Maritain cites of what the Catholic Church has received for its support of Italian Fascism is the fact that "the Ballilas have been constrained to concede Sunday to religion and the family." This mitigates the fascization of these babes in arms on all other days of the week. M. Maritain might have also cited the additional fact that Mussolini has not withdrawn the rights of Christian burial to the victims of the Ovra.

one would expect from a pious Christian but from a French patriot. One can respect the motives of the French patriot. But one cannot respect a rationalization of French patriotism in terms of Catholic theology. It is truly sad to observe in M. Maritain's Christian apologetics for the cause of the Allies the lamentable disregard of the very distinctions he has so seriously urged upon us until now. In order to appreciate the gravity of M. Maritain's intellectual sins—for the intellectual life has its virtues, too—it is necessary to recapitulate briefly the argument of his *True Humanism*, approved by the Catholic censor, and compare it with the text of his article on the war, approved by the French censor.

In the first, the Catholic Church is presented as the only genuine alternative to secular totalitarianism. The capitalist democracies are scorned for their bourgeois humanism, for their degrading cults of profit and comfort, and their anarchical conception of freedom. They receive particular condemnation for preparing the way for the worst features of totalitarianism. The totalitarian cultures are regarded as historically legitimate heirs of the vicious errors of bourgeois democracy, and as morally legitimate revulsions against this unendurable heritage. They show a praiseworthy concern for the souls of men but they have taken the wrong road to salvation. They exemplify "virtues gone mad." Their errors cannot be corrected by a return to the spiritual indifference of bourgeois humanism but by an acceptance of the Catholic way of life which will preserve the positive features of the totalitarian cultures, Italian, German, or Russian, while pruning the deplorable excesses that flow from a false metaphysics.

And now let us hear M. Maritain in defense of the war.

"The thing which I want to say at once and that I want to cry from the house tops is that the spiritual situation of Europe has completely changed and that the salvation of Europe has begun ... the striking indication of this change is the Russo-German alliance. It has completed the unmasking of the enemy.... Everyone now realizes that ... there is only one revolution; and this revolution is in essence directed against the first principles of all Christian civilization, against everything which indicates the mark of God on man, against everything which implies respect for the human person, for justice and for truth, against everything which relates to greatness and liberty of the human soul.... The declaration of war against Germany by England and France on Sunday, the third of September, was not simply an action that had become politically necessary. It was also an admirable evidence of the strength of soul and of the moral greatness of these two countries.... The world saw that the democracies ... were willing to remain faithful to the reason for their existence ... that the men of France and England, of those two ancient Christian lands, risked in the perils of a hellish war both their lives and their dearest goods and the incomparable heritage of civilization of which they are the guardians" (*Commonweal,* Oct. 13, '39).

Yesterday France and England, according to M. Maritain, were capitalist democracies accursed by bourgeois humanism; today they are "those ancient Christian lands," guardians of "the incomparable heritage of civilization." Yesterday, the atheism of bourgeois man, of Stalinist totalitarianism, of Fascism, were three different forms of the same essential heresy; today, by a verbal transsubstantiation, the atheistic bourgeois democracies become protagonists of the Christian principles they had shamelessly flouted for more than a century. Yesterday, M. Maritain was hopeful that with the extension of the Popular Front and the signing of the Franco-Soviet pact, the Christian truths held in captive by the state philosophy of Stalin might yet convert their captors; today Stalinism is not only the creed of the unregenerated but of the unregenerate. Had the war broken out with either Hitler or Stalin on the side of the Allies, it is reasonable to assume that M. Maritain would soon find an essential difference between these twin forms of totalitarianism. And how fervently must M. Maritain pray for the continuance of Italian neutrality! For if *totalitarian* Italy, that most ancient of Christian lands, joins the defenders of Christian civilization, it will spoil the lines of his apology; and if it joins its sisters then we will have the strange spectacle of a totalitarianism, presumably tamed by the papacy, waging war against the principles of Christianity.[7] A cruel dilemma only one degree less cruel than the fate of an apologist called upon to explain the possible support of Christian principles by Mohammedan Turkey, not to mention China and Japan.

So many questions crowd the mind concerning M. Maritain's

[7] Since the above was written, Italy has joined with Germany in war against the Allies, and the Italian Church has blessed Mussolini's arms.

Christian defense of Allied victory that it is difficult to know where to begin. We might question him about the application of the first principles of Christian civilization by France and England to the natives of India and Indo-China. We might inquire why he so lightly disregards the danger he himself cites that war may bring many features of totalitarianism to the old Christian countries. We might ask why, if he believes that Europe has already been saved for Christianity by baptism of fire, he is stanchly opposed to a peace without complete military victory. But all this is foreign terrain for M. Maritain and we wish to question him in his own terms. How is it possible for capitalist democracies thrice accursed by bourgeois humanism, metaphysical nominalism, and educational secularism to become the defenders of "the first principles of all Christian civilization"? [7a]

There is only one answer that M. Maritain, as a Catholic, can make to explain the conduct of M. Maritain, as a French patriot. Despite the spiritual negations of capitalist democracy, the latent strength of true Catholic principles, which exist in a distorted form even among the Christian heresies, has at this decisive moment transformed the character of the culture and opened new possibilities for a new Christendom. Overt or hidden, it is Catholic principles, and *only* Catholic principles, which are the true guardians of the Christian birthright of mankind. The Church can be relied upon to combat totalitarianism.

And yet when M. Maritain wrote his Catholic apologia for Allied victory in a "just war," he was not unacquainted with the Pastoral Letter of the Bishops of the Catholic Church of Germany which said:

"In this decisive hour we admonish our Catholic soldiers to do their duty *in obedience to the Fuehrer* and be ready to sacrifice their whole individuality. We appeal to the Faithful to join in ardent prayers that Divine Providence may lead this war to blessed success." (*New York Times*, Sept. 24, 1939.)

Will M. Maritain tell us once more that this is an action "produced within" the Church but "not involving" the

---

[7a] This is not to be construed as a criticism of M. Maritain's defense of the cause of the democracies against Hitlerism but only of the grounds he offers. Cf. the Appendix to this chapter.

Church? Let us hope so, because since it involves a mystery it does not insult our intelligence and outrage our moral sensibilities as does the answer he actually gives. "It is entirely understandable," he writes in another issue of *Commonweal*, "that the bishops of the countries at war should exhort their respective peoples to serve their countries loyally." An evasion which lacks even subtlety. Does loyalty to one's country, then, demand loyalty to whatever "criminal dreamer" whose "lust for power and savage aggression" (the words are M. Maritain's) orders them into battle? And have the Catholic bishops merely exhorted the Faithful to be loyal? They speak of the duty of *obedience to the Fuehrer*. They speak of the duty of *sacrificing their whole individuality* to him. But this is precisely the kind of abomination which M. Maritain has condemned in the name of *the Church*, authentic Christianity, integral humanism.

All this, according to M. Maritain, is entirely understandable; and he adds that it is "naïve" to be scandalized by it. What is understandable? The war of the Allies, M. Maritain is convinced, is a "just war," demonstrable as such by eternal Christian principles. How is it understandable that a just war on one side of the Rhine, should be considered an unjust war on the other side of the Rhine by Catholics who enjoy the same grace of papal benediction and the same light of revealed principles as their fellow-Catholic, M. Maritain? Is justice, then, as Pascal suggests, bounded by a river? Would it be understandable if M. Maritain, as a Catholic, supported an unjust war? Why is it more understandable that the Catholic Bishops of Germany should support an unjust war? And why is it "naïve" to be scandalized by the division among Catholics? Because to be scandalized implies that one has taken the principles of integral humanism seriously? Or because it implies that one is not acquainted with the long record of such division? Or because it implies that it lacks intelligence to expect Catholic principles to be administered in any other way except realistically, i.e., with an eye to organizational fortunes rather than to justice or sanctity?

M. Maritain himself has exposed the hollowness of his integral humanism. A French patriot need not be driven to such desperate expedients to justify his action. Whether we accepted his reasons or not, we could understand them. For they would not involve transcendental mythology.

4. *Science, Atheism, and Mythology*

One of the central terms in M. Maritain's critique of modern culture is "atheism." Almost all of our current evils and errors are reduced to expressions or consequences of atheism. It is the root of Marxian fallacy in theory and Marxian inadequacy in practice. Insofar as M. Maritain finds occasion to criticize totalitarian regimes, he traces their excesses not to false principles of economics or politics but to their "atheism." This atheism, he reminds us, is the logical outcome of bourgeois free thought. In many places M. Maritain seems to suggest that the Deists, many Protestant sects, all humanists except integral humanists, are atheists, too. Even the "bourgeois liberal," as a type, no matter how great a play he makes of morality and a spiritual point of view, "is a deist and an atheist; it is he who has taught their atheism to his pupils and heirs, the communists" (*True Humanism*, p. 72).

How such broad divergences as democratic socialism, capitalism, and Stalinism can flow from a negation of a theological principle, M. Maritain leaves unexplained. But here as elsewhere by a carefully cultivated ambiguity M. Maritain uses one term to cover at least two different doctrines which logically do not involve each other—the one, a theological proposition which denies the existence of god or gods, as well as divine creation or governance of the world; the second, a theory of personality or human value. In the strict sense, many people can be atheistic without ceasing to be religious. In fact, there are religions which are atheistic. Unfortunately, M. Maritain employs the term "atheism" in such a variety of contexts that it is difficult to find what common nucleus of meaning he gives it. It often serves as an epithet of denunciation rather than of description. Sometimes it means disbelief in the Gods of Catholicism, sometimes disbelief in any gods, sometimes devil worship, or irreligion, or anti-personalism, or just plain immorality.

Where M. Maritain discusses atheism as a doctrine which denies the existence of God, his procedure is very illuminating. He does not attempt to prove the existence of God although we may suspect he accepts the Thomistic proofs, all of which are logically invalid. Instead, he tries to demonstrate the horrible practical consequences of atheism. Atheism is false because consistently lived, it must lead to suicide. "It is not by accident, it is by a strictly necessary effect, written in the nature of things, that every absolute experience of atheism, if it is conscientiously and rigorously followed, ends by provoking its psychical dissolution, in suicide (*True Humanism*, p. 53).

Even *if* it were a practical consequence of atheism, it would not prove that atheism is false. But why does M. Maritain insist that consistent atheism leads "by a strictly necessary effect" to suicide? M. Maritain's reasoning is so shockingly bad that it is hard to account for it even in the interests of apologetics. He takes over, literally and completely, the argument of the mad Kirillov in Dostoevski's *The Possessed*. "If God exists all things depend on him and I can do nothing outside his will. If he does not exist, all depends on me and I am bound to display my independence. . . . For three years I have been seeking for the attribute of my divinity and I've found it; the attribute of my divinity is independence. . . . I shall kill myself to prove my independence and my new terrible freedom." Dostoevski, even without benefit of St. Thomas Aquinas, is credited with the profound metaphysical insight that one must believe either that God exists or that one is himself God. If God doesn't exist, then I must be God, and if I am God, I can only prove it by committing suicide.

It is hard to take this with a straight face but it would be discourteous to M. Maritain's high seriousness to take it otherwise. Very well, then. If God does not exist, it does *not* follow in the least that everything depends on me. Why should the only alternative to belief in a myth be a form of romantic madness? Even if God does not exist, I am still dependent in many ways upon other things and other people who do not depend for their existence upon me. If to exist means to be dependent upon something, it still does not follow that I must be dependent upon God. If to exist means to be independent of some things in some respects, it does not follow that I must be independent of all other things in all other respects, that I must be "absolutely independent," whatever that may mean. And if the absolute independence of Kirillov demands that he commit suicide, then the absolute independence of a Divine Power demands that, analogically understood, it, too, commit suicide.

The whole reference to Dostoevski is unfortunate, and on more grounds than one. The intellectual pattern of Dostoevski's reactionary genius, although softened by pity, is not compromised, as in M. Maritain, by doctrinally unmotivated gestures towards liberalism and democracy. And his psychological insight penetrates even more deeply than M. Maritain realizes into the sophistic compulsions of those who desire to find logical reasons for beliefs based upon arbitrary faith. The sophism, whose conclusion is that atheism entails suicide, which M. Maritain borrows from Kirillov, Dostoevski puts into the mouth of a madman. The more plausible sophism that belief in an omnipotent and benevolent God leads to self-destruction in a world of evil, Dostoevski puts into the mouth of Ivan Karamazov, the most powerful intelligence among his characters. Ivan is a believer whose Euclidean understanding cannot grasp the reason why the innocent should suffer in a world created by an omnipotent and benevolent God. As he explodes every justification theologians have advanced for the existence of evil, he concludes, "It's not God that I don't accept, Alyosha, only I most respectfully return Him the ticket." Neither the sophism of Kirillov nor the sophism of Karamazov has any place in a discussion of the arguments for God's existence.

The problem of evil does not exist for naturalists. Nor for those Marxists who are genuine naturalists and not believers in a benevolent *Natur-Dialektik*. When M. Maritain reproaches Marxism for its atheism, he therefore shifts to another alleged consequence of disbelief in the existence of God, viz., its atheistic conception of man and human nature.

The "atheistic" conception of man is regarded as profoundly inhuman because it views him as a natural and social creature but not as a personal one. It sacrifices man to "the monism of collective life" which bestows prosperity upon him only after it has deprived him of essential dignity. Marxist humanism, according to M. Maritain, operates with a philosophy of the human being as tropistically determined by constant biological needs and varying historical ones. From that philosophy we can never derive the sense of human self-respect and human freedom which are central to Catholic integral humanism.

M. Maritain will probably be surprised to learn that it is in the name of that very human dignity and independence, which *he* treats as spiritual abstractions, that Marx rejects not only liberal capitalism but Catholicism. M. Maritain has had his forerunners—the great Lamennais who towers above him as well as a whole flock of petty German consistorial councilors who lack his subtlety. On one of the occasions when the latter urged the working classes to unite with Church and Throne against the liberal bourgeoisie, Marx reviewed briefly those "social principles of Christianity" which had taken eighteen centuries to develop.

"The social principles of Christianity justified the slavery of classical days; they glorified medieval serfdom; [8] and, when necessary, understand how to defend the oppression of the proletariat. The social principles of Christianity proclaim the necessity for the existence of a ruling class and an oppressed class, and remain content with the pious wish that the former will deal charitably with the latter. The social principles of Christianity assume that there will be a consistorial compensation in heaven for all the infamies committed on earth, and therewith justify the continuance of these infamies. The social principles of Christianity explain that the contemptible practices of the oppressors against the oppressed are either just punishments for original sins and other sins, or trials which the Lord in his infinite wisdom has ordained for the redeemed. The social principles of Christianity preach cowardice, self-contempt, abasement, submission, humility, in short all the qualities of the canaille; and the proletariat, which will not allow itself to be treated as canaille, needs courage, self-respect, pride and sense of personal dignity even more than its bread. The social principles of Christianity are mealy mouthed; those of the proletariat are revolutionary." (*Gesamtausgabe,* Abt. I, Bd. 6, p. 278.)

There is rhetoric in this, and a patent failure to appreciate the positive accomplishments of the Christian heretical movements. But here as elsewhere, Marx is concerned to defend human personality—its dignity and independence—against vulgar materialistic views, on the one hand, and authoritarian spiritualistic views, on the other. For Marx, man is not born

[8] This judgment is confirmed, in more sober language, by the distinguished medieval historian, G. G. Coulton, in his *Medieval Panorama* (1938): "The Church never fought against the *principle* of serfdom, any more than she had done against the principle of slavery under the Roman Empire" (p. 86).

with a "soul" or "human personality." He achieves it. Marx's social philosophy is an attempt to discover, and to help to bring into existence, the social, cultural and educational conditions under which all men and women may develop significant human personalities. M. Maritain's belief in a "personality" which can exist independently of physical, biological, historical and cultural conditions is a consequence of a bad psychology and still worse metaphysics.

M. Maritain is right in asserting that Marx's critique of religion is the basis of Marx's entire philosophical approach. He is wrong in identifying that critique of religion with atheism. He fails to understand in what way Marx's critique of religion is the basis of all his other critiques. There is one clue to Marx's anti-religious position which M. Maritain, together with others of even greater acuity of social perception, has not read properly. We know that Marx was continuously charging that avowed atheists like Bruno Bauer and Max Stirner had not liberated themselves from religious dogmas. He takes Feuerbach to task for the same reason although he regarded him more highly than any of the Young-Hegelians. Why?

The answer is that for Marx the essence of the religious attitude is to be found in the *method of hypostasis* no matter what the objects hypostatized are. For Marx any introduction of *abstractions*, whose origin and reference are allegedly transcendental rather than historical, and which are presumably tested by intuition rather than by their functional use in concrete experiential situations, is religious. Literally it is super-naturalism. Marx's critical method is *scientific method* used to disclose those problems and interests of men which are concealed by the introduction of unanalyzable abstractions. He is always asking: What is the earthly and empirical basis for unearthly and non-empirical dogmas? In the abstractions of theology, he finds a fetishism of words which conceals specific historical and organizational needs. In the abstractions of jurisprudence, he finds a fetishism of principles which conceals the genuine power distributions in society. In the abstractions of economics, he finds a fetishism of commodities which conceals the fact that men today are controlled by the very forces of production which they themselves create. Each set of abstractions is accompanied by a set of practices. Since these abstractions are non-empirical and non-historical, the only meaning that can be assigned to them is in terms of these very practices. Wherever abstractions are worshiped, whether it be in theology, politics or physics, the task of scientific (materialistic) method is to locate the concrete situation in which they were first introduced, to observe the practices (Praxis) which they set up, and their subsequent career in estopping more fruitful modes of procedure in similar situations.

It is in Marx's scientific critique of abstractions that his irreligion lies and not in the village atheism with which it is often confused by many Marxists and most non-Marxists alike. This critique of abstractions constitutes the gravest challenge to M. Maritain's philosophy and theology. For it cuts all dogmas at their root, especially those based on what is called analogical knowledge of proportionality, and reveals them as the conceptual instruments of systematically cultivated *obscurantism*.

Take, for example, the dogma of divine creation, so necessary for M. Maritain's theology. To create is a natural and historical process and in its usual sense implies either an end or an intent or both. When we say that an individual creates, we mean that it is an act in time, upon material which antecedes the action, by means of instruments which are at hand in a given place even though they may have been previously created. For M. Maritain, God creates the world together with the antecedent material and the instruments of creation. How is this creation to be understood? Not metaphorically but analogically. The metaphorical sense of creation is obviously derived from the activity of men as when we speak of the "creative gusts of spring," (or of "smiling skies" derived from "smiling men"). The analogical concept of creation as applied to God, however, has a meaning which in *principle* is not derived from, or reducible to, the creative activities of men. Nor are *divine* creation and *human* creation two different modes of creation, for in that case "creation" as a term would have a univocal, not an analogous meaning, and what is in question here is the analysis of the term "creation," rather than the term "divine" whose meaning has difficulties of its own.

Strictly speaking, we cannot predicate properties of God

whose meanings are derived from human activity, without sub-
jecting him to the same empirical tests as we apply to creatures
of space and time. If we do this, God is anthropomorphized and
all statements about him become false. If we do not do this,
there is no possible way by which statements about God can be
tested, and they become meaningless. It is in order to escape
the dilemma between uttering false or meaningless statements
about God, that the analogy of proportionality is introduced,
since it enables theologians to say that our knowledge of him
is "inadequate." But this is no help, for if the concept "inadequate" is taken literally, the position is self-contradictory since
it presupposes some true knowledge of God; and if it is taken
analogically, the entire position is begged.

For Marx the function of intelligent analysis of creation or
of any other abstraction is to put an end to mystery: for M.
Maritain it is to prepare the mind to accept mystery. From
mystery to miracle is one step, and from miracle to authority
another. And if we recall that for M. Maritain our analogical
knowledge of God, for all its inadequacy and limitation, is
more reliable than *any* other knowledge we have, more certain
even than our knowledge of "the beating of our own hearts,"
the true measure of his denigration of scientific method becomes
apparent.

5. *Appendix: A Comment and Rejoinder*

In what I take to be a reply to one point in the foregoing,
M. Maritain has responded with the following words:

"A critic blinded by many resentments reproached me with having
spoken of England and of France as two ancient Christian countries
and with having recalled that the force which created Europe has its
purest sources in the Gospel, whereas in several of my earlier books
I condemned the inhumanity of modern capitalism. . . . Where has he
ever seen me confuse with the capitalist system two nations whose
heritage of culture took shape long before the advent of that system?"
("Ten Months Later," *The Commonweal*, June 21, 1940.)

M. Maritain has failed signally to grasp the point at issue.
It is not his defense of the democratic cause in the present
war to which I objected. Nor to the historical accuracy of the
reference to England and France as "ancient Christian lands."

I did and do object to the reasons he gives for supporting their cause, for reverting to the fact that they are ancient Christian countries whereas up to the outbreak of the war, he criticized them for violating the principles of "true humanism," if anything, even more severely than he did Italy, Germany, and Russia. That England and France are ancient Christian countries is as undeniable as it is irrelevant to the present conflict. After all, are not Italy and Germany also ancient Christian countries whose heritage of culture took shape long before the advent of the capitalist system? If England and the France which has not surrendered, are fighting in behalf of the heritage of *Christian* culture, and if Italy and Germany are fighting against it, then why have the Catholic Church of Italy and Germany blessed the anti-Christian arms of the *Duce* and the *Fuehrer?* And this with the benefit of M. Maritain's protective understanding!

The truth is that Italy and Germany are waging a cultural and political counter-revolution against the ideals of the French Revolution which even in their imperfect forms were still actualized in England and pre-Petain France. In behalf of a different conception of order, M. Maritain is also opposed to the ideals of the French Enlightenment and Revolution, not to speak of the Reformation. It is the conjunction of these ideals with the development of modern capitalism, he maintains, which has debauched the ethos of Christianity. The theological *parti pris* that lurks behind M. Maritain's position is apparent from the fact that even now, in his rejoinder, he links *Luther* with Hitler, and asserts that the German people cannot be free unless they liberate themselves from the incubus of both.

As one who believes that it is the duty of every liberal, progressive and socialist to support the capitalist democracies in their struggle against Hitlerism, I deplore the effort to provide a theological motivation for such support, on the ground that it is ill-conceived in theory and divisive in practice. A far more adequate and unifying justification is that a victory over Hitler offers at least an opportunity, if democratic political forms are preserved (a difficult but not insuperable task), to bring our other institutions more and more into line with the promise of the great American Dream. The ideals of the American Dream are still substantially identical with those of the

French Revolution. Both presuppose a type of secularism to which M. Maritain is hostile.

Criticism of the effects of capitalism upon the material, cultural, and psychological life of the great masses is not incompatible with a valiant, even heroic, desire to conserve and extend whatever is genuinely democratic in the faith and works of Western culture. In supporting the life and death struggle of England (which is America's struggle, too) against Hitlerism, I do not see, therefore, that I am committed to an endorsement of whatever economic and social practices prevail at the moment in that country. Nor am I committed to a belief in the declaration made some time ago by a pious but uncritical supporter of England: "The British Commonwealth is the flower of justice and liberty. It is the product of the Bible, not the bayonet." Great Britain *is* a capitalist country. It *is* an imperialistic empire. But it is also a political democracy and all that that implies. The prospect of preserving what it has, its wide variety of freedom, is sufficient to justify coming to its support, without rhetorical phrasemongery, theological or otherwise. The further prospect of checking the spread of Fascism, and in the course and consequence of that struggle extending democracy to other phases of its life and to all its lands, should inspire democratic socialists, as it has the English Labour Party, to seek the leadership in the struggle.

This policy may fail. But before it is condemned, critics should formulate a realistic and practical alternative.[9]

9 For further elaboration of these points, Cf. my "Is Nazism a Social Revolution?" and "Socialism, Commonsense and the War" in the *New Leader*, July 20 and Sept. 2, 1940.

CHAPTER SEVEN

WHAT IS LIVING AND DEAD
IN MARXISM

OF MARXISM AS of Christianity it is easy to say that it has never been tried. There is some justification in speaking of Christianity in this fashion because, literally interpreted, it can never be applied. But by its own proud profession, Marxism is not merely a set of ideas but the theoretical expression and guide of an historical movement. Its validity can be tested only in historical practice. If events pass it by, that is to say, neither confirm nor invalidate it, one may still appeal to the pristine integrity of doctrines which, because they have never been understood, have never been acted upon. Such an appeal, however, is tantamount to a confession that these doctrines are historically irrelevant. And it is a good Marxian dictum that what is irrelevant for purposes of historical understanding and action is historically meaningless. For Marxism as the theory and practice of achieving socialism is not chiefly a method of reading history but of making it.

1. *The Crisis of Marxism*

The debacle of Marxist movements throughout the world may be only temporary. But at present their eclipse is almost complete. The "bankruptcy," "collapse," "degeneration" of Marxism is the theme of innumerable articles and books, Even its "autopsy" has already been written, albeit prematurely. By itself the vogue of this critical literature testifies little concerning the actual state of affairs. From one point of view it indicates that Marxist theory, like every doctrine so often declared dead but which must be buried again and again, has considerable vitality.

More impressive evidence of the debacle of Marxism is to be

derived from a direct examination of the dwindling influence of Marxist movements on contemporary social and political affairs. Such a survey will show that more than material power and strategic position have been lost. Confidence in the ideals of socialism has been undermined in quarters which had taken their validity for granted. For the first time in a century the Marxist movement in every country of the world seems to have lost that sense of direction and assurance which had sustained it in previous crises. Articles of faith and doctrine have been abandoned in a precipitate scramble for slogans and formulae that will work for a day, a week, or a month.

History itself has turned out to be the most deadly revisionist of Marxist theory and practice. Illusions which were already hoary in the time of Marx have been refurbished and set up as guides to political practice. The Stalinists, who have long since betrayed the ideals of socialism, still call themselves Marxists, just as in the past many groups that surrendered their Christianity still insisted that they were Catholics. Others, proud of their orthodoxy, are compelled to say as they run from the brutal blows of reaction, that it is all happening according to the principles of Marxism. Win or lose, their doctrines are right. Every defeat is an additional confirmation. "Events did not catch us unawares," writes Trotsky, "it is necessary only to interpret them properly."

The current moods of wholesale denial and skepticism are no more illuminating than uncritical reaffirmations. Those who in blind fury destroy the altars of the gods who have forsaken them are just as religious as the devotees who still remain rapt in their worshipful ignorance. They will find other idols and other Churches. They will not assay for themselves what is valid and invalid in the doctrines of Marxism for fear of discovering that what they have treasured is fool's gold.

In this chapter I wish to inquire into those doctrinal aspects of contemporary Marxist movements which seem definitely invalidated, and those aspects of the Marxist tradition, broadly conceived, which may still be integrated into a sound synthesis. Whether such a synthesis is *called* Marxist or not, is immaterial, as is the question whether it is "what Marx really meant."

2.   Science, Ideals, and Scientific Method

Everyone is acquainted with the proud boast of Marxism that it alone is "scientific socialism." Whatever the limitations of its conception of science, there is no questioning the *desire* of Marxists to be scientific, i.e., to base their judgment and action on verifiable evidence about the nature of man and the world. Scientific knowledge and valid knowledge were synonymous in Marxist literature. No popular movement ever surpassed Marxism in the intensity of its verbal appreciation of science both as a cultural force and as a basis upon which to project a philosophy of life.

The limitations of the orthodox Marxist conception of science were threefold—historical, analytic and functional. What it meant for anything to be a science was determined by the nineteenth century formulations of Engels which were already antiquated at the time he penned them. It was a deistic view of the world without Deity in which terms like infinity, necessity, universality were used in emotionally free but intellectually unprecise ways. The conclusions of science were celebrated but its methods hardly studied. And sometimes even these conclusions, as in anthropology and biology, became intellectual fixtures of the Marxist mind despite their untenability in the light of new scientific advances.

Analytically, the limitations of the orthodox Marxist view of science flowed from its lack of methodological clarity. It would assert: "Marxism is not a dogma" but it never made clear what the difference was between a dogma and an hypothesis. It looked to experience, but only to confirm Marxist pronouncements, not to test them. We search in vain in the canonic writings of the pre-war or post-war periods for any indication as to what empirical evidence Marxists were prepared to accept as constituting even a possible refutation of their doctrines. Yet without a clear conception of what would constitute a possible refutation of any particular view, we are without a clear conception of what would possibly constitute a confirmation. No adequate distinctions were drawn between what might be, what would be, what must be, even what we would like to be. "Cause," "condition," "occasion" were used interchangeably. The economic factor, usually undefined, was declared "fundamental," in an uninterpreted sense, in a "last analysis" or "long run" which remained unanalyzed.

The functional drawback of the Marxist conception of science was the most fateful of all its limitations, for it prevented Marxists from making clear to themselves the relation between their goals, the whole cluster of socialist ideals, and the means by which these goals were to be furthered. It is untrue to say that Marxists were not conscious of their socialist ideals or that they explicitly identified them with whatever the historical process brought forth. Before the first World War, the propaganda of the Marxist movement was infused with moral passion and idealism. It is true to say that with the coming of the Bolsheviks these ideals were taken for granted and policies were checked, when they were checked at all, by their bearing only on the conquest of power, and not in the light of the socialist ideals by which power was to be justified. For Lenin the proletarian power was its own justification. Whether the state power *in fact* was proletarian, needed no further proof in his eyes other than his own consciousness that he and his party "expressed" the "real" needs of the proletariat. If he had any doubts he settled them with the same decrees with which he silenced opposition parties.

Thinking back· more than twenty years to American pre-war days, I recall the distinction which even youngsters in the socialist movement made (so invariably as to seem almost a stock response), between government ownership and socialism. The novice who defined socialism as *government ownership* of all means of production, distribution and exchange would be carefully corrected. The post office and water works were government owned; even if the whole economy were organized and owned by the government, it would be a far cry from socialism. Socialism, we used to say, was collective ownership and *democratic control* of the basic means of production. Perhaps the influence of the I.W.W. with its exaggerated distrust of the state was reflected in this attitude; but whatever the causes of our belief, the ideals of personal and cultural freedom, of social and educational democracy, were considered as integral to socialism.

The ideals, then, were there; but not the habit of taking bearings by them or the courage to revise them in the light of what Marxists found themselves actually doing. Despite their vaunted scientific philosophy, Marxists never scrutinized their professed goals in terms of the programs and methods which they claimed the situation exacted from them, never criticized their ends-in-view by the consequences of their means in action. No matter what they did, no matter what the consequences of their doing, socialism was a valid ideal which would be somehow and sometime realized. The ideal of socialism, therefore, functioned as an absolute, as something that could always be saved despite the appearances. At most Marxists were scientific about means toward limited objectives, never about ultimate ends, and yet their own *theory* stressed the interrelatedness of ends and means.

This fear of revising their ideals—a revision which is a natural phase of the process of understanding and criticizing them by consequences in action—led, on the one hand, to a terminological fetishism, and, on the other, to a vicious, because unacknowledged, revision of socialist ideals in practice. Socialism could not be touched, harmed or discredited no matter what Marxists did or how historical events turned out. It fulfilled all the qualities of a dream.

Human beings will always dream. Dreams have their consolations, and sometimes, like religions, they may express edifying fairy tales. But to mistake a dream for a sober hypothesis about existence and history is madness. What is still living in Marxism, or more accurately, what can be brought to life in the thinking of Marxists, is the tradition of scientific criticism of all social dreams, so that the wishes behind them can be adjudged reasonable or unreasonable in the light of their contexts, and the possibilities and costs of achieving them. It is only then that dreams become ideals.

How much of traditional Marxism will remain after it is scientifically purged, cannot be foretold in advance. Even if everything cannot be saved, it is unlikely that nothing can be used. For psychological and historical reasons it may be necessary to discard the word "Marxism" as an identifying term.

3. *Critique of Capitalism*

The perennial source of strength of all socialist movements is the inequities and inequalities of capitalist economy. By themselves, poverty, insecurity, unemployment, war, and their cultural effects do not constitute an argument *for* socialism, for there is always the abstract possibility that as bad as capitalism is, socialism may be even worse. But they are a compelling argument to look for something better, and insofar as Marxists can demonstrate that no fundamental improvement in these respects is possible under capitalism, they constitute the most powerful of all arguments *against* capitalism.

Stripped of the metaphysics of its value theory, the Marxian critique of capitalist economy still retains its validity. It is economically impossible for capitalist production under existing social and technological conditions to guarantee profits, employment, and an adequate standard of living for the working population, where "adequate" is not taken absolutely but relatively to the potential resources of wealth that are either not utilized or destroyed.

All proposals to effect recovery under capitalism turn out to be variations of three main lines of action—all of them sooner or later bound to fail, according to Marxist theory, because they cannot insure a profitable return on capital investment which is the only inducement to new investment.

a. Increases in prices relative to wages. This may re-establish profits in certain industries for a limited period. But before long a decline in the purchasing power of the consumers results in overproduction and depression. A decrease in wages relative to prices has the same effect.

b. Increase in wages relative to prices. This cuts the rate of profit to a point where there is no inducement to continued production. It also intensifies the quest for labor-saving devices in order to reduce costs, resulting in a higher incidence of technological unemployment. An increase of prices relative to wages likewise increases costs and reduces profits. An increase or decrease of both wages and profits cancel each other out.

c. Government spending on a large scale with no extensive regulation of prices or wages. This leads either to inflation or to increase in taxation which cuts profit and discourages new investment.

From this it by no means follows that capitalism is doomed to an automatic economic collapse. It can stagger along from crisis to crisis, "solving" its difficulties by destruction of materials, restriction of production, armament economics, and as a last resort, by war. The whole concept of "breakdown" is a mechanical and inept analogy. The transition from capitalism to another form of society, if it is made, is a *political* act, although not only a political act. This is recognized *on paper* by almost all Marxists. Were it taken seriously, it would follow that political prognosis could not be conceived as a corollary or addendum to an economic analysis. In actuality, however, instead of honestly facing the difficulties of political prognosis, and scientifically mastering as many of the relevant elements which time and the exigencies of intelligent action permit, stubborn intellectual habits persist. The future is read off on the basis of a simplistic economic monism. No matter how stormy the political weather, we are comforted with the assurance that some day all will be peace, plenty and freedom.

4. *Theory of the State*

Despite elements of exaggeration, and Utopian belief in its eventual disappearance, the Marxian theory of the state is fundamentally empirical. Many followers of Marx have attempted "to prove" that the state is an instrument of the ruling class by *definition;* but in the writings of Marx, this proposition appears as a generalization of analyses made of the specific activities of legislative bodies, courts and the executive arm. Where there are conflicting interests, and where the regulation and the adjudication of these disputes are obviously the concern of the state power, it is legitimate to inquire in whose interests the state acts. And in principle, a determinate answer to such an inquiry can always be given.

Unfortunately, empirical analyses of state activity have rarely been undertaken. At best they can only yield answers of *degree* for various historical periods. Conclusions to the effect that the state "for the most part" or "in the main" serves as an instrument of the dominant class have little propaganda value. More important, they are formally irrelevant to the question of whether the state *here* and *now* and in respect to *this* proposal will act to further or frustrate the interests of a particular class.

Where Marxists have made a beginning at empirical analyses, their work has usually suffered from a threefold defect. They have often assumed, even when they have disclaimed doing so, that it is *only* economic interests which determine state activity; they consequently either discounted the influence of religious, racial, and sectional interests, or interpreted the latter as *mere* disguises of economic interests. Their conception of what constitutes a class has been so vague that no matter what the evidence, it could be claimed as a vindication of their thesis. Thus, if the farmers by high-pressuring the legislators, gained their point at the expense of the city consumer, or if one group of industrialists lost their advantage to another group by repeal of some discriminatory legislation, or if a government service or tax policy adversely affected a private monopoly, or if a Labor Relations act, helpful to workers, was adopted in the teeth of organized opposition by employers—all this would be taken as confirmation of the view that the state was an instrument of *the* dominant class. In these cases, it is explained, the "ruling class" yielded to pressure in order to escape more drastic demands being made upon it. But the fact that the "ruling class" could be made to yield is just as significant in understanding the nature of the state as its reasons for yielding. The third and crassest error was to assume that in a collectivized economy, differences in economic interests would disappear and therewith the necessity for any state power. This was more than a monstrous piece of question-begging. It estopped thought precisely at the point where it was most urgent, i.e., in relation to the question of how liberties and rights, which historically had developed with an unplanned capitalism, were to be preserved and extended in a planned collective economy.

Underlying all these errors was a momentous confusion between what may be called the *substantial* conception of the state and the *functional*. According to the latter, the state is what it does, and in any definite period, what it usually does gives it its class character. According to the former conception, the state consists of a set of institutions whose *essential* nature is class-determined even when it expresses this nature in the most varied ways. The legislature, the courts, the army, police and militia *cannot* change their nature by functioning differently or for different purposes. Now, historically, Marx may have been justified in asserting that in a given situation in a given country the state institutions, in virtue of their traditions and personnel, could not function to achieve socialist purposes, and that the workers and their allies, therefore, could not rest with capturing the state machinery but had to destroy it. But Lenin converted the conclusion of a specific analysis into a dogma and asserted that by its very nature, the existing state could never under any circumstances change its nature by new uses and new functions. He *defined* the state in such a way as to preclude this possibility. The result was that the road to power everywhere and everytime, in advance of specific historical situations and empirical analyses, was declared to be the road of dual power. This was a command concealed as a description or prediction. The slogan *Soviets partout!* became universal, and the enormous advantage in democratic countries of winning and using Parliaments in order to transform them into the instruments of socialist ideals and purposes was not even considered. Instead Parliaments were regarded as mere sounding boards from which to proclaim to the community their complete futility—a sentiment enthusiastically acclaimed also by Nazis and Fascists.

The confusion on this point was obscured by the completely independent question of whether the transition to socialism could be achieved peacefully. From Marx's point of view, it might be achieved peacefully; but peacefully or not, always democratically. According to Lenin's revision of Marx, the transition to socialism *cannot* be achieved either democratically or peacefully.

5. *The Party as Instrument*

Socialism is not inevitable. It is something to be accomplished when objective conditions are ripe. But how? By men and not by economic forces. Men may accomplish this spontaneously and with only a dim consciousness of what they are doing, or deliberately and through organization. The only form of organized political action we know is the action of a political party, a fact which is not altered by speaking of political "groups" or "associations." The character and functions of a political party are such that, if there are genuine alternatives of action, and there usually are, ideals may be perverted and instruments may corrupt ends. Nonetheless, to rely upon the spontaneous action of the masses, as a substitute procedure, in the hope of achieving the desirable features of political action without the risks of political bureaucracy, is unintelligent. Belief in the spontaneous and sustained wisdom of the masses is the sheerest mysticism. History is not like a gigantic roulette wheel which can be put into motion again and again until the favored number is drawn. Nor is it, as most believers in spontaneity hold, the unfolding of a benevolent cosmic dialectic.

For good or for evil, then, to the extent that social revolutions are political revolutions, they are organized by political parties. It speaks well for the scientific *intent* of Marxism that concern with the nature of the instrument—the political party —by which the socialist movement is to be led, has always been in the forefront of theoretical discussion. I say scientific *intent* because, here as elsewhere, the scientific analysis was cut short whenever conclusions emerged whose implications seemed to threaten the ends in behalf of which the party as a political instrument was to be used. Differences concerning the conception of the socialist party, its relation to the class, and its vocation of leadership proved to be the most *fateful* of all the causes of the Russian Thermidor.[1] The party was conceived only as instrument by which political power could be won, not as an instrument by which socialism could be achieved.

Despite its concern with organizational questions, the Marxist movement, particularly its most militant wing, showed itself singularly unaware of the far-reaching dangers to a democratically functioning socialism in the conception of a party of professional revolutionists. Its eye was fixed on the problem of how power could as soon as possible be wrested from those who had it, and not on the consequences to socialism of a view according to which a minority political party constitutes, by its

[1] *Cf.* below, the chapter on "Reflections on the Russian Revolution."

own edicts, the vanguard of a class which in turn "expresses" the interests of humanity. The warnings of the syndicalists and the anarchists, the profound arguments of Mosca, Pareto, and Michels before the Russian Revolution, the criticisms of Martov, Rosa Luxemburg and others after—were all disregarded. There is no more eloquent testimony of the practical ruthlessness and theoretical naïveté of Lenin than his reply to those dissident communists who warned against the cult of political leadership which was involved in the Bolshevik substitution of the dictatorship of the party for working-class democracy. "The mere presentation of the question," he says, "[of] 'dictatorship of the Party *or* the dictatorship of the class' is . . . childishness . . . evidence of the most incredible and hopeless confusion of mind." To contrast the dictatorship of leaders and the dictatorship of the masses, he adds, "is ridiculously absurd and stupid." It is worse. It is "repudiation of the Party principle and Party discipline . . . *for the benefit of the bourgeoisie*. It is to carry out the work of the agent-provocateur." [2] His discussion never even reached the level of an argument.

Lenin's naïveté was the reflection of his inability to imagine that *his* conception of the best interests of the workers could ever in fact be different from what their best interests actually were. His indignation was a reaction to a criticism which in virtue of his naïve Messianic faith, he could not interpret otherwise than as an attack upon *his* personal integrity. Stalin was the price that Lenin paid for this naïveté. And if we recall one of Lenin's own favorite maxims: "A political leader is not only responsible for the way he leads but also for what is done by those he leads," Lenin's responsibility for Stalin is absolute. Given this naïveté, it was perfectly natural for Lenin to charge that the Workers' Opposition which fought for more democracy *within* the Soviets was trying to overthrow the Soviet Power. It was perfectly natural for Lenin to hold that anyone who deviated from the consistent communist line (as *he* interpreted it), must end up as a Kronstadt mutineer, and that every Kronstadt mutineer, a "hero of the Revolution," when he aided the Bolsheviks, was now *malgré lui* a White Guardist. [3]

2 *Selected Works*, Vol. X, Eng. ed., pp. 80 ff. Italics in original.
3 *Op. cit.*, Vol. IX, pp. 105, 121, 131-2.

A final illustration of this simple-minded infamy will show the lengths to which Lenin was prepared to go. After the New Economic Policy had been introduced into Russia, Otto Bauer, one of the leading theoreticians of Western Social-Democracy, and a stanch opponent of any intervention into Russian affairs, wrote, "They are now retreating to capitalism; we have always said that the revolution is a bourgeois revolution." At which Lenin indignantly exclaims: "And the Mensheviks and Social-Revolutionaries, all of whom preach this sort of thing, are astonished when we say that *we will shoot those who say such things*." [4] One does not know whether to be more repelled by the actual murder of his working-class opponents because of their opinions than by the self-righteousness with which Lenin carried it out.

The alternative to the Leninist conception of the political party is not the traditional Social-Democratic conception. The latter assumed that a party dedicated to the heroic task of transforming existing society could succeed with the same organizational forms, the same leisure-time holiday effort, the same evaluation of electoral gains, which characterized capitalist parties for whom politics was, by and large, a business. The genuine alternative to the Leninist conception of the political party is a party not less disciplined but more flexibly disciplined in virtue of a better grasp of both scientific method and the democratic process. Its task will be to guide, and not to dictate, the organized struggle for socialism in such a way that "the conquest of power" becomes a phase in the unfolding of democratic institutions and tendencies already present in the community. It recognizes and respects the relative autonomy of the arts and sciences from politics, and thus avoids both the horror and foolishness of a "party line" in anything but politics. It is built around principles and not a cult of leadership. Its perspective is neither one of blood and thunder nor of milk and water. It must yield to none in realism which means nothing more than applied intelligence. It therefore will have no doctrinal dogmas, acceptance of which is a prerequisite of membership. Its confidence will extend to a point where it is prepared to take account of the dangers and obstacles which its

4 *Op. cit.,* Vol. IX, p. 842, my italics.

own organized activities may create, even with the best of intentions, to the successful consummation of socialism.

6. *The Anatomy of Revolution*

Such a conception of the political party must face at least
two severe criticisms. One is drawn from the alleged laws of
social revolution according to which revolutions cannot be won
except by a monolithic party which strives for a monopoly of
political power. The other is drawn from another set of alleged laws, psychological and historical, according to which
socialists (democrats) can be victorious, but socialism (democracy) never. We shall consider the first objection in this section, and the second in the subsequent one.

The difficulty of contending that there are "laws of social
revolution" lies in the ambiguity of the key terms and, once
they are univocally defined, in the indecisive character of the
evidence that they actually obtain. To begin with, the denial
that we possess verifiable laws of social revolution must not be
taken to assert that social revolutions are uncaused. There may
be a multiplicity of causes of such complexity that we cannot
reduce them to general statements about invariable relationships between events. Moreover, what do we really understand
by a "social revolution"? In the strict Marxist sense, a social
revolution is a change in property relationships in the mode of
economic production. Most discussions of social revolution,
however, include political revolutions which do not involve
changes in property relations. Even Marxists refer to the Paris
Commune as an attempted social revolution although it made
no effort to introduce socialism.

Professor Brinton in his *Anatomy of Revolution* tries to cut
the Gordian knot of definition by saying that "since the movements with which we are concerned are commonly called revolutions, they may be so called once more." The only, but fatal,
difficulty in this approach is that our choice of specimens is so
wide that we can easily make a selection which would reveal
quite a different set of simple uniformities from those Professor
Brinton derives. If we take a functional approach to the question of property, i.e., in terms of actual control rather than
paper decree, then the Fascist and Nazi revolutions must also

be regarded as social revolutions. The German and Italian (and Russian) bureaucracies own the instruments of production in a more absolute fashion than the bourgeoisie in any capitalist democracy. These two revolutions fall outside the purview of Professor Brinton's survey and are rarely considered by Marxists as a test of their laws of social revolution. It is questionable whether any "law" according to which revolutions can be won only by a monolithic political party striving for a monopoly of political power, can be established except for illustrations already selected to conform to this "law."

Interestingly enough the Marxist conception of "historical laws" makes generalizations of this sort extremely risky. Marx does not deny that there are laws of production which hold for all epochs and without which production in any epoch is impossible. But he insists that "the conditions which generally govern production must be differentiated in order that the essential points of difference be not lost sight of in view of the general uniformity which is due to the fact that the subject, mankind, and the object, nature, remain the same." [5] These general laws of production do not tell us what the economic laws of slavery, or of feudalism, or of capitalism are. Similarly, even if there were laws of social revolution, it would not necessarily follow that the laws of capitalist revolution and the laws of socialist revolution would be the same. Nor, if there were laws of socialist revolution, need they necessarily take the same form in countries as different as France, Russia, China and the United States.

All this was ignored or overlooked by the Leninists. It can be easily demonstrated that they based their conception of how political power was to be won on their study of the French revolutions of 1789, 1848, and 1871 (the Commune), and the attempted bourgeois-democratic Russian Revolution of 1905. Professor Brinton errs grievously when he asserts that "the Bolsheviks do not seem to have guided their actions by the 'scientific' study of revolutions to an appreciably greater degree than the Independents (Cromwellians) or the Jacobins. They simply adapted an old technique to the days of the telegraph and the railroad train." As a matter of fact, all the leading ideas of the Bolsheviks were drawn from their fancied

---

[5] *Introd. to Critique of Political Economy*, Kerr ed., p. 269.

"scientific" study of previous *bourgeois* revolutions. To be
sure, there was the element of improvisation, including the public denial of their principles, and other Machiavellianisms. But
this, too, was provided for by their organizational theory. After they won, their theory became canonic doctrine for *all* parties of the Communist International. They were shrewd enough
to say on paper that since the conditions of the Russian Revolution could not be repeated elsewhere, there would be
corresponding differences in strategy and tactics in other
countries. But in fact the same tactical line, down to the very
details of slogans and phrasing, was always imposed at the
same time in all countries.

The success of the Bolsheviks by no means proved that their
theory was scientific. For they won power, not socialism. Even
if they had achieved socialism—an extremely unlikely event in
view of their methods—this would not have proved that their
methods could succeed elsewhere.

One further consideration, of no little importance, is overlooked by Leninists when they speak of the laws of revolution.
It is an oversight also committed by Professor Brinton in his
Anatomy of Revolution, a witty and readable book which shows
genuine insight into all questions concerning social revolutions
except the important ones. This is the influence of *knowledge*
of the theories guiding those who lead social revolutions upon
the methods by which such revolutions are combated. In no
country of the world where the Bolshevik theory of the conquest of power is known by their opponents are the Bolsheviks
likely to win again if they act on their theory. Present-day
Stalinists, of course, who are merely the border guards of the
Soviet Union, have no interest in winning power, except if and
when it becomes necessary to safeguard the Russian bureaucracy. But other species of Leninists are doomed to failure
precisely because of their unscientific disregard of the specific
factors in each historical situation and of their underestimation
of the historical effects of knowledge and ignorance.

7. *The Fetishism of Power*

The most powerful arguments against the possibility of
democratic socialism have been advanced in the writings of

Mosca, Pareto, Michels and Nomad.[6] These arguments are all the more impressive if we recall that they were formulated long before the rise of totalitarianisms, and in a period when social optimism was as general as pessimism is today. They carry, therefore, the additional weight of predictions that appear to have been at least partially confirmed. In the light of recent events, the position taken by these thinkers has been revived in many quarters. If it is sound, then the social philosophy of Marxism is a pernicious illusion, a variant of a Utopian dream which must cost mankind dear wherever an attempt is made to realize it.

Mosca's thesis is a simple one and recommends itself with a high initial plausibility to anyone who has had some political experience. It asserts that political power in actuality never rests upon the consent of the majority, that irrespective of ideologies or leading personalities, all political rule is a process, now peaceful, now coercive, by which a minority gratifies its own interests in a situation where not all interests can receive equal consideration. As Mosca puts it: "Political power always has been, and always will be, exercised by organized minorities, which have had, and will have, the means, varying as the times vary, to impose their supremacy upon the multitudes." In peaceful times, the means are public myths and legal frauds; in a crisis—force. Whichever side wins, the masses who have fought,.bled and starved, lose. Their "saviors" become their rulers under the prestige of new myths. The forms of mythology change but the essential content of minority control and exploitation remains. This is put forth by Mosca as a "law" of all social life which can be demonstrated to the satisfaction of everyone except the dull, the pious, and candidates for political leadership. It is a "law" accepted by every political partisan as obviously true for other organizations but as a slander when applied to his own.

Mosca's "law" appears in Pareto under the principle of "the circulation of the élite." Belief in the homogeneity of society is a fable for simpletons. According to Pareto, differences between groups, and conflicts between their interests, are always more pervasive than the harmonies which idealistic

6 Mosca, G., *The Ruling Classes;* Pareto, V., *Mind and Society,* esp. Vol. IV; Michels, R., *Political Parties;* Nomad, M., *Apostles of Revolution.*

philosophers discover, more often than not, by definition. Every society divides roughly into two classes—an élite which includes all who enjoy the fruits of recognized excellence in virtue of their strength, cunning, valor, wealth, social origin—the lions and the foxes—and a non-élite which comprises the rest of the population—the sheep. The élite in turn subdivide into a governing élite and a non-governing élite which mutually support each other. A governing élite, like the poor, we always have with us. Whenever its members lack qualities of vigor, will, discipline and *readiness to use force in an emergency*, new members are recruited from the non-élite, those who prove that they are not sheep after all. When this does not happen, the reins of power are torn from the hands of the ruling class by a revolution headed by a counter-élite. "History is the graveyard of aristocracies." But aristocracies there will always be. Power may be taken in the name of humanity, democracy and freedom. It can only be wielded by a few.

Michels reaches the same conclusion through considerations that are more empirical. Political power in behalf of any ideal, no matter how exalted, can be won only by organization. All organization, no matter how democratically conceived, inevitably involves the emergence of a leadership which in the last analysis controls the organization. If it is defeated it is replaced, not by a functioning democracy, but by a new leadership. All democratic movements, therefore, are self-defeating. They are doomed by "the iron law of oligarchy." According to this law "the majority of human beings, in a condition of eternal tutelage, are predestined by tragic necessity to submit to the domination of a small minority, and must be content to constitute the pedestal of an oligarchy."

In the interests of clear analysis we must distinguish between the descriptive generalizations of Mosca, Pareto and Michels concerning the actual uses and abuses of political power in the past and present, and the theoretical explanations they offer of them. As descriptive generalizations, their conclusions, after differences in the forms of political rule have been properly noted, are largely valid. It is true that every political organization is in effect run by a minority. It is true that vital lies, chicanery, and naked force have been almost always the three props of all political rule. It is true that all

successful mass movements—even with democratic ideologies—
have compromised some of their basic principles, sometimes all
of them. The history of Christianity, German Social-Democracy, and Russian Communism indicate in a dramatic and
focal way all this and more. But in explaining these phenomena and in predicting that the future *must* be always
like the past, Mosca falls back upon a psychological theory
of human nature as something given and fixed independently
of its social context. Almost every one of his major explanations and predictions involves an appeal to an original nature,
conceived as essentially unalterable despite its varying expressions. Mosca's antiquated terminology, has, and can be,
brought up to date by translation into the language of dynamic
psychology and psychoanalysis. But the controlling assumptions are the same. The laws of political power are frankly
characterized as psychological. They flow from unchangeable
elements in the nature of man. Mosca had no hesitation in
sometimes referring to them as "wicked instincts." It is from
this conception of original sin that his direst prophecies flow.

The same is true for Pareto, and in a lesser degree for
Michels. The whole significance of Pareto's doctrine of the
constancy of residues is summed up in the sentence: "The centuries roll by and human nature remains the same." Michels
weakens the force of his arguments, which are drawn from
the technical indispensability of all leadership in all political
organization, by deducing therefrom the conclusion that "the
majority is permanently incapable of (democratic) self-government." Even Crane Brinton, who is reluctant to state propositions in outmoded psychological terms, concludes his study
of revolutions with the remark that "in some very important
ways the behavior of men changes with a slowness almost
comparable to the kind of change the geologist studies." Instead of saying "human nature never changes," Brinton is
saying "almost never"! As far as historical understanding is
concerned, the qualification is not very significant.

The fact that the argument from human nature must be
invoked to support the sociological law that democratic socialism is impossible is *prima facie* evidence that the entire position
is *unhistorical*. If it is true that history without sociology is
blind, it is just as true that sociology without history is empty.

For the sake of the argument, everything Mosca and Pareto claim may be granted except when they speak in the future tense. The genuine problems of power are always *specific*, are always rooted in the *concrete needs* of a *particular* people at a *determinate* time. Any conclusion based on their finding (Michels is in a different category) about the futility of social struggle and revolution is a *non sequitur*. It betrays political animus, for to cultivate abstract suspicion of the excesses of all political power is often to encourage acceptance of the customary abuses of existing power. Insofar as the conclusion concerning the futility of revolution is grounded, it must be derived from other empirical, non-psychological, considerations. Michels provides some of these considerations but it is noteworthy that he does not base any counsel of inactivity or despair upon them.

The belief that there is an invariant core of properties which constitute the "essential" character of human nature, rests on gross data drawn from history and a faulty technique of definition. Habits, historical traditions, and social institutions play a much more important role in political behavior, and are more reliable in predicting the future than any set of native impulses, residues, instincts or urges. By isolating the latter from their objective cultural setting, selecting from among them an alleged impulse to dominate, to be selfish, to fight, love or flee, the pattern of human nature can be cut to suit any political myth. The whole conception has received its definitive refutation in John Dewey's *Human Nature and Conduct*.

8. *The Uses and Abuses of Power*

Despite the fact that "the laws" of Mosca, Pareto, and Michels, when presented in psychological dress, have no empirical warrant, they can be reformulated *with supporting historical evidence*. Stated in such a way, they bear relevantly on particular situations in which intelligent choice is possible between accepting a given form of political rule, with its known evils, and struggling for a new form of political rule, with its menace of new evils. In such situations, these "laws" function as guides or cautions to possible dangers that attend the transference of power from one group to another. The task then becomes one of devising safeguards—an occasion for experiment, not for lamentation. And most safeguards do not make accidents impossible, they make them less frequent or less fatal.

Sometimes the prospect of social gain by change in political power may be so small that in face of our knowledge of the dangers of social revolution, we can easily reconcile ourselves to our existing condition no matter how deplorable. For example, if all that can be said of the gains of the French and Russian Revolutions is, to cite Brinton's wry speculation, "that it took the French Revolution to produce the metric system and to destroy *lods et ventes* and similar feudal inconveniences, or the Russian Revolution to bring Russia to use the modern calendar and to eliminate a few useless letters in the Russian alphabet," then to undertake revolutions would be criminally stupid. But the gains of the revolutions, as Mr. Brinton well knows, were much more extensive. Whether they were worth the price is another question. Whether the price was necessary is still another. Whether we must *continue* paying the price, or even a higher one, is a third question.

These questions must always be posed in a specific context. The present context is one in which we must consider the price that *may* have to be paid by an attempt to achieve democratic socialism. To the Marxist, indeed, to any intelligent person, that question presupposes another: What is the price of the *status quo?* If that price is war, it is hard, but not impossible, to conceive of any loss of life, freedom and happiness attendant upon the abuse of power under socialism which will be worse than the losses suffered in a large-scale war. Further, we are now in a position to anticipate more adequately the probable sources of corruption and oppression under socialism, and to construct theoretical and institutional safeguards against them.

Without the consciousness of the dangers of a collectivized economy and the recognition of the necessity of establishing safeguards for freedom, criticism, personal independence, and all the other basic practices we associate with a functioning democracy, the case for socialism, it seems to me, is lost. For it would lead to another variant of Stalinism which costs too much no matter what its dubious gains. Russia under Stalin has lost many more dead than she lost in the World War under the Czar. No mass misery in her entire history, including the famines, begins to equal the distress and absolute political despotism which the Russian masses have endured in the last generation. As André Gide said, writing in the years before the great purges began, "In no country of the world . . . is thought less free, more bowed down, more fearful (terrorized), more vassalized."

We turn now to a brief survey of the dangers against which socialists must safeguard themselves. The first sphere of conflict and possible oppression in a socialist society—any socialist society—is the sphere of economic life. This may shock those uncritical socialists who believe that economic injustice is possible only under a system of private ownership of means of production. It is apparent, however, that under no system operated by finite creatures in a finite world can all men be equally served in everything. What is just as important, they cannot be equally served at once. Consequently there will be some differences in standards of living, no matter what level the productive forces of society will reach. To deny this is the veriest Utopianism. If Marx's dictum for a classless society be taken literally "From each according to his capacities, to each according to his needs," instead of as a guiding principle to reduce differences in living conditions (*while increasing their absolute minimum level*), it is a will o' the wisp. Differences there will always be; and because there are differences, conflicts. The kind of conflicts, their extent and intensity will depend largely upon the presence of specific mechanisms which will both reflect and negotiate the conflicting interests of different groups of producers and consumers. Among these mechanisms are working-class and professional organizations, trade-unions and guilds, *that are genuinely and permanently independent of the government.*

The second sphere of possible abuse of authority in a socialist society is administrative. Every administrator entrusted with responsibility for making decisions that may affect the jobs, pleasures and life careers of other human beings, may function as a tyrant. The greater the area of administration, the greater the danger. Especially, when efficiency is a desideratum, is it easy to palm off injustice as a necessary evil.

Here, too, the situation is one that must be met, for better or for worse, by contriving checks and controls. A vested interest on the part of the qualified worker in a job must be publicly recognized. Where administrative action affects civil or industrial rights they must be subject to review by democratically elected commissions, *independent of party affiliation.*

Finally, there is the multiplicity of individual psychological factors which make for oppression. It is extremely questionable whether there is any such thing as the love of power in the abstract. There is a love for a variety of things which, to be achieved or retained, require power in varying degrees. For some, the exercise of power is a compensation for frustration; for others, it is a way of acquiring prestige, glory, a sense of vitality or importance; for almost everybody, a temptation to favor those we like and overlook those we despise. Everyone has his own list of people whose absence he believes would be a boon to the world. But what follows from all this? Nothing that need dismay anyone who is not a saint or a fool. Here, as everywhere else, once we surrender the dogmas of an unalterable human nature or inevitable laws of organizational progress or corruption, we can do something to mitigate, counteract, and establish moral equivalents.

Whether we are talking of pain or injustice or power, there is no such thing as *the* problem of evil except to a supernaturalist. There are only evils. The more we know about the pathological lust for power, the conditions under which it thrives, the instruments it uses, the myths behind which it hides —*and the more public we make that knowledge*—the better can we cope with the problem of taming it. Skepticism is always in order; but no more than in science need it lead to paralysis of activity. More knowledge is required but we know enough to make at least a beginning.

Most of that knowledge is a knowledge of what to avoid, derived, in the main, from a close examination of Germany and Russia. It is clear that no monopoly of the instruments of education, including the press and radio, can be tolerated. More positively, the primary emphasis of all educational activity must revolve around the logic and ethics of scientific method. The meaning of democracy itself must be so conceived as to show that the methods of intellectual analysis to resolve conflicts of policy between minorities and majorities are an integral part of it. Freedom and authority can live together happily only in a society where scientific method is applied not merely to problems of physical control but to questions of human value.[7]

9. Historical Materialism

Despite theoretical recognition of the plurality of factors in history, Marxism as a political movement has tended to assign to the mode of economic production an overwhelming determining influence upon politics and culture not borne out by a scientific study of the facts. It has failed to realize that the economic organization of a society is often compatible with different alternatives of political rule and cultural behavior. This failure entailed an insensitiveness to the operation of other factors, including, as we have already pointed out, the historical effects of knowledge and ignorance, upon future events. Tested, therefore, by its ability to predict political and cultural changes, traditional Marxism has not been very successful. That other social theories have not been more successful, is hardly an extenuation because Marxism has claimed to be the *only* scientific theory of social change.

Two conspicuous illustrations of the disproportionate influence assigned to the mode of economic production may be cited. Until recently most Marxists deduced the nature of the cultural superstructure of socialism—politics, law, and the family, religion, art and philosophy—as a simple corollary from the character of socialist production. To say that they "deduced" anything is, in a sense, an exaggeration. It is more accurate to say that they took these matters for granted. The change in productive relations of itself guaranteed that social life, and even the soul of man, would be harmonious, just and free. Concern with the constitution of the socialist commonwealth, with the problems of cultural and educational direction, with the possibilities of collectivist tyranny, was dismissed as, at best, a time-wasting absorption in empty possibilities. Often, reflections of this kind were considered as hampering the

<hr>

[7] Cf. my *John Dewey: An Intellectual Portrait,* Chap. VII, John Day, New York, 1939.

struggle for political power, instead of being evaluated for their bearing upon the way the struggle must be conducted in order to achieve the ideals of democratic socialism.

Even a more glaring example of the overemphasis of economic factors is the political position of Leon Trotsky, the most "orthodox" of contemporary Marxist-Leninists. Because he assumes that the Russian *economy* is socialist, he is prepared to defend the invasion of any democratic country by Stalin's armies, and the imposition of Stalin's absolute and bloody totalitarianism upon their citizens, including the proletariat. Trotsky does this not because he approves of Stalin's bureaucratic regime, fortified, as it is, by frame-up, purge and cultural terror. Nor because he approves of the wisdom of such invasions. But solely because he expects the productive relations to be socialized. Even if the cultural and economic lot of the workers is worsened by this change, Trotsky is certain that the dialectical necessity of socialized economy will inevitably result in secondary political revolutions which will sweep Stalinism away. This mystic faith has nothing in common with a scientific analysis of politics but it is consistent with that view of historical materialism which is common to all schools of Marxist-Leninism.

If the truth be told, the very statement of the theory of historical materialism in the writings of canonic expositors suffers from several types of ambiguity which make it difficult to know how to go about testing its validity. Among them may be mentioned the equation between productive relations and productive forces, the shift from necessary to sufficient conditions, the meanings of the term "basic" and the phrase "in the last instance" in such statements as "the mode of production basically determines a culture in the last instance," etc. Here an important work of clarification must be done. The greatest obstacle to the task of clarification is the persistent contention among orthodox Marxists that they command a dialectic method which permits them to entertain without embarrassment doctrines that appear to others as downright inconsistencies. The insoluble difficulties in the orthodox Marxist conception of dialectic will be analyzed in detail in the chapters of Part Two.

10. *The Critical Historicism of Marx*

The social philosophy of Marxism has been repeatedly declared to be historical. Historical in a two-fold sense. First, in the obvious sense, that it arose in a definite historical period to articulate the interests and direct the struggles of the international workingclass. Second, in that it stresses what was once *not* a commonplace, viz., that all cultural activity, all norms and standards of social theory and practice are bound to a time and place.

If we take the term "historical" in the first sense, then to say that Marxism is historical is to state a fact. But what follows from it is by no means clear. Does Marxian socialism express the interests of the working class only or of the community as a whole? If of the community as a whole, why does it claim to be a class doctrine and why is the class struggle the central feature of that doctrine? If in liberating itself from the bonds of capitalism, the workingclass liberates the rest of humanity—as Marx himself asserted—then it would be just as true to say that in liberating itself from the bonds of capitalism, the rest of humanity liberates the workingclass.

Sometimes Marx speaks as if the rest of humanity, or that portion of it which finds its apparent present interests in irreconciliable opposition to those of the workingclass, does not truly appreciate what its "real" interests are. These are alleged to be harmonious with the "real" interests of the workingclass. Here Marx follows Hegel who follows Rousseau in the distinction between the general and individual will. The chief trouble, leaving the metaphysics aside, with this distinction between the apparent and real interests of the community, is that the same grounds which lead Marxists to make it, justify them in introducing a similar distinction between the real and apparent interests of the workingclass, i.e., between what the workers think they want and what Marxists *know* they really want. This distinction introduces the thin edge of totalitarianism into Marxism which Lenin drove home to a disastrous conclusion. It is diametrically opposed to Marx's oft-expressed view that the workingclass is the architect of its own political fate and that its victory must be democratically achieved with the uncoerced support of the majority of the population.

The only intelligible inference that can be drawn from Marx's writings on this point is that only the workingclass is in a position to lead successfully the struggle for socialism. The reasons adduced by Marx are many. Primary among them are that its most pressing difficulties—unemployment, insecurity, relatively low standard of living—cannot be met short of socialism, whereas this is not so true or as obvious, for other groups; and second, its strategic position in industry gives labor, once organized, a tremendous striking force both of defense and offense. Marx did not assert that the workingclass *alone* can achieve socialism but that it must constitute the chief base of a movement, uniting different groups of the population, to bring it about.

Let us grant for a moment Marx's claim that the workingclass is, and has been, in a position to lead a successful socialist movement. Unfortunately, being in a position and being able to move from that position are two different things. The test of events has shown that the workingclass has been petrified in its position of potential movement. Grant that if the workingclass does not lead the socialist movement, democratic socialism will not be achieved. True as that may be, it is no assurance that it will ever actually take the lead. The causes of the failure of socialist labor to win allies from middle class and professional groups, or even, in many countries, to align most of the workers under its banner, may be in dispute, but the facts themselves are incontrovertible.[8] The liquidation of peasants and intellectuals during the counterfeit socialist Russian revolution enhances, of course, the difficulties of united action between the workingclass and other sections of the population. No one really knows today how such fruitful united action is to be achieved. The time for it is very short, indeed. New political genius is necessary to develop the techniques of co-operation and persuasion.

The second sense in which Marxism is historical does not justify a belief in the relativity of truth as that phrase is cus-

---

[8] In the United States, a *Fortune* poll indicates that most American workers believe that Henry Ford, the arch-opponent of labor unions, has done more for them than their own trade-union leaders.

tomarily interpreted in popular literature. If we examine Marx's procedure, we will observe that his historical approach is not a substitute for scientific method but a concrete application of that method to the question of "universal" social laws and "abstract" ethical ideals.

As we saw in a previous section, Marx does not deny that certain uniformities of social behavior may be observable in all societies. What he insists upon is that for purposes of understanding and action in any historical period, an investigation must be undertaken of the historically differentiating factors in that period which may bear upon the extent and validity of the supposed uniformities. When we are dealing with the subject matter of history, we discover that there are many more variable factors that are relevant for our purposes than is the case in the materials of the natural sciences. The basic pattern of inquiry is the same in both fields. Whatever differences appear are differences not in general method but in the specific natures of what is being investigated. At any definite time, the conclusions reached by Marx are either true or false, once meaning can be assigned to them. To call them "historical" truths or errors does not add or take anything away.

Insofar as abstract ethical ideals are concerned, Marx follows the basic outline of Hegel's critique of Kant, substituting naturalistic theories of mind and human interest for Hegel's spiritualistic ones. The good and the right, or the better and the more just, are not expressions of arbitrary fiat drawn from intuition, revelation or authority. Nor are they empty tautologies deduced from purely formal rules. They are evaluations and commitments based upon *knowledge* of (i) all the relevant interests involved in a particular situation, (ii) how they are related to the state of productive forces and relations, (iii) the alternatives of action open to men, and (iv) the consequences of the respective actions. The historical approach to ethical ideals is nothing more than intelligent criticism of ideals. And all ideals are subject to criticism. The process of criticizing ideals may include *more* than what Marx believed necessary. But it must include at least that. Only those are in fundamental opposition to Marx's critical, historical approach, who believe that some ideals or standards are above or beyond criticism at any time or place.

It should be noted that what is living and sound in Marx's critical historicism, as well as in his "rationalism" and "humanism" (discussed in the subsequent sections) are to be found not so much in contemporary Marxists or Marxist movements as in the thought of individuals who, identifying Marxism with Marx, naturally regard themselves as utterly opposed to him. The most outstanding figure in the world today in whom the best elements of Marx's thought are present is John Dewey. They were independently developed by him, and systematically elaborated beyond anything found in Marx. If ever a democratic socialist movement succeeds in striking roots in American soil, it will have to derive one of its chief sources of nourishment from the philosophy of John Dewey.

11. *The Rationalism of Marx*

Few of Marx's leading principles have been so severely criticized as his alleged rationalism. Not many have taken the trouble to specify what they meant by it. Marx is not a rationalist, if that means the belief that "reason" constitutes the structure of things or that it is the impelling force in human behavior and history. Marx is a rationalist in that he believes that rational or scientific method is the only method that can be successfully employed wherever we seek understanding and control. It is in this sense that he is a true child of the enlightenment. There is nothing that cannot be scientifically investigated, nothing to which scientific method is irrelevant whether it be the stars in their courses or human beings entangled in their emotions. The determinants of human behavior may be as far from "reasonable" as one pleases, but it is only by the use of reason that we can discover the fact. Passion and faith may move mountains but who can say whether they will set them down at the right place? They are not by themselves expressions of reason but after they are submitted to critical analysis and their historic causes and consequences investigated, they may become reasonable.

The charge that Marx and Marxism suffer from too much rationalism seems peculiar when one recalls that only a generation ago they were criticized for being much too sentimental. As everyone knows who follows the day by day activity of Marxist groups, it is marked more by zealotry than intelligence, more by narrow organizational loyalty than cool appraisal of events. Slander is a weapon more often employed than argument, and hate the ruling emotion. One may justifiably expect more of Marxist groups but it is doubtful whether these unlovely qualities are uniquely characteristic of them alone. It was not because they lacked enthusiasm that Marxists lost out to Fascists in Europe. It was partly because they lacked the courage to act boldly at the height of their power, partly because their doctrines were inflexible, and their specific practices unintelligent.

As for Marx himself, his irascible personality is hardly reconcilable with the view that human beings do, or should, live "a reasoning life" if that is contrasted with a life of reason. His one chronic lapse into rationalism, in the exaggerated sense, seems to be his optimistic assurance that all workers could read *Capital*, and that anyone who read it without prejudice, would therewith be convinced. However, if to be rational means to be intelligent, then it is sufficient to remark that since genuine intelligence knows its own limits, it is absurd to charge that anyone can suffer from "too much intelligence."

The most conspicuous illustration of Marx's legitimate rationalism is to be found in his theory of social organization. He believed that under existing historic conditions society could be organized by an intelligent plan. One of the purposes of such planning would be to increase human security and liberate men from the manifold anti-social consequences which flow from those unplanned and unorganized economic activities that constitute what is metaphorically described as our present social "system." Marx can claim to have inherited the bequest of classic rationalism as expressed in the social insights of Plato and Aristotle with much greater justification than those of his critics who rant with mystic fervor about the Graeco-Roman Whole. For the harmonious organization of natural impulses under the control of reason which according to Plato and Aristotle are essential to the good life, is conditioned, according to Marx, by the harmonious organization of natural and economic resources under the rule of intelligence. To be intelligent means to plan. And an intelligently organized society is one which is socially planned. Since the profit "system" makes *social* planning impossible, the intelligently organized society must be one in which the profit motive in the major spheres of economic activity has been abolished.

One of the primary justifications of a planned society is its promise to achieve a social and personal *security* not realizable under regulated or unregulated capitalism. But as we have come increasingly to realize, there are various kinds of security, all compatible within limits, with a planned society. There is the security of a co-operative enterprise of free men; there is the security of an army machine; there is the security of a jail. No philosophy of a planned society is complete without an indication of what and whom we are planning for. We are, with good warrant, suspicious of those who speak of security, and *only* of security, for human beings can be secure and yet shackled—securely shackled. There is no wisdom in staking one's life and fortunes in a struggle for an abstract ideal of security unless we know something about the kind of men and women we hope to see developed, and the price that we may have to pay for that security. To these questions Marx replies with a theory of man which indicates that economic security is not the be-all and end-all of the good society but the conditioning framework for the activities of free, creative, critical and adventuring human beings. This brings us to another fundamental principle of Marx's social philosophy which has been ignored by his critics and caricatured by many of his professed followers—Marx's humanism.

12. *Marxian Humanism*

Criticism of Marx's social philosophy has alternated between the charge of soulless materialism and demonic spiritualism. Familiarity with the early philosophy of Marx would dispel misconceptions of this kind. It is saturated with a Feuerbachianism which brims over with terms like "humanity" and "justice" and "brotherhood." His critique of Feuerbach sought to give these abstract terms a material content in the present historical period and not to deny the possibility of giving meaning to them. As a matter of fact, they pervade even his technical works in economic theory and are always in evidence when he makes a political appeal. I shall state three specific expressions of Marx's humanism. If they have an air of novelty, this only re-enforces the necessity of making sharper distinctions between Marx and contemporary Marxist movements.

(a) The first is Marx's recognition that property (not *capital*) and personality are indissolubly connected. Despite his rejection of the use which both Kant and Hegel make of their philosophy of property, he agrees with them that the possession of some property—articles of use and enjoyment— is necessary to the enjoyment of personality. There can be no effective freedom if we can call nothing our own. Without the possession of some things, whose nature and extent depend upon the historic period, the only personalities we can develop are those of saints or ascetics for whom the whole of life is a preparation for death. William James somewhere makes the same point in tracing the way in which our personalities extend to our clothes, books, and other personal effects.

The juridical essence of property is the right not so much to use as to exclude others from what we have. Consider the right of property, Marx argues, in the basic instruments of production in the modern historic period where the independent craftsman and journeyman are anachronisms. No one can reasonably claim that property in these things is necessary for the development of personality. They are not personal objects of use but impersonal instruments of social utility, operation of which provide the livelihood of the masses. The right of private property in instruments of production carries with it the power to exclude the masses from their use, a power exercised whenever business becomes unprofitable. Since this use is necessary to existence, such a right means power over the very lives of those who exist by using them. In other words, Marx recognized that power over things, more specifically the tools and resources of labor, means the power to hinder, thwart, and sometimes destroy human personality. It was this insight, together with the desire to free human beings from the arbitrary control which variations in the rate of profit exercised over them, that led him to his detailed studies of the nature and effects of capitalist accumulation. Before him, in the interests of human personality, men had fought for liberation from a secularly armed, *religious* authority. With the expansion of the productive forces of capitalism and the growth of enlightenment, men turned against the traditional forms of *political* despotism as incompatible with the "rights of man." It is as a phase of this struggle in the interests of human personality that we must understand Marx's proposal to end *economic tyranny*—a tyranny no less onerous for being, in the main, the unconscious result of unplanned economic behavior. He believed that it was possible by scientific husbandry and democratic control to provide abundance, freedom from economic care, for *all* members of the community.

(*b*) Another expression of Marx's humanism is to be found in his ideal of *the whole man*. Under conditions of modern life, there are two kinds of specialization—one freely chosen by individuals who seek appropriate outlets for their creative energy, and the other imposed upon man by the uncontrolled machine process and the necessity of earning a living. The second kind of specialization reduces man, so to speak, to a part of himself, it *depersonalizes* him, and leads him to think of his life as beginning just where his work ends. The individual thus finds his life segmentized so that there is no commerce between his desires and his deeds, his play and his labor, his ambition and his opportunities. The natural process of growth is replaced by accidental shifts of energy and interest which build no meaningful pattern. Sooner or later, the worker finds himself, when not unemployed and at loose ends, sunk into a mechanical routine whose monotony is punctuated by bursts of passion against whatever scapegoats convention, and those who interpret so-called public opinion, create for him. Or he lives in the dimension of make-believe which requires no active participation of any kind on his part.

Marx's ideal of the whole man entails a conception of labor which gratifies a natural bent at the same time that it fulfills a social need. In this way what appears in our present social context as onerous drudgery is capable of acquiring a dignified status. Welcoming, as he does, the division of labor because it makes possible those levels of productivity in the absence of which there can be no equality of abundance, Marx is distrustful of the psychological effects of over-specializations of any kind, even those voluntarily acquired. An artist who can paint but cannot think, a thinker at home with abstractions but blind to color and deaf to sound, an engineer aware of the slightest flaw in steel and stone but insensitive to the subtle and complex character of human relationships, indeed, any individual who can do a particular job well and nothing else—all these for Marx are creatures who are only partly men.

It is patent that Marx was overly optimistic about the potentialities of creative achievement in men, both as individuals and as a collectivity. Always partial to the great classic ideals of antiquity, he adapted to an age of scientific technology the Greek conception of harmonious, all-around self-development. He does not, however, expect men to be revolutionized by doctrinal conversion or by education in a society which sharply separates school from life. In an early philosophic work, he writes, "By work man transforms nature," and adds in *Capital*, "By transforming nature [and society], man transforms himself." The process is gradual but neither automatic, inevitable nor universal.

(c) A more striking expression of Marx's humanism, and one particularly noteworthy today in view of the Bolshevik-Leninist distortions of his meaning, is his *democratic* conception of social control. This constitutes an unambiguous answer to the question: What kind of security, what variety of socialism, did Marx think worth planning for? Marx envisaged the active participation of all members of the community to a point where the vocation of professional politicians would disappear—a rather naïve hope but one which bears testimony of his pervading faith in the democratic process. He refused to consider man merely as a producer, a living instrument employed to implement directives laid down for him from above, acquiescent to any sort of totalitarian rule if only it guaranteed him a minimum of creature comforts. The "producer" for Marx was also a user; and it was the decision of the user which ultimately determined the basic objectives of production. That was why Marx looked to the organization—the free organization—of producers and consumers to provide the effective political unit of the future.

Marx's objections to the "clerical socialism" of his day apply even more aptly to the national socialisms of our own day in Germany, Russia and Italy. It is not only another form of economic servitude for the masses but a state of spiritual slavery. "But the proletariat," Marx confidently declares, "will not permit itself to be treated as canaille, it regards its courage, self-confidence, independence, and sense of personal dignity as more necessary than its daily bread." As a prediction, this has turned out to be tragically wrong; as a declaration of an ideal, it expresses what Marx believed, and what millions today still continue to believe, worth fighting and dying for.

Certain things follow at once from Marx's humanistic democracy. (i) Any criticism of existing democracy, no matter how imperfect, is justified only from the standpoint which seeks to extend the processes of democracy in personal, social, and political life or which seeks to bolster it against reaction. (ii) Socialism cannot be imposed upon the community from above by dictators who are always, so *they* claim, benevolent and wise, but who can be neither because of their fear of criticism and love of power. "The emancipation of the workingclass can only be accomplished by itself." (iii) Just as evident is it that the dictatorship of a minority political party which has a monopoly of all means of publication, education, housing, employment, and which, in effect, owns the instruments of production, is a police state not a socialist democracy. (iv) Under certain conditions, socialism without democracy—which is really no socialism at all—may be worse, much worse, than any capitalism that abides by the forms of political democracy.

Marx was a tough-minded realist. He anticipated stubborn opposition to the advance of the democratic process by an influential minority whose immediate interests, prestige and posts of power would be adversely affected in the course of it. If it resorted to violence to nullify the popular mandate, it would be swept from its place by the iron broom of revolution. But, and he was always careful to make this clear, such action would require the support of the great majority of the community; it would not be the work of a minority of self-delegated saviors, or a putsch, or the private creation of one political party.

Like all the revolutionists of the 19th century, Marx thought of the revolution as a progressive historical event. Beneath the cross-currents of the political struggle, he saw in the socialist revolution a profoundly conserving force rather than a destructive one. It conserved, first of all, the great technical achievements of capitalism. These were to be used, in peace and not merely in war, to their full capacity, as a foundation upon which to build the structure of a new economy of human welfare. It preserved, even where reinterpretation might be undertaken, the cumulative cultural wealth of the past, carefully treasuring everything of genuine beauty and truth in the arts and sciences of the recent and remote past. The vicious nonsense of "the Bolshevization of culture," one of the most far-reaching and fateful slogans of the Russian Revolution, would have been set down by him as nothing more than a form of militant barbarism. Thirdly, the revolution was conceived by him as something which would preserve and extend the civil rights and liberties which had been won during the Protestant Reformation and French Revolution and which Marx regarded as an essential portion of the bequest of the past. Greater intellectual and cultural freedom, as well as a larger area of independence in personal life, were to be fortified by removing the economic restraints which previous religious and political revolutions had left untouched.

All this provides us with a triple criterion by which to determine, in any given case, whether a revolution has a genuine socialist content or whether it marks merely the change by which a group of lean bureaucrats replaces the fat. First, is the standard of living of the great masses of people higher than their standard of living under the most highly developed capitalism? Second, is the level of cultural activity and creation higher, or at least more inclusive, than what has hitherto been the rule under capitalism? Third, do the citizens of the community enjoy *at least* as much freedom of thought, speech and action, as much freedom to criticize and disagree, as they possessed under the most enlightened of capitalism? Unless it be the case that in respect to all three of these questions, the answer is emphatically in the affirmative, the socialist revolution, as Marx conceived it, has not been achieved.

13. *Means and Ends*

If we evaluate the validity of Marx's ideas in the light of predictions which follow from them, we reach some interesting conclusions. Insofar as they bear upon what may be called the instrumental presuppositions of socialism—the economic structure of the new society which emerged within the shell of the old—they are, by and large, true. Insofar as they bear upon the question as to whether the generous social and political ideals of socialism would, as a matter of fact, be realized within this new institutional framework, they are almost completely false. Insofar as the failure of these ideals to be realized reflects upon their adequacy as leading principles of social life, judgment must be suspended.

Consider to what extent the following, more or less explicit, predictions of Marx and his followers have been realized: the concentration and centralization of capital and economic power, the ever closer alliance between government and economy, the development of rationalization of industry, the place of technological engineering, the mechanization of agriculture, the contraction of the free market and the growth of monopolies—in short, the features of what we know as corporate economy. Let us make no mistake about it. Despite local variations, the fundamental tendency of economic development shows substantially the same pattern in England, France, and the United States as in Germany, Russia, Italy and Japan.

Consider, on the other hand, the poignant disparity between the predictions about the political, social and cultural ideals, which were to be realized within the new economy, and what we find in sober fact. If we chart the situation as it exists today in all countries, we discover that there exists an inverse relation between the degree of integration of economic life and the degree of democracy in social and political life. There is both irony and pathos in a situation in which socialists of many countries look back with nostalgia to the freedoms of the capitalistic democracies they had once considered their mortal enemy.

The means of socialism, its economic instrumentalities, have proved not to be integral with the ends of socialism, as most Marxists have hitherto considered them. Obviously, the political methods of Marxism have also been found wanting, for reasons already discussed.

What, then, are we to conclude? Our conclusions will satisfy neither those who have already written autopsies of Marxism nor those doctrinal diehards who would count history well lost provided they did not have to declare Marxism wrong.

Our first conclusion is that the failure of socialist ideals to develop within the economic framework which makes them possible is, in the main, due to *the failure of men*. Not "the dialectic," whatever that is, not the level of productive forces, not the "laws" of the class struggle, are responsible but men. The debacle of Marxism represents a colossal *moral* failure—a failure of intelligence and courage. The lack of a positive moral philosophy among all the Marxist movements of the world and the substitution of organizational piety for a genuinely scientific study of the problems of social change, has revenged itself upon them.

Marxism as a movement is dying, and in many countries is already dead. Yet there is a living kernel in the thought and ideas it failed to develop. As a program of scientific activity in behalf of socialist ideals, fortified by the lessons of experience, rearmed with deeper moral and psychological insights, and prepared to learn what it really means to be scientific, these ideas still constitute a promising social philosophy. Embraced by the labor movement, farmers, professional groups, and their allies, whether under the name of Marxism, or as is more likely, under another name, it may once again become a living force. If no "Marxist" movement arises, these ideas will undoubtedly fructify political and social research; but as a program of action, it will be remembered only as an historical possibility, as something that "might have been," and take its place beside the great ghostly IFS of history. For the history that has already been made in its name has been made by its counterfeits—German Social-Democracy and Russian Bolshevism.

If a "Marxist" movement, as here understood, i.e., an organized activity to achieve, by applied intelligence, economic security, political freedom, and opportunities for cultural development in an essentially socialized economy, does not arise, then we must conclude that democracy as a way of life is incompatible with the structure of modern economy.

We cannot resign ourselves to this conclusion until several more efforts have been made in the coming generation.

CHAPTER EIGHT

REFLECTIONS ON THE RUSSIAN REVOLUTION

MORE THAN twenty years have elapsed since the Russian Revolution of October, 1917. From some perspectives twenty years may be regarded as a day in world history. But when a day is so long and crowded with events as the period from 1917 to 1938, its close provides an appropriate time for stock-taking. The grim news which has been coming out of Russia for the last few years makes such stock-taking an inescapable necessity for all except blind devotees and professional cynics. What happens in Russia makes a difference not only to subjective hopes and fears, not only to the objective course of events, but to the personal decisions of many well-meaning people. Integrity cannot be achieved by action alone, even when it is successful action. A faith which cannot withstand searching analysis must lead either to sentimentalism or fanaticism.

Like other people who worship at one altar, revolutionists are not given to raising critical questions about their "axioms." That in the eyes of others these axioms may appear as prejudices is regarded as perfectly normal. In fact, another axiom exists, linked up in some confused way with the theory of historical materialism, according to which such "prejudices" are discounted in advance by attributing them to a blindness born of social position or vested interest. It is a rare occasion when a revolutionist achieves the singular combination of enforced leisure, intelligence, and distance, that enables him to look at his first principles. In recent times the nearest approach to this kind of critique is to be found in Leon Trotsky's *The Revolution Betrayed*. It is long on the first two qualities and a little short on the third, but I take it as the point of departure for my own discussions because it raises all the important questions even if its analyses leave something to be

142

desired. Whatever its limitations, it is far and away the best argued of any recent writing of orthodox Marxism and superior in every respect to the excited polemics which have since come from Trotsky's pen. No one can pretend to a considered judgment on the Russian Revolution who has not read and studied it carefully.

1. *Russia after Twenty Years*

It is a commonplace of scientific inquiry that statistical conclusions are worth no more than the methods which have been used in gathering them; and that their significance always depends upon what they are *compared* with. In every regime which permits no opposition and brooks no criticism, official figures are rightfully suspect. (According to official Stalinist theory, "statistics cannot be neutral" for statistics is a "class science.") An atmosphere in which inefficiency can be converted by administrative decision into the capital offense of sabotage is not conducive to objective reports. From time to time even the Soviet press is full of bitter denunciation of officials—always in subordinate positions—who have falsified their figures in order to escape the obloquy of not fulfilling their assigned norms. But no matter how profound one's skepticism of Russian statistics may be, certain facts appear clear. During the last ten years industrial production and capital investment have increased many times over. In the fields of electric power, agriculture, aviation, and almost every branch of heavy industry Russia has made giant strides forward. Leaving aside indices of quality and per capita productivity, Russia easily challenges comparison with the advanced capitalist democracies of the West. In a brief but masterly chapter, Trotsky, despite his methodological caution, does more justice to the achievements of the successive five-year plans than the raucous battalions of erstwhile "friends of the Soviet Union" who carry on as if they had never seen a factory or power station before.

The significance of this industrial advance, however, depends upon how it is reflected in living standards, and again with what these standards are compared. If we compare the living standards of the average unskilled industrial or agricultural worker with his forbears of prerevolutionary days, we get one conclusion. If we compare them with the living standards of the American or English worker, we get another conclusion. And if one does the first, then again it depends upon what years are taken for purposes of comparison. Shall it be 1933, when between four and six million people starved to death, or 1936, or 1928, or 1940, a year of very acute shortage? [1] Further, there is always a difficulty in establishing comparisons between historical periods which are technologically quite different from each other. To what extent does electricity compensate for hideous living quarters, and modern, even if defective, plumbing, for a restricted fare in a factory kitchen? So far we have no method of reducing these things to commensurable terms.

Grant for a moment, in the teeth of the evidence, that the lot of the Russian worker is better than that of the prerevolutionary worker. What is that supposed to prove? The superiority of socialism? But the lot of the workers in any advanced industrial society can be shown, with the same warrant, to be better than their estate in some earlier phase. This becomes clearer if we shift the basis of the comparison to the living conditions of workers under American capitalism. Not even the most rabid partisan could seriously maintain that the average Russian standard of living even approximates the American. And if we take into consideration the actual purchasing power of the rubber ruble which is used for internal purposes of exchange, it is no exaggeration to say that many recipients of relief in industrial American centers receive more than is earned by the average Russian worker. If the present standard of living of the Russian masses is supposed to evince the superiority of "socialism," I should like to see a proof that such a standard could not have been reached by the normal processes of Russian "capitalism." As far as real wages is concerned, the worker under Czarism was better off than he is under Stalin.

The whole question of living standards, aside from its technical aspects, throws an interesting light on the history of the

[1] Cf. the detailed report of Mr. Spencer Williams, who for more than ten years served in a sympathetic capacity in Moscow as the representative of the American-Russian Chamber of Commerce, *New York Times*, April 14, 1940.

Russian Revolution. Not so many years ago, official communists and their sympathizers praised the Russian Revolution not for the material gains which had been won by the Revolution but for its great cultural and political steps forward. No attempt was made to gloss over the miserable living conditions of the masses. These were attributed to the backwardness of Russian economy. Continuous improvement was expected but no one dreamed of calling the emergence from an economy of hunger, "socialism." Today the cultural and political features of the early years are gone almost in their entirety. To boast of the problematic increase in the material welfare of the Russian masses is to use a very poor argument for socialism. For although the lot of the workers in other countries may appear relatively worse compared to the total social product they create, it is still much higher, defined in absolute figures of pro rata consumption, than that of the Russian worker.

Trotsky is so eager to do justice to Russian accomplishments of the last few years that he overstates their significance. "Socialism has demonstrated its right to victory, not on the pages of *Das Kapital*, but in an industrial arena comprising a sixth part of the earth's surface—not in the language of dialectics, but in the language of steel, cement and electricity." By his own account, all that has been achieved has been the industrialization of the country following the pattern of capitalist development in the West. That Russia has done this in a shorter time period than capitalist countries is not surprising. Except in organization, she was a follower and not an imitator. In technique she borrowed and acquired through purchase more than she discovered. In contradistinction from other borrowers, she has not improved on that technique. With an eye on England, it took Germany fifty years to become a great industrial power: with the entire capitalist world as a model, it took Russia twenty. From a purely industrial point of view, Russia at most has done as well as Western capitalism, which Marx in the *Communist Manifesto* praised for transforming the face of the earth and creating works in comparison with which the seven wonders of the world seemed everyday affairs. Before Trotsky can call the Russian achievements a victory of socialism, he must first show that the process of capital accumulation has not been accompanied by the same degree of exploitation as in capitalist countries, and that the political control which has directed the Russian economy has actually been an expression of the democratically arrived at decisions of the Russian masses. These are necessary conditions for any form of socialism. They are not sufficient, as we shall see. But at any rate it is clear that Trotsky begs the whole question by pointing to the passage of Russia in double quick time from an agrarian to industrial economy as evidence that "socialism has demonstrated its right to victory." The real struggle for socialism only begins at that point.

2. In What Sense Betrayed?

That the phrase quoted above is rhetorical is suggested in the body of Trotsky's book as well as by the title. Its theme song is that the revolution has been betrayed and that it is problematic whether socialism will be introduced in the future. Some critics of Trotsky have demanded that he produce proofs of "calculated treasonable actions of the bureaucracy." Such a demand is disingenuous on its face. For what Trotsky means is that the ideals of the Russian Revolution and of international Marxism have been betrayed by present policies, not that the leading cadres of the existing regime have sold out to anyone. Enjoying absolute power to whom could they "sell out"? Those who have challenged Trotsky to establish personal culpability where he does not assert it, are themselves not loath to use the term in the same sense in analogous situations. For example, the actions of Social-Democracy in 1914 are commonly referred to by its political opponents as a "betrayal" of the ideals of Marxism. No one in his senses, however, would maintain that calculated or personal treason entered into the situation. Indeed, the evidence shows that at the very moment when Social-Democracy was supporting capitalist governments and enlisting wholeheartedly for the duration of the War, its leaders sincerely believed that they were furthering the cause of socialism. None the less, their betrayal had a political meaning, recognized even by erstwhile opponents of Social-Democracy as "a return to patriotism."

But has Trotsky established a case for his contention that the Russian Revolution has been betrayed? Put in its mildest form we may say that if what was done in 1914 constituted a betrayal of socialism, then there can be little doubt that the Russian regime and its agency, the Comintern, have likewise betrayed the ideals of socialism. For there has not been a single deed committed by Social-Democracy in its social-chauvinist mood which has not been surpassed in perfidy in the recent history of Russia and the Comintern. Until August, 1939, Communist Parties throughout the world called for the most vigorous support of all capitalist governments which were not overt enemies of the Soviet Union. In the United States, for example, their chauvinism took such a turn that it was sometimes difficult to distinguish their verbal effusions from the patriotic rhodomontade of the Sons and Daughters of the American Revolution. Since the Soviet-Nazi Pact, the Communist Parties, on instructions from Moscow, first declared that the Second World War was an imperialist conflict, and then, as the alliance between Germany and Russia became stronger, that England and France were the chief aggressors.[2] Even before 1939, the Communist International, on instructions from the foreign office of the Kremlin, had abandoned the fight against Italian Fascism. In Italy the Communist Party conception of a popular front extended so far to the right that it even included "good" fascists as opposed to bad. It declared that "it adopts as its own the Fascist Program of 1919" (*International Press Correspondence* [official Comintern organ], Vol. 16). In Spain, Stalin shared with Franco the dubious honor of burying the beginning of a democratic, socialist Spain.[2a]

---

[2] In its official May Day proclamation on May 1, 1940, the Communist Party declared, in bold face type, "British imperialism has today become the chief center of world reaction and the chief instigator for extending the imperialist war into a world war." What Goebbels says one week, the Stalinists repeat the next.

[2a] The truth about the Kremlin's role in Spain has been obscured by the figureheads behind whom the disruptive work was carried on. But the revelations of ex-Premier Caballero, and Srs. Ariquistain and Prieto, as well as those of General Krivitsky, even after allowance has been made for *parti-pris*, are decisive on this question. The chief techniques employed by the Stalinists, on orders from the Kremlin, to get rid of their anti-Fascist working-class opponents, were denunciation of them as "agents of Franco," and if this did not avail, assassination. Evidence in point is the unfounded charges made against the leaders of the P. O. U. M. which led to their arrest, and the assassination of A. Nin and other working-class militants. These techniques were and are practiced in every country of the world through the apparatus of the Communist International, particularly in what was formerly Czecho-

Such expressions of betrayal are in a familiar style. But the ruling group in Russia has made its betrayal of socialism even more poignant by adding others which in virtue of its historical position are uniquely its own. Almost all of the liberating ideals of the Russian Revolution have been abandoned to such an extent that the identification of its cultural and political institutions with those of other totalitarian countries is inescapable to the critical mind. The very limited functional and functioning workers' democracy of the early years has been openly replaced by a minority one-party dictatorship which is in turn subject to the dictatorship of a small faction organized around a still smaller clique. The relatively free, heated but comradely discussion of principles and basic policies *within* the Communist Party has given way to a cult of personal leadership endowed with absolute power. The sycophantic adulation of Stalin exceeds anything known in world history. No Russian Czar ever demanded or tolerated a homage so organized and extravagant. The critical temper—an integral part, one would imagine, of "scientific" socialism—has been driven underground. Differences in income and living conditions between different strata of the population parallel class differences in capitalist countries. Those whose views even remotely approximate the ideas and ideals of the Bolsheviks who led the October Revolution are defamed and executed as fascist spies, saboteurs, and poisoners of little children. Harold Denny, the correspondent of the *New York Times*, reports in uncensored dispatches that the lot of genuine Communists is worse in Russia than in any other country of the world. For they are being literally exterminated—before Stalin's pact with Hitler, as "agents of Fascism," today, as "enemies of mankind."

If this does not constitute a betrayal of the ideals of the Russian Revolution and of socialism, which has always stressed scientific method, intellectual and personal liberty, and material security for all, nothing can. Many things have become

slovakia and Poland, and in the Western world, Mexico. Fenner Brockway, leader of the Independent Labor Party of Great Britain, has recently published detailed evidence, based on the relevant documents, that the Communist Party of Great Britain has secretly denounced to the British government numerous anti-Nazi refugees, who have broken with Stalinism, as "Nazi spies." *Cf.* British *New Leader*, May 23, 1940.

clearer since Trotsky completed the manuscript of his book more than two years before its publication.[3] In their light, his insight on many questions borders on prescience. He has no difficulties in proving the facts of betrayal as he states them— really, as he understates them. His difficulties begin in explaining or accounting for the facts.

3. The Causes of Betrayal

The betrayal of the Russian Revolution was consummated during the regime of Stalin and against the strenuous opposition of Trotsky. But why did Stalin triumph? Trotsky's answer is incisively expressed in the sentence, "The leaden rump of the bureaucracy outweighed the head of the revolution." The bureaucracy constitutes Stalin's social base. And the bureaucracy—what explains the fact that instead of being a servant of the masses it has become their uncontrolled master? So far as I can gather, Trotsky adduces four main reasons for the transformation of the bureaucracy into a ruling stratum. First of all, the tardiness of the world revolution enabled the bureaucracy to consolidate its position of power without undergoing the purifying process of sacrificial action. Secondly, the best cadres, those for whom socialism was not merely a doctrine but a mode of life and feeling, were decimated by the civil war. Thirdly, a psychological let-down after heroic years of struggle weakened resistance to the virus of personal ambition and careerism. Finally, the sickness and death of Lenin removed the only personal force which could possibly have stemmed the tide of reaction.

But Trotsky's main stress is upon another thesis from which the rise of bureaucratism follows as a corollary, and in relation to which the four reasons enumerated above are merely contributory. This thesis is that so long as an economy does not make material well-being possible for all, so long as its productive forces and cultural development generate material want, the rise of a bureaucracy is literally inevitable. This position is so important and, as I shall attempt to show, in such striking contradiction to Trotsky's other explanations, that I cite some key passages.

[3] The book was published in 1938.

"The tendencies of bureaucratism, which strangles the workers' movement in capitalist countries, would everywhere show themselves even after a proletarian revolution. But it is perfectly obvious that the poorer the society which issues from a revolution, the sterner and more naked would be the expression of this 'law,' the more crude would be the forms assumed by bureaucratism, and the more dangerous would it become for socialist development. The Soviet state is prevented not only from dying away, but even from freeing itself of the bureaucratic parasite, not by the 'relics' of former ruling classes, as declares the naked police doctrine of Stalin, for these relics are powerless in themselves. It is prevented by immeasurably mightier factors, such as material want, cultural backwardness and the resulting dominance of 'bourgeois law' in what most immediately and sharply touches every human being, the business of insuring his personal existence." (*The Revolution Betrayed.*)

In fact, Trotsky does not hesitate to attribute to this social law a character of "iron necessity" which physicists of our day are chary of ascribing even to their best warranted generalizations.

"If the bureaucracy arises above the new society, this is not for some secondary reasons like the psychological relics of the past, etc., but is a result of the iron necessity to give birth to and support a privileged minority so long as it is impossible to guarantee genuine equality."

And if it be unlikely that genuine equality (whatever that may mean) can ever be established in a finite world, where not everything can be manufactured at once and distributed at once, and where wealth and poverty are always relative to each other, it would follow that Trotsky's law becomes absolute. It turns out to be another variant of the well-known "iron law of oligarchy," made famous by R. Michels and others, according to which socialists may be victorious but socialism never.

The crass philosophical contradiction which underlies Trotsky's reasoning here and elsewhere I shall examine subsequently. At present I wish to consider the concrete illustration provided by Trotsky's specific causal analysis and its implications. If Trotsky's "law" holds good, in his own terms it is inevitable that the bureaucracy should have developed into a privileged minority even if the best cadres had *not* been mowed down and Lenin had *not* died. Even if socialism had been victorious in the West after a prolonged civil war, matters could hardly have been appreciably different. Only the *forms* of bureaucratic usurpation would have altered. For it is obvious that on the most optimistic perspective the conditions of genuine equality could not have been guaranteed for a long time—at least, for a sufficiently long time to give the bureaucracy an opportunity to develop stubborn roots. Particularly in Russia, matters would not have been economically very different from what they are now. More heroes would have been produced, not more goods. A proletarian dictatorship which would plan its economy for Europe as a whole might have saved Russia some years of hunger. It could not have equalized economic disparities between the various parts of Europe; "bourgeois law" would still obtain for distribution of objects of consumption, and the European Thermidor would be on its way.

Consider now the four causes enumerated for the Russian Thermidor and their relation to Trotsky's basic thesis. It is difficult to tell whether Trotsky regards them as falling within the same necessitarian sway as the law of bureaucratic crystallization in backward economies. In places he speaks as if he does, particularly in discussing the psychological reaction and let-down which follows the first phases of all revolutions. But certainly he cannot believe that the death of Lenin and the decimation of his comrades-in-arms was socially "inevitable." And were he to assert that the failure of the proletarian revolution in the West was likewise socially inevitable, he would be compelled to admit that the Bolshevik conquest of power was based on a mistake, and Plekhanov, Kautsky and Martov would be vindicated against Lenin and Trotsky. As a matter of fact, however, Trotsky's moral and political castigations of reformism and Social-Democracy only make sense on the assumption that "productive forces"—the motor power of his social necessity—on some of the most crucial occasions of history, are *not* decisive, neither in the first nor in the last instance.

It is difficult to understand how Trotsky can seriously juxtapose his basic thesis with his ancillary reasons. If the former is valid, the latter are superfluous except to explain merely parochial phenomena. If the former is valid, then and only then does the title of his book become pure rhetoric, for "betrayal" has no meaning, even as a social concept, except as it presupposes the grounded possibility of another type of action. But major alternatives of social action are precisely what Trotsky's law excludes. In at least two vital places Trotsky is caught in the trap of orthodox Marxism. If he adheres to the fetishism of "productive forces" as all-determining (always decisive in the "last instance"), then the Russian Revolution should not have been undertaken, and failing revolutions in the West, it was foolishness even to begin to build socialism in an area recognized as the weakest link of capitalism. If his law of emergent bureaucracy is sound, then his indictment of the Stalin regime reduces itself to the personal objections of a sensitive intelligence to Stalin's manners. Yet Trotsky, with some justice, still glorifies the early years of the Russian Revolution; and although his own fate and that of his family have been unutterably tragic, no personal tone is heard throughout his entire analysis of the brutal and bloody course which Russia has taken under Stalin's rule.[3a] Wherever Trotsky's position is supported by empirical evidence, its implications are in flat contradiction to the orthodox Marxism by which he unnecessarily seeks to justify it.

After this it may seem strange for me to write that Trotsky does state, in my opinion, the relevant reasons for the Soviet Thermidor. But he does not acknowledge them to be such. They are mentioned as incidental *effects* of the complex of causes discussed above. I shall return to them in a subsequent section.

4. *Philosophical Inconsistencies*

Trotsky is not the only orthodox Marxist theorist whose philosophy is a compound of methodological naïveté and popular science. But it is more apparent in his case because his honesty before the facts leads him in specific analyses to conclusions irreconcilable with the dogmas of dialectical materialism whose chief fount is Engels. He writes:

"Marxism sets out from the development of *technique* as the fundamental spring of progress, and constructs the communist program upon the dynamic of the *productive forces*. If you conceive that some

---

[3a] Trotsky's assassination, the news of which reached me as I was correcting the galleys of this chapter, is the culmination of one of the most implacable manhunts ever organized against a human being. Stalin has killed more of his opponents in foreign countries than all other dictators combined.

cosmic catastrophe is going to destroy our planet in the fairly near future, then you must, of course, reject the *communist perspective* along with much else. Except for this as yet problematic danger, however, there is not the slightest scientific ground for setting *any* limit in advance to our technical-productive and cultural possibilities." (*The Revolution Betrayed.* Italics mine.)

In other words, the development of *technique* and productive *forces*, barring a cosmic accident, is bound to lead to communism. This communism is of a kind such that materially more than enough of any type of goods can be produced, which is indeed necessary in order to guarantee genuine equality; and such that culturally, as Trotsky elsewhere says, "the average human type will rise to the heights of an Aristotle, a Goethe, or a Marx. And above this ridge new peaks will rise" (*Literature and Revolution*).

Trotsky does not stop to inquire what causes the development of technique and productive forces. Evidently these are not self-caused. And if they depend upon other things, then their development is contingent, unless Trotsky extends the necessitarian chain, to these other things. This would lead him to a stick-beat-dog-chase-cat-catch-rat kind of causation which to boot imperils his materialistic starting point. However, it is not necessary to raise difficulties of this sort as well as those involved in his ironic concession to cosmic accident—difficulties that are fatal to his monism. All we need do is to confront this optimistic assurance in the benevolent character of productive forces with Trotsky's conclusions in discussing concrete problems in Germany, China, Russia, and Europe generally. In these cases it is always something done or left undone—a mistaken policy, a corrupt leadership, stupidity, narrow self-interest—which is responsible for events. Of course, all of these phenomena, according to Trotsky, in some way or other reflect social antagonisms which are produced by economic contradictions. But this addendum is merely theoretical piety, for, like Engels, Trotsky attributes to them a relatively autonomous character which brings his systematic monism toppling about his ears. Yes, "economic contradictions produce social antagonisms," but these "*in turn develop their own logic, not awaiting the further growth of the productive forces*" (italics mine). In other words, these factors have efficacy, and although not uncaused they are autonomous in respect to productive forces. What remains of the monism?

There is only one possible reply open to Trotsky as an orthodox Marxist theoretician—a reply to which Trotsky, the clear-eyed historical analyst, makes a perfect rejoinder. As a theoretician, his reply is that productive forces operate on the whole and in the long run; that the workingclass may be defeated in its struggle for socialism once, twice, many times; but that as a result of what humans do or leave undone, the inexorable processes of history will work themselves out in time until the classless society is achieved. Ah! but what is it that he says to those sentimental friends of Russia who think with their viscera and who pass off every criticism of Stalin's despotism with the statement that despite bloody purges and the betrayal of all socialist ideals, some day socialism will completely triumph in the Soviet Union? "Time," retorts Trotsky, "is by no means a secondary factor when historic processes are in question. It is far more dangerous to confuse the present and the future tenses in politics than in grammar" (*The Revolution Betrayed*). What is it that he said to those who, capitulating without a struggle, left Hitler to the bitter fate which the productive forces of Germany had in store for him? To these "cretins and cowards," he pointed out that Hitler might decide the fate of Europe for generations. What is it that he said twenty years ago to those of his comrades who opposed the October Revolution? Together with Lenin, he replied, "What *we* do in the next two or three days might determine the future of the socialist revolution." Whether it is the policies of Chiang Kai-shek in China or of the popular front in France or Spain, Trotsky is continually whipping socialists who lag behind events and who expect history to give them a free ride to Utopia.

Now Trotsky cannot eat his scientific cake and have it, too. Not even with the help of the transubstantiations vouchsafed by the dialectic logic. His orthodox Marxist theory invalidates his specific analyses, and conversely. Rarely does Trotsky deduce a concrete proposal of *action* from the level which the productive forces have reached. When they do enter it is usually as a rationalization of defeat. They do not compel anything to be: they merely prevent things from being. Trotsky, the metaphysician, speaks of the iron necessities of the laws which govern the development of productive forces: Trotsky, the empirical historian, is given to weighing evidence on the delicate scales of probability, evaluating alternatives, considering the large and small "ifs" of history, making predictions on the assumption that human intelligence and action—yes, and even morals—make a difference to the course of events. Were his metaphysics sound, his whole scientific procedure would be unintelligible.

My criticism of the fundamental inconsistency in Trotsky's philosophical position is undertaken not as an exercise in formal logic, but in order to clear the way for a presentation of what I regard as the most relevant causes of the Russian Thermidor. Since they are not directly bound up with the level of "productive forces," they are exposed to the charge by Trotsky and other orthodox Marxists of being merely "incidental"—political, cultural, or what not. It becomes necessary, therefore, to show that when he is analyzing a problem rather than developing an ideology, it is precisely these factors which very frequently are given determining weight. That Trotsky proclaims his metaphysics to be science must not mislead us. It is a linguistic archaism. The truth of the matter is that it is much nearer to religion than to the logic of experimental science. Even the sentence in which Trotsky seems to say the opposite confirms this. In defending the position that the development of technique *must* produce communism (barring always the intervention of the heavens themselves), he writes: "Marxism is saturated with the optimism of progress, and that alone, by the way, makes it irreconcilably opposed to religion." This optimism is based on the view that the world is such that sooner or later man's highest ideals must find realization: that the dialectic processes in *nature* and in *society* guarantee the victory of socialism. Far from being irreconcilably opposed to religion, this is only another variety of religion. Those who hold such a view differ from professed religionists only in what they call progress and in the events concerning which they are optimistic. Indeed, so far as I can see, the only doctrine which *all* religions as well as idealistic philosophies have in common, is that human ideals are fortified by some "friendly" force, principle, or structure, in the nature of *things*. It is no accident that the belief in a *Natur-Dialektik* is the foundation stone of the theology of dialectical materialism.

5. *The Nature of the State*

In politics as in other practical fields, problems cannot be settled merely by definition. The theory of politics, however, is pre-eminently a field in which people operate with disguised definitions. The beginning of wisdom and political clarity is to recognize the difference between statements which are "true" by convention and definition, and statements which are in the nature of predictions and whose truth depends not upon our sweet will but upon the actual state of affairs. Orthodox Marxism has long been proud of its realistic theory of the state. But the history of the Russian Revolution has shown that this theory needs radical revision. It fails to provide even a handle to the present Russian state. Whatever predictions of Russia's course that have been made on the basis of it are either quite definitely false or subject to important qualifications. These difficulties emerge in a most garish light when we confront the provisions of the new Russian constitution with the orthodox theory. Since the Russian government is committed to both, the contradictions appear to be nothing short of grotesque, and Trotsky has easy work in establishing the theoretical bankruptcy of Stalin and the present crop of Red professors. I state some of the central contradictions.

(i) According to Marxist theory, the state is an instrument of a dominant economic class. In a genuine classless society, there can be no state; the regulatory functions of government become an integral part of the productive processes. Today, by official edict, Russia is declared to be a genuinely classless socialist society. At the same time, not only is the existence of the state recognized but its strengthened character is an occasion for celebration. The Communist International adopted a resolution on August 20, 1935, which proclaims that "the final and irrevocable triumph of socialism and the all-sided reinforcement of the state of the proletarian dictatorship is achieved in the Soviet Union." This sentence, from a Marxist point of view, represents a contradiction in terms.

(ii) According to Marxist theory, the differentiating factor in the exercise of *state* coercion, as distinct from the coercion of public opinion, mores, and spontaneous expressions of self-defense, is the existence of special bodies of armed men standing over against the rest of the population. Where such special bodies of armed men are found, their invariable, if not exclusive, function is to protect the economic interests of a dominant class. Russia, according to Stalin, has already reached the first stage of communism in which classes are no longer to be found. Yet the G.P.U. (under its different names) and the Red Army are bigger, if not more powerful, today than ever before in their history.

(iii) According to Marxist theory, the "dictatorship of the proletariat" is in reality a workers' democracy which gradually gives way to complete political and social democracy for the entire population under socialism. The Russian Constitution —advanced as the basic document for a socialist society—not only leaves "in force the regime of the dictatorship of the working class" (Stalin) but expressly provides in Section 126 that the *Communist Party* is to be "the directing nucleus of all organizations of the working people, both public and state." There is nothing new in this form of dictatorial political control by a minority. But it is the first time in history that it has ever been written into a constitution. To my knowledge, never before has such a mode of political rule been called democratic except on the occasion when Hitler referred to Nazi Germany as a democracy "in a higher sense."

For Trotsky and other orthodox Marxists, these disparities between Marxian theory and Russian practice testify to the extent to which the existing regime is un-Marxian; they do not invalidate the theory. In fact, they confirm it, for the nub of the theory is the contention that the state power, as distinct from purely administrative institutions, is an instrument of class domination. Which class does the dominating? The proletariat. Which class is dominated? The capitalist class? But there is no capitalist class in Russia. The proletarian state suppresses proletarians. In whose interests? In the interests of a group of people who do not fit into the scheme of orthodox Marxian class categories but whose exercise of the state power is more ruthless than even under Czarism. As we shall see in the next section, no stretching of the conventional Marxian class definitions will be adequate to cover the facts. Where there are no classes, there can be no class struggle; where there is no class struggle, there is no need for the state. How, then, account for the existence of the Russian state and its domestic practices?

Both Engels and Trotsky assert that it is not enough that "class domination" disappear but that "the struggle for individual existence" must disappear before the state disappears. For Engels "class domination" and "the struggle for individual existence" go hand in hand. The latter flows from the former. Trotsky recognizes a certain lag. "It is true that capitalist anarchy creates the struggle of each against all, but the trouble is that a socialization of the means of production does not yet automatically remove the 'struggle for individual existence' " (*The Revolution Betrayed*). Excellent! This means that the "struggle for individual existence" can go on even after the instruments of production have been socialized. Who struggles against whom? Obviously, those who have power against those who have not, those who have more against those who have less. Trotsky makes fun of the Philistine who "considers the gendarme an eternal institution. In reality, the gendarme will bridle mankind only until man shall thoroughly bridle nature." How thoroughly must man bridle nature in order to eliminate all struggle for individual existence? More important than the struggle for individual existence is the struggle for *better* individual existence. And as important as the struggle for better individual existence, once subsistence has been assured, is the struggle for power, for prestige, for deference and place. No matter how thoroughly man may bridle nature, he may still oppress man, sacrifice people to efficiency, and seek compensation for personal frustration by imposing an arbitrary will upon others. We do not have to assert that this is certain and eternal. We can assert, however, that this is far more probable than the eschatological Utopianism with which many "scientific" socialists oppose it.

It is one thing to assert that the diminution of coercion is an ideal which a socialized economy strives to realize more widely than ever before. It is an entirely different thing to assert that the elimination of state coercion follows with historical inevitability from the abolition of private ownership in the means of production. Even if it were true that there are no struggles between economic classes in Russia (which we will have reason to deny subsequently), the existing regime is a gruesome illustration of how bloody and fierce state oppression may be. There is an important difference between proclaiming the decrease in state power as an *ideal* and asserting it as a historic *law*. In the first case, it puts us on guard against bureaucratic excesses, leads us to look twice and three times at every coercive measure allegedly justified as a merely transitional procedure. In the second case, the belief that some day in some way the state *must* wither away makes people less sensitive to brutalities in the present, more ready to solve negotiable problems by force than intelligent compromise, and serves as a blinding fiction which obscures the facts of discrimination and repression in popular consciousness.

6. *Are There Classes in Russia?*

The question of the nature of the Russian state involves the important question of whether there are classes in Russia. Here again most of the disputes rage around definitions. Now, as I have undertaken to show elsewhere,[4] the simplest semantic analysis of the concept of "class" in classical socialism, reveals that its applicability is restricted to societies in which there is private ownership of the means of production. Under socialism, under communism, and even during the transitional period, classes do not exist, by *definition*, so long as we define a class by its role in the production and distribution of wealth. Everything "belongs" to everyone, and the socialization decrees are taken to be evidence of it. But there are other conceptions of "class" to be found in the writings of Marx and the literature of Marxism, according to which a class is defined in terms of its social position and political power, its privileges or lack of them, in short, its standard and conditions of living. In fact, for political and moral purposes, the first type of approach to "class" is justified only because in societies where the instruments of production are owned by a few, it illumines the patent inequalities in the conditions of life.

Even the apologists for the Stalinist regime admit that the

4 *Partisan Review*, April, 1938.

differences between the incomes and living conditions of the polar strata of the Russian population are enormous. They are typified in the differences in the standard of life, say, of a day-laborer and an executive of a trust. The admission of these differences is glossed over with the assurance that as production increases, the differences will be eliminated. Unfortunately, the whole trend of the Soviet economy shows that the increase of production has intensified and not diminished the differences in standards of living. There is absolutely no evidence by which we may conclude that an increase of production automatically eliminates gross inequality in standards of living where the actual *distribution* of the social product is not determined by the democratic decision of the producers themselves.

Trotsky, despite his searching inquiry into the social inequalities of Russian life, agrees with the present regime in regarding Russia as basically a workers' or proletarian state. This means, for him, merely that the productive forces of society have been socialized, not that those who do productive work in Russia democratically determine social policy. He substitutes economic categories for political, and juridical categories for economic, as if they were identical. Yet his own concrete analysis, which, until the Russian invasion of Finland, revealed penetrating insight and scrupulous regard for fact, indicates how irrelevant the socialization of property can be both to the economic status of the worker and to his political status in the community. "The transfer of power to the state changed the situation of the worker only juridically" (*The Revolution Betrayed*). That is to say, as far as an equivalent return for his labor goes, or his right to determine the general social purposes for which the surplus product, not returned to him, should be invested—*the worker can be just as much exploited when the instruments of production are owned in common as when they are not.* Compulsory speed-up has replaced the right to strike in Russia; and Stalin openly proclaims that "the [Communist Party] cadres decide everything."

To say that Russia is a workers' state but not a workers' democracy is to fall a victim to the fetishism of productive relations, the central mystical doctrine of orthodox Marxism. The consequence is that socialism as a democratic way of life becomes incidental to socialism conceived as a juridical scheme which may really leave differences in standards of living unaffected, and strengthen, by fiction and force, the political and economic power of the ruling bureaucracy. No one has said this better than Trotsky himself, despite its manifest inconsistency with both his premises and his conclusion.

"If a ship is declared collective property, but the passengers continue to be divided into first, second, and third class, it is clear that, for the third-class passengers, differences in the conditions of life will have infinitely more importance than that juridical change in proprietorship. The first-class passengers, on the other hand, will propound together with their coffee and cigars, the thought that collective ownership is everything and a comfortable cabin nothing at all." (*The Revolution Betrayed.*)

To make the picture complete, as it applies to Russia, we must add that the crew and captain take their orders only from the first-class passengers, who periodically get rid of malcontents—those that think too much of differences in power and living conditions—by making them walk the plank.

The stock response made by the defenders of the existing regime is a feeble exegetical attempt to show that socialism is not the same as equalitarianism. The above account does not assume that they are. Neither are capitalism and equalitarianism one and the same. What, then, is the differentiating characteristic of socialism? Article 12 of the new Stalin [5] constitution reads:

"In the U.S.S.R. the principle of socialism is realized: 'From each according to his ability, to each according to his work.'"

If this is socialism, then Western Europe and America, from the time of early capitalism on, have been socialist. For reward according to work has been the basic principle of wage payment under capitalism. Equalitarianism when defined as equal consumption of equal allotments of goods and services is neither possible nor desirable. But from this it is a far cry to the defense of inequality of incomes whose extent may be gauged by the admission of Sidney Webb, the most uncritically

---

[5] Called the "Stalin" constitution but prepared by the Committee of 31, and written by Bukharin. Of this Committee of 31, almost all have been liquidated.

extravagant non-party apologist of the Stalin regime, that "the maximum divergence of individual incomes in the U.S.S.R., taking extreme instances, [is] probably as great as the corresponding divergence in incomes paid for actual participation in work, in Great Britain, if not in the U.S." (*Postscript to Soviet Communism.*)

Reference to Marx's dictum in his *Critique of the Gotha Program* to justify these inequalities is downright abuse of a plain text. For there Marx is pointing out that *even when equality of wage payments exists,* since individuals are unequal in respect to needs and responsibilities, inequalities must result. In principle, Marx allowed the possibility of some variation in wage payments in a workers' democracy but like all socialists of his time, and indeed like the leaders of the Russian Revolution down to 1923, his bias was for equality of wage payments. In distinguishing the way in which the representative institutions of the Paris Commune differed from those of capitalist democracy, he makes much of the fact that all administrative functions are to be performed at workmen's wages. And it is well to remember that for Marx, the Paris Commune was "the political form at last discovered under which to work out the economic emancipation of labor" (*The Civil War in France*).

But it is not a question of Marx's meaning here save as it is invoked by apologists as an authoritative source to cover up the perpetuation of gross economic and social inequalities under "socialism." Diligent analysis of the facts of history, and upon the objects of reflective interest, constitutes the test of desirability and not any words of Marx. It is clear that there can be no actual equality in what people have and enjoy in any society. But it is not at all clear in what way this justifies placing a mansion at one man's disposal and a corner of a room at another's; giving one the power, in virtue of economic income, to marry, divorce, and control the size of his family and denying it to the other; opening up special social and educational opportunities to the children of the first and restricting it for the children of the second.

If Russia is a class state but not a workers' state, what kind of class state is it? The sense in which we are now using the term "class" will be obvious when we point out the connection between property and power. Even on the traditional Marxist theory, it is recognized that the very meaning of *ownership* is social and that individuals own things only to the extent to which the state stands ready to exclude others from their use. Ownership without this kind of control is empty. It is a personal claim and not a social right. Whoever has the recognized power to exclude others from the use of the instruments of production, in effect owns the instruments of production. In Russia today, the bureaucracy of the Communist Party, to whom alone the Red Army, the police, and the G.P.U. owe responsibility, can by administrative decree exclude any worker or any group of workers from the use of the instruments of production. By controlling their jobs, their living quarters, their power to move from one part of the country to another, their press, school, trade-union, club and every other association, they control their lives more absolutely than any country in the world. But the Stalin Constitution reads differently! So does the Constitution of the U.S. which provides free suffrage for all men irrespective of color in the North and South. To identify what is read in an official document with what actually obtains in fact is a good definition of political cretinism. Those who read the Stalin Constitution apparently do not read the Stalin press, which, despite its zeal to put the best democratic face upon minority party oppression, shows every day how glaring the discrepancy is between the paper privileges of the Russian workers and their actual rights. Things have come to such a pass that Russian workers are liable to loss of position, bread cards, living quarters, and are even subject to criminal prosecution, for unexcused absence from work. Their immediate overseers are threatened with imprisonment and liquidation for failing to report infractions of these new decrees by workers.

Here is not the place to document the absolute control which the Russian Communist Party bureaucracy, unchecked by genuine democratic processes, exercises over the lives and jobs of the Russian workers and peasants. Trotsky, at any rate, as well as all other independent observers, does not dispute it. The question is whether this absolute power over "socialized" property justifies the ascription of ownership, and, further, whether the owners constitute a genuine class.

Once we exclude the orthodox Marxian definition of a class, which by its own law of contextual significance cannot apply to Russia, no valid objection can be raised against considering the Russian bureaucracy as a definite social class. This definition is adequate to the known disparities in Russian life between standards of living, distribution of political power, and social prestige. On the basis of it, we can illumine the history of the Russian Revolution and predict subsequent developments. It explains what the bureaucracy does and leaves undone both in its domestic and foreign policy. And as to whether this constitutes "ownership," an affirmative answer follows not only from the definition of ownership in property but from comparison with systems of "state capitalism" (or "state socialism").[6] True, it differs in many respects from other forms of state capitalism, actual and ideal. Its bureaucracy has no stocks and bonds and it does not transmit its power to its biological heirs. But it does not need stocks and bonds, for it alone directs the accumulation and investment of capital and takes the necessary toll for its own standards of living without let or hindrance by the working population. Its hierarchy is not recruited from its biological heirs as yet but from its ideological heirs, i.e., those who combine the qualities of submission to the top cadres and ruthlessness to all others in a manner approved by the Political Committee of the Communist Party. In the most unbridled capitalist democracy there are many things that the Rockefellers and Morgans and their interlocking directorates cannot do. As directors of the incorporated economy of the U.S.S.R., the hierarchy of the Communist Party is all powerful. If its ownership appears different from that of other countries, it is only because of the absoluteness of its character, the ideological rationalizations which accompany it, and its official holiday invocations to the ideals of socialism it has long since abandoned in practice.

---

[6] No currently accepted term is available for describing the Russian system. More important than terminology are the facts. Russia is not a capitalist state in the conventional sense, nor a workers' state, nor a socialist state. Perhaps it would be best to characterize it as a totalitarian state in order to bring out, despite differences in historical origin, its similarity with Germany, which also escapes classification if we employ only the conventional terms "capitalist," "socialist."

7. *Democracy and the Dictatorship of the Party*

If the foregoing analysis is valid, the key to Russian economy, to the evolution of Russian culture since the early years of the revolution, to its ghastly purges and juridical frame-ups, is to be found in the character of the Russian state power. The Russian state is marked by the concentration of all political and economic power in the hands of the Communist Party. Other political parties of the working class are forbidden, even in the "democratic" Stalin Constitution. The organization of factions within the Communist Party is punishable by exile to concentration camps or by death. The Soviets and Parliament have the same function in Russia as the Reichstag in Germany—emphatic rubber stamps for policies decided by the Political Committee of the Party. Begun as a dictatorship of a class, the Russian Revolution developed through the dictatorship of the Communist Party into the dictatorship of the Secretariat. Questions of causation are always tangled knots, but I think it can be established that, given the conditions in which the Russian Revolution was begun, the only *controllable* factor that led to the degeneration of the Russian Revolution and its Thermidorian regime was the abrogation of working-class and peasant democracy, signalized by the suppression of all other political parties and the concentration of all power in the hands of the Communist Party.

Let us cast a glance in this light at the various reasons given by Trotsky for the Soviet Thermidor. The immaturity of the productive forces, the belatedness of the world revolution, the decimation of the best fighters and the idealists, the weakening of morale, the death of Lenin—none of them was in the control of the Bolshevik party. And if together they constitute a sufficient explanation of the Thermidor, then degeneration and betrayal were unavoidable no matter who was at the helm or what political forms prevailed. Trotsky, however, is far from establishing a direct and relevant connection between any or all of these factors and the corruption of socialist program and ideals in the Soviet Union. But there is one factor which he does mention as having a direct bearing upon the emergence of Stalinism from Bolshevism, whose importance, however, he immediately proceeds to deny by subordinating it to those mentioned above. "It is absolutely indisputable that the domination of a single party served as the juridical point of departure for the Stalinist totalitarian system. But the reason for this development lies neither in Bolshevism nor in the prohibition of other parties as a temporary war measure, but the number of defeats of the proletariat in Europe and Asia" (*Stalinism and Bolshevism*, 1938).

Domination here is a weak word. A political party can *dominate* even in a democracy which offers it a mandate after the give and take of free discussion. What Trotsky means is the exclusive *dictatorship* of the party, and on other occasions he has not hesitated to say so. The more forcibly the Communist Party exercised its dictatorship over other working-class parties, the more pervasive became the dictatorship of the Secretariat within the Communist Party itself. Times without number Trotsky has maintained that had genuine democratic processes prevailed in the Soviet and in the Party, Stálin's policies would not have prevailed. That is to say, were there Soviet, or even Party, democracy, Stalin's policies would not have prevailed *even though* the revolution was delayed, Lenin dead, and the productive forces undeveloped. Trotsky's policies were quite different from those of Stalin's and they were based every whit as much upon recognition of the objective situation in Russia and in the world generally. But on Trotsky's own analysis, the failure to adopt them was due *not* to the common objective situation but to the absence of workers' and party democracy. Were Trotsky to deny this, he would be admitting that the defeat of his policies was necessary, inevitable, and justifiable, and the denial would make nonsense of his eloquent criticisms of the strangulation of the Soviets and Party under Stalin. Despite his cosmic optimism, even Trotsky acknowledges that there will always be some periods in which the objective situation is unfavorable, as was true in 1924. Where contrary policies are advocated to meet the situation, absence of workers' and party democracy means that the policy of those who have the dictatorial power in their hands will be adopted, irrespective of whether it is an intelligent one or whether it leads to a *cul de sac*. Even if we assume identity of interests between the dictators and the rank and file, we cannot assume

infallibility on the part of the dictating bureaucracy in adopting appropriate measures to realize the common interests.

On every concrete question on which Trotsky has been defeated in Russia, the proximate cause has been, not the level
of the productive forces at home or the political situation
abroad, but the denial of equal rights of assembly, agitation,
and publication to him and to his followers, and the persecution, imprisonment, and often the execution of those of his
followers who have tried to exercise these rights. Had Trotsky's
policies been turned down in a genuinely functioning workers'
and party democracy, the factors he mentions might be relevant in explaining why the electorate refused to give him its
confidence. But as it was, Stalin's policies, which led directly
to the Thermidor, prevailed because the dictatorship *of* the
party was transformed into a dictatorship *over* the party.

It does not require much perspicacity to realize that the dictatorship of a political party cannot for long be effective without its own internal organization becoming dictatorial. The
necessity of *controlling* the mass of the population over whom
the party wields a dictatorship, of effectively combating enemies, real and alleged, of imposing a uniform ideology, compels
the party to assume a military, sometimes called monolithic,
structure. The interests of the non-party masses which cannot
be openly expressed because of the absence of free political institutions, naturally tend to express themselves in differences
within the party itself, in factional groupings of various sorts.
But the dictatorship of the party cannot be effectively wielded
unless the facts and appearance of division in its own ranks are
concealed from the non-party masses. To conceal this division
and to parade the maximum amount of unity, the ruling group
in the party must regulate and control the expression of opinion
among the rank and file. It must exercise an even stricter supervision of the party press than it does of the non-party press.
Now in order to exercise the proper supervision the leading
group must itself be unified. Dissidents are isolated, gagged
into silence, exiled, deported, and shot. The rule of the leading
group must be fortified by a mythology which glorifies "the
leader," "the beloved disciple," "the man of iron" who tops the
pyramidal structure and whose word on any subject is law.
Opposition of any kind is equated with treason. Decisions are

"unanimously" approved; failure, no matter for what reason, becomes sabotage; silence today, a sign of betrayal tomorrow; the instruments of one purge become the victims of another. Historical variations may appear at some points in this evolution from the dictatorship *of* a political party to the dictatorship *over* the party. The general pattern of Russian development, however, fits the facts: from the outlawing of other working-class political parties, to the prohibition of factions in the Communist Party (in March, 1920), to ruthless police terror against *all* dissidents under Stalin.

8. *The Sources of Stalinism*

Although he denies that the explanation of the present political regime in Russia is to be found in its natural evolution from party dictatorship to dictatorship of the secretariat, Trotsky gives himself great pains to show that the dictatorship of the party is no part of the theory of Bolshevism, and that its rise in Russia, and the concomitant absence of workers' democracy, "was a measure of defense of the dictatorship [of the proletariat as a class] in a backward and devastated country, surrounded by enemies on all sides." In this way, he seeks to refute those Marxist critics who lay the totalitarian form of the Stalin regime and its bloody excesses at the door of Bolshevism as well as those non-Marxist critics who see in what has transpired in Russia a final judgment upon the whole tradition of Marxism. Trotsky's reply to this point is crucial not merely because of its bearing on the understanding of the Russian Revolution but because of its significance for the entire socialist movement.

I propose to show that Trotsky's reply is ambiguous, that although he denies that the dictatorship of the party is an integral part of the doctrines of Bolshevism, his theories of the conquest of power and of the relationship between the revolutionary party and the working masses are such that they entail an acceptance of party dictatorship. I shall begin by showing that it is false, in fact, to say that the prohibition of other working-class parties in Russia was a temporary exigency adopted because of peculiar Russian circumstances, but that it followed from the Bolshevik theory of leadership and conquest of power. I will then argue that these theories are incompatible with the ideals of democratic socialism which are *professed* by those who hold these theories and used as justification for them.

That the Bolsheviks considered the dictatorship of the proletariat to be the dictatorship of the Communist Party is evidenced by (1) the existence of a polemic literature, long before the October Revolution, and to which Trotsky himself contributed, charging them with that view; (2) the critique of groups like that of Rosa Luxemburg, which shared the international social program of the October Revolution but protested against the abrogation of Soviet democracy; (3) their oppressive treatment of other working-class organizations, press, and leaders even before the country was rent by civil war; (4) the substantial identification of the dictatorship of the party and the dictatorship of the class in the theoretical writings, after 1917, of Lenin, Trotsky, Bukharin, Zinoviev, and Stalin; and (5) most important of all, as far as this specific point is concerned, the program of the Communist International, which left no room for doubt that the Communist Parties of their respective countries would liquidate at the first opportunity other working-class parties. Despite Trotsky's claim that the one-party dictatorship was the result of the Russian backward economy and other local conditions, the Theses and Resolutions of the Fourth Congress of the Communist International which were mandatory upon *all* Communist Parties *everywhere*, specifically state that the dictatorship of the proletariat can only be achieved by a purely Communist government. At most other forms of working-class government must be regarded as a starting point of the struggle for party dictatorship.[7]

---

[7] "The Communist International must anticipate the following possibilities:
(1) A Liberal Workers' Government, such as existed in Australia, and likely to be formed in Great Britain in the near future.
(2) A Social-Democratic 'workers government' (Germany).
(3) A Workers' and Peasants' government—such a possibility exists in the Balkans, in Czechoslovakia, etc.
(4) A Workers' government in which Communists participate.
(5) A real proletarian Workers' government which the Communist Party alone can embody in a pure form. . . .
"The other two types of workers' government (workers' and peasants' government, and workers' government—with participation of Communists) are not proletarian dictatorships, nor are they historically inevitable transition forms of government towards proletarian dictatorship, but where they are formed may serve as starting points for the struggle for dictatorship.

To be sure, in order to gain additional support, the Bolsheviks were willing to permit other political groupings to enter the government with them (the Left Social Revolutionaries) provided that they agreed with the immediate Bolshevik program and left them in control of the Ministries of War. They were always prepared to unite with other groups which accepted the immediate Bolshevik program and leadership. But just as soon as any other political group of the working class began an opposition to them even within legal forms, and especially when such opposition proved effective, repression set in. It is quite true that some of the activities of the non-Bolshevik working-class parties exceeded the limits of Soviet legality, but it is even truer to say that the Bolsheviks themselves defined and changed these limits at will. For every act of violence against Bolshevik leaders, there were hundreds committed against their political opponents.

Even before the Allied intervention, the Bolsheviks operated with a very simple classification as far as working-class opponents were concerned. Those who agreed with them on specific points and offered their co-operation, together with some known world-figures who like Kropotkin abstained from politics, were unmolested, and in official propaganda exploited as illustrations of how benign the Bolsheviks were to working-class opponents. All others were simply classified as bandits and subjected to a ruthless reign of terror. Time and again when the Bolsheviks were bombarded with protests by foreign working-class organizations against their treatment of imprisoned Mensheviks, Social Revolutionists, and Anarchists, their reply was that these people were not political prisoners, even though

Only the workers' government, consisting of Communists, can be the true embodiment of the dictatorship of the proletariat." (*Resolutions and Theses of the Fourth Congress of the Communist International;* italics mine.)
If we take this together with the Bolshevik thesis that power can be won only by *an armed insurrection,* then it goes without saying that the Bolsheviks never envisaged the possibility that the purely Communist government—alone able to carry out the revolution—would be *democratically* elected by the population or that after the revolution they would tolerate the existence of any working-class party which opposed their undemocratic seizure of power.
The openness with which this was proclaimed varied with the strategical exigencies of the moment, but see for the U. S. William Z. Foster's *Towards Soviet America* (1932), p. 275. "Under the dictatorship, all the capitalistic parties—Republican, Democratic, Progressive, Socialist [*sic!*]—will be liquidated, the Communist Party functioning alone as the Party of the toiling masses."

the overwhelming majority of them were guilty of nothing but differences of opinion.[8] The official press would often indignantly deny that these political groups were even socialist. Whatever working-class groups differed from the Bolsheviks were regarded as "conscious or unconscious tools of capitalism." By this simplistic thought process the Bolsheviks could identify themselves with the working class as a whole and justify their suppression of any working-class group which disagreed with them.

By their curiously mystical, but highly convenient, doctrine that the Communist Party knew better than the working class itself what was good for it, the Bolshevik leaders could pretend that any workers who disagreed with them were agents of the enemy. But among themselves they spoke quite frankly about imposing their will upon the working class when it was in a reactionary mood. They, of course, were the *sole* judges as to when that mood was reactionary. Shortly before the Tenth Congress of the Communist Party in 1921 and *before* the Kronstadt uprising, Karl Radek declared before the Communist fraction in the War College of the Red Star—the men who subsequently were used to tame "the reactionary spirit of the masses" at Kronstadt:

"The Party is the self-conscious advance-guard of the working-classes. We are now at a point where the laboring masses, at the end of their endurance, refuse any longer to follow an advance guard which continues to lead them to battle and sacrifice.... Ought we to yield to the clamors of the workingmen who have reached the limit of their patience and their physical endurance, but who are less informed than we are about what is for their true advantage? Their state of mind is, at times, frankly reactionary. The Party has decided that we shall *not* yield, that we must impose our will to victory on our exhausted and dispirited following. Grave events are impending. You must be ready...." [9]

This is not to maintain that in the early years of the Revolution no democratic processes whatsoever existed within the

---

[8] Bukharin used to say "jestingly" that the Bolsheviks believed in the existence of many political parties—one in power and the others in jail. When Berkman and Goldman visited Lenin to protest against the imprisonment of anarchists, he declared with a straight face that no anarchists were jailed but only bandits. *Cf.* Goldman, *Living My Life*, N. Y., 1931, p. 764.

[9] Quoted by Brig. Gen. A. Barmine, *Memoirs of a Soviet Diplomat*, London, 1938, p. 118.

Soviets. Compared to their complete absence from 1924 down to the present, they loom large. Nor can the existence of genuine democracy within the highly centralized Communist Party during the early years be disputed. But the tendency towards complete domination of the Soviets by the minority Communist Party, reinforced by a thousand and one sanctions that the possession of state power bestows, was there from the very beginning. Nothing demonstrates this more clearly than the attitude of the Bolshevik leaders to the slogans of "freely elected Soviets" which were raised by their working-class opponents after the October Revolution. This was really nothing more than another form of the slogan "All Power to the Soviets" under which the Bolsheviks had marched to the conquest of power. But because, here and there, some Cadets took up the slogan in hope that under its cover they could carry on anti-Soviet propaganda, *all* who made the demand for democratically elected Soviets, including the heroic Kronstadt sailors, were regarded as counter-revolutionists. It was in Lenin's own time that *Pravda* proclaimed that "All Power to the Soviets" had been replaced by "All Power to the Cheka."

In their international program, the Bolsheviks permitted a certain flexibility in the *details* of how power was to be conquered and consolidated. In non-Russian countries, the higher level of technology and culture, it was hoped, would make some of the measures adopted in Russia unnecessary. But the decision as to which measures were suitable, and which not, was to be the sole responsibility of the Communist Parties. Indeed, the Bolshevik leaders often wrote as if they owed no allegiance to the Soviets, presumably the representative body of the working class, save when the Soviets accepted the Bolshevik program. A conflict between the Soviets and the Party, after power had been won, was to them literally unthinkable. When Trotsky, in discussing the relation of the Bolshevik party to the Soviet, writes: "The fact that this party subordinates the Soviets politically to its leaders, has, in itself, abolished the Soviet system no more than the domination of the conservative majority has abolished the British parliamentary system," [10] his own analogy tells heavily against him. The Tories can be, and have been, turned out despite the limited character of Brit-

[10] *Cf. Stalinism and Bolshevism.*

ish democracy. The situation is more analogous to that of Germany. The Nazis "dominate" the German Reichstag no more than the Communist Party the Russian Soviets and Parliament. And yet Trotsky would be the first to maintain that the "domination" of the Nazis has certainly abolished the German parliamentary system.

That the identification of the dictatorship of the party and the class is an integral part of the Bolshevik theory, and not a removable appendage, must be the inescapable conclusion of any critical inquiry into its party documents and historical practice. Article 126, the prize joker of the Stalin Constitution, which lays down as the law of the land that the Communist Party is "to constitute the guiding nucleus of all organizations, both social and governmental," states candidly what was already true in the time of Lenin.

Before proceeding to uncover the premises from which this identification flows, it is important to call attention to the fact that there is not a single line in the writings of Marx which justifies this identification. Whatever other kinship exists between Marxism and Bolshevism, on this crucial point they are poles apart. Classical Marxism conceives of the socialist revolution as an extension of existing democratic processes, political as well as social, as a movement which may be influenced by minority groups but which is not subject to dictatorial rule by a minority of self-appointed saviors.

The assumptions from which the identification of party and class dictatorship flows as a corollary are: (1) that the Communist Party constitutes the vanguard of the working class as a whole; (2) that it is the vanguard because it has knowledge of the genuine interests of the working class; (3) that if the workers do not recognize the claim of the vanguard to leadership, it is because of (a) the stultifying influence of capitalist propaganda, or (b) the existence of other working-class political parties, whose lack of knowledge or integrity leads them into becoming "tools" of the bourgeoisie, or (c) the emergence of special interests among skilled workers who prefer the Philistine securities of the present to the glorious promise of the future; and (4) that no revolution can be won except under the "leadership" of a political party which directs the campaign for the conquest of power.

In respect to the first point, *every* working-class party considers itself to be the vanguard not only of the class but of the new society it is striving to achieve. Secondly, in so far as the claim of any party to be the vanguard is based on knowledge, unless it regards itself as infallible, which would be ridiculous in view of the record of mistakes of all parties, then it cannot legitimately use that claim as a basis for suppressing other working-class organizations. Once admit that the party may be mistaken on some key policies and that opposing parties may be right, then devotion to the interests of the working-class as a whole, far from justifying the absolute suppression of political opposition, would, at the very least, make for its toleration. Montesquieu's warning injunction is still valid: "*Le malheur d'une republique—c'est lorsqu'il n'y a plus de brigues.*" Third, to impute blanket ignorance and absence of integrity to political opponents is pure *argumenta ad hominem* and therefore always open to the *tu quoque* response. Not so, however, is the belief that there is a heterogeneity of interests in the working class as such, and that different political parties represent them. If this is true, then no longer can any political party claim to be the vanguard of the class as a whole but only a section of it. Of which section? Unless the political party is to say that it knows what the "real" interests of the workers are better than they do themselves (the traditional argument of all benevolent and not-so-benevolent despotisms), the answer is that it represents only that section of the working class which in the course of free discussion and experience gives it its confidence. That there is a heterogeneity of interests in the working class is true not only in the period preceding the socialist revolution but after. The anomaly, therefore, would be the domination of one party. Once it is granted that we have diversity of interests within the working class, the way is open to raise the pointed question concerning the special interests of the political party itself, when in power, as opposed to the interests of those whom it allegedly represents. Special interests of power-holding groups grow up consciously and unconsciously. There are, of course, no guarantees against the abuse of power even when rulers are democratically elected. But the suppression of other working-class parties and a monopoly of propaganda are already evidence of that abuse. No political party, therefore, which advocates such measures is worthy of confidence.

The fourth and final assumption is the most important. Although we may dismiss, as a shocking abuse of terms, the simple equation which the Bolshevik theorists draw between "leadership" and "dictatorship," the nub of their position is that the conquest of power is impossible without a party dictatorship. At this point, they cast phraseological evasion aside, turn upon their critics, accuse them of making a metaphysical fetish out of democracy, and demand to know by what other methods the battle for socialism can be won. Our answer at this point must be brief. If it is a battle for socialism, then it is a battle not only for higher production but for the democratic way of life in industry, politics, and education. The interdependence of ends and means which Trotsky himself has recently stressed in a brilliantly-written but woefully inconsistent study [11] forbids the use of any means whose consequences invalidate the end. For Trotsky, as distinct from Stalin, not all means are justified but only those which *genuinely* lead "to the liberation of mankind," or more concretely, "to the abolition of the power of man over man." The history of the Russian Revolution has demonstrated that a minority one-party dictatorship has led to an increase of the power of man over man, to a power exercised more brutally and accompanied by greater servility than anywhere else in the world. There is every reason to believe on economic, psychological, and historic grounds that a one-party dictatorship would lead to similar results everywhere in the world today. The presence of a superior productive technique would confer no immunity; it would merely make the engines of repression more efficient. But for a political party to forego the chance to take power, comes the crushing retort, may mean a lost revolution! Possibly. Yet some things are much worse than a lost revolution. A betrayed revolution! A lost revolution is a defeat in one battle of an enduring war: a betrayed revolution invalidates the fundamental principles in behalf of which the war is waged, dispirits and makes cynical an entire generation, and far from removing the arbitrary power of man over man secures it more firmly.

[11] *The New International*, June, 1938.

There are other alternatives of action which do not necessarily lead to a lost or betrayed revolution. If the liberation of the working class can only be achieved by the working class itself, a dictum of Marx which Trotsky repeats, it must cut itself free from the leading strings of all political prophets. It cannot be dragooned into socialism for its own good. When the occasion arises, its own representative institutions must decide on specific ways and means of achieving their goals. This does not mean that political parties are unnecessary. They are the appropriate instruments of articulating differences in interests. They may offer a program and leadership, but just as soon as they reach out for a monopoly of political power, education, and propaganda behind the back of representative political institutions of the producers and consumers, it is time to build barricades against them. Like any other group, the working class will sometimes follow bad advice and ignore good. That is its right. The infallibility of the masses cannot be counterposed to the infallibility of the leaders. But if there is no faith in the capacity of the masses to learn from their own experience, socialism is a willful illusion.

9. *Stalinism, Czarism, and Democracy*

In so far as this chapter leads to any conclusions, they are involved in the previous section on democracy and party dictatorship. A final word is necessary, however, with reference to a type of extenuation which many who are opposed to party dictatorships within their own country make for the totalitarian regime in Russia. After all, they say, Stalinism with all its oppressions and evils is better than Czarism. And some day Stalinism, too, will be buried in the graveyard of dictatorships. Now it cannot be too strongly emphasized that the Bolsheviks did *not* overthrow Czarism but the bourgeois democracy of Kerensky, and that after the suppression of the Kornilov revolt, in which the Bolsheviks aided Kerensky, the danger of a Czarist restoration was extremely remote. Nor is it a question of whether the Bolsheviks should have taken power but *how* they took power and its consequences. Viewed in the perspective of twenty years, those who approve of the present regime in Russia must maintain at least four propositions: (1) That real wages and living conditions generally of the Russian workers and peasants are much higher today than under Czarism. (2) That the dictatorial regime has accomplished more by its system of "state capitalism" from 1917-1938 than could have been achieved by bourgeois democracy in that period. (3) That the millions of corpses which it piled up in the course of consolidating its power, the sacrifice of political liberty, cultural freedom, and spiritual independence, were not too high a price for the assumed differential benefits. And (4) that no other policy, of a democratic nature, could have achieved, at the very least, the same material gains at a lesser human and cultural cost. The first proposition is highly questionable; the second proposition is extremely difficult to prove, even if the first be granted; the third depends upon one's scale of values (although we should expect the liberal to regard human values as more important than increase in efficiency); the fourth is demonstrably false, and if taken literally would make it impossible to criticize the Stalin regime on any count—heights of faith to which even Sidney Webb cannot rise.

It may be that Stalin's dictatorship will fall as a result of the opposition which his hydra-headed terror will raise up against him.[12] Attempts to extenuate his rule, however, constitute a strange avocation for liberals. For the question is not

[12] The absence of any *organized* opposition to Stalin in Russia has been somewhat of a mystery to political observers. This mystery disappears if we understand the way in which the civil population is compelled to participate in the espionage system, devised by a bureaucracy which has learned the lessons of a century-old Russian underground movement.

As explained to me by Generals Barmine and Krivitsky, who were in a position to know, the system operates as follows: A and B are workers in a factory, office, or agricultural collective. B drops a hostile remark about the authorities before A. Or he grumbles bitterly about conditions. A ignores the remark. A week later A is summoned to the local office of the G. P. U. (N. K. V. D.) and asked why he did not report B's subversive remarks. He is released with a warning that failure to do so again will result in a loss of employment (and bread card), living quarters, and in possible banishment to a notorious concentration camp, together with penalties for his immediate family. The incident is given wide circulation in the place it occurs. Thereafter if A (or any other worker) hears C make a disloyal remark, he fears that he may be the victim of another provocation and so rushes off to report. Even if A is in genuine agreement with C, he is led by elementary caution to report him out of fear that the latter may turn out to be another B. Each half of the population is thus set to watch and report on the other half. Could anything be more devilishly ingenious?

The only drawback of the plan from the standpoint of the authorities is that many individuals attempt to pay off personal grudges by false denunciations. The very frequency with which the Russian press reports punishments for false denunciation indicates the prevalence of the system.

whether the regime of Stalin will forever endure but whether
it will be replaced by another dictatorship or by a representative democracy of the Russian masses.

10.   *Stalinism and Trotskyism*

In so far as the blanket identification of Trotskyism and
Stalinism is concerned, the following considerations point to
the necessity of a nicer discrimination. To the extent that a
ruling bureaucracy takes color and stamp from its leader,
there can be little doubt that whatever political course Russia
would have taken under Trotsky, its history would have been
free from some of the terrible features which can be laid directly at the door of Stalin and his immediate circle; the extermination of from four to six millions of Russian peasants
by administrative decree; crude juridical and extra-juridical
frame-ups,[13] the only line of manufactured goods in which
Stalin's slogan "to catch up with and surpass America" has
been realized; deadening repression of the critical and creative
spirit in art, letters, and many fields of science. An oft-re-
peated and incisive dictum of Lenin states that "a political
leader is responsible not only for his policy but also what is
done by those he leads." From this point of view, all of these
excesses must be laid at Stalin's door even if some of these acts
were performed by his subordinates.

But there are other aspects of Stalinism less ghastly in
their immediate impact, but just as dangerous to the ideals of
socialism as those already enumerated. These flow from the advocacy of a minority party dictatorship during the transition
period—in reality, a period which never ends—from capitalism
to socialism. To the extent that Trotsky held this view, Trotskyism and Stalinism, despite their antipodal differences on
"the permanent revolution" or "socialism in one country," are
politically one and the same. Despite the cultivated ambiguity
of Lenin on party dictatorship, this was his view, too. Today,
since Trotsky no longer *defends* party dictatorship in princi-

---

13 On this point *cf.* my discussion in Common Sense, Jan., 1938; "Liberalism
and the Case of Leon Trotsky" in *The Southern Review*, Autumn, 1937; and
"Corliss Lamont, Friend of the G. P. U.," in the *Modern Monthly*, April, 1938;
also *Not Guilty*, the report of the Dewey Commission of Inquiry into the
Moscow Trials, N. Y. (Harpers), 1938.

ple, and interprets his past adherence to it as an exigency of historical circumstances, the identification of Stalinism and Trotskyism would appear impermissible. But until he takes a more positive stand and *attacks* it in principle, there will always be some suspicion that after all, potentially, Trotskyism is capable of developing into Stalinism.

From some points of view it may plausibly be argued that Trotskyism has already developed into Stalinism, that they are socially identical twins fathered by Leninism. As far as Russia's foreign policy is concerned, Trotsky, even when he criticizes Stalin's blunders, calls for unconditional defense of the U.S.S.R. and active aid to the Red Army even when it is depriving workers in other countries of their lives and liberties. Thus, he has called upon the workers of Poland and Finland to help the Red Army and G.P.U. in their brutal invasions. Further, despite Trotsky's latter-day theory, his own organizational *practices* smack of Stalin's techniques. It is amusing to observe how he handles serious opposition of any kind to his authority and doctrines in his own political grouping. First he uses cajolery. Then he reviews the past of those with whom he disagrees to show that even when they were in apparent agreement with him they represented a different and dangerous tendency. This tendency is invariably characterized as having fallen under the influence of the class enemy, so that, in effect, those who disagree with him are labeled as agents of the class enemy. If that does not bring capitulation, they are expelled on one or another ground, and the erstwhile comrades of yesterday are denounced as swindlers, thieves, and saboteurs. It is not hard to imagine what Trotsky would do to them, if he had state power. Whatever he did, it is certain he would do it more intelligently than Stalin. But the difference would not rise to the level of a new principle. This suggests that Trotskyism is Stalinism *manqué*.

*　　　*　　　*

The socialist movement originally appeared in Western Europe as the heir of the great traditions of political democracy which were imperiled by the absence of corresponding democracy in social and economic life. Its program, its axioms, its faith—called for better and more democracy, not less. The fate of the Russian Revolution is impressive testimony of a negative sort that no set of economic arrangements, from which democratic control is absent, can ever achieve the moral and material promise of the socialist ideal.

The socialist movement originally aspired to develop a scientific social philosophy as a guide to action. But almost from the very outset it was saddled with a metaphysical heritage. This heritage took the form of a belief in dialectical laws and dialectical method, with the result that gradually the scientific intent of socialist theory receded into the background. In Part Two we come to grips with dialectical beliefs, and beliefs in dialectic.

SCIENCE AND MYTHOLOGIES
OF REASON

CREDO

CHAPTER NINE

DIALECTIC AND NATURE

THE SOCIAL importance of a philosophy is measured by the number of people who hold it, the practices it is used to justify, and the habits of thought and valuation it leaves in its wake. From this point of view the philosophy of dialectical materialism is easily one of the most important social doctrines of our times. Sometimes the scope of this philosophy is restricted to the realm of social and cultural phenomena; sometimes it is identified with a systematic elaboration of the principles of scientific method; but most often its adherents interpret it as a set of doctrines which describes the fundamental characters of existence in the large as well as in the small, enabling us to formulate laws that operate in nature as well as in human and social activity. An examination, however, of the writings of those who profess to be dialectical materialists in this last sense shows that they are unified more by a community of allegiance than by a community of meaning. This becomes apparent when one seeks a clear answer from them to the questions: "What is dialectic? How is it related to scientific method? What does it mean to say that dialectic is found in nature?"

Aside from the fancied political implications of the doctrine, the sweeping theoretical claims made for it, the insistence that the dialectic is universal, that it is not merely a method of proof but an instrument for winning new truths in the sciences,[1] that it transcends the limitations of formal logic and opens new horizons of research—all warrant the closest analy-

---

[1] "Es ist schon ein totaler Mangel an Einsicht in die Natur der Dialektik, wenn Herr Dühring sie für ein Instrument des blossen Beweisens hält, wie man etwa die formelle Logik oder die elementare Mathematik beschränkter Weise so auffassen kann. Selbst die formelle Logik ist vor allem Methode zur Auffindung neuer Resultate, zum Fortschreiten vom Bekannten zum Unbekannten, und dasselbe, nur in weit eminenterem Sinne ist die Dialektik...." Engels, *Anti-Dühring*, 12th ed. (1923), pp. 186-7.

sis. For if these claims are true, then the neglect of this philosophy by natural scientists is nothing short of reprehensible.

The chief sources of the views we are to consider are Engels' *Herrn Eugen Dührings Umwälzung der Wissenschaft,*[1a] better known as *Anti-Dühring*, and his *Dialektik und Natur* published posthumously in the *Marx-Engels Archiv*, Bd. II. The philosophical writings of Plekhanov, Kautsky, Lenin, Trotsky, and Mehring and the minor figures in the orthodox tradition contain little on these themes not already to be found in Engels.

What I propose to do is (i) to distinguish the various senses of the term "dialectic" in the major writings of Engels; (ii) to determine whether they are mutually compatible; (iii) to analyze the so-called universal laws of dialectic and the illustrations offered of each; and (iv) to investigate whether there is any sense in which the dialectic can serve as a corrective, supplement, or substitute for scientific method.

1. *Seven Meanings of Dialectic*

I. DIALECTIC AS UNIVERSAL AND OBJECTIVE

For Engels, as for Hegel, the laws of dialectic are both objective and universal. Every field of knowledge, the objects known as well as the processes by which they are known, is subject to their sway. What, indeed, can be more comprehensive than Engels' statement that "the dialectic is nothing more than the science of the general laws of motion and development of nature, human society and thought"? (p. 144.) The illustrations offered are drawn from mathematics, physics, chemistry, biology, geology, history, and philosophy.

Engels does not assert that the knowledge of these laws by itself is sufficient to give mastery over things, for these laws are "unconsciously operative in nature and history" and their discovery in specific situations presupposes the possession of specific knowledge. But whenever man thinks correctly, he thinks dialectically, and whenever he controls things, he does so only by adapting himself to the dialectic processes implicit within them. The failure, however, to take explicit note of

[1a] All references below are to the 12th ed., Berlin and Stuttgart, 1923.

these laws probably—and an open disregard of them, necessarily—will lead to error. Like the laws of grammar and correct usage they operate as restrictive conditions. People may speak correctly without a knowledge of the rules of syntax; but for difficult constructions they are a help, and when deliberately flouted, soon re-establish their necessity in facilitating communication or make way for new rules. In passing, it should be noticed that the admission that there is undialetical thinking, even as a psychological fact, invalidates the claim made for the universality of dialectic. But we shall return to this later. It is clear, then, that one important sense of the term dialectic makes it *a constitutive principle in everything*, a pervasive ontological character of anything that ·is or may be conceived. Therefore, once we have acquired genuine knowledge of any situation, we can show that it conforms to the laws of dialectic. But at this point we are confronted by a difficulty. Engels emphatically maintains in defending Marx against Dühring that the former "does not dream of attempting to prove" the historical necessity of capitalist accumulation and decline by the laws of dialectic. "On the contrary: after he has historically proved that in fact the process has already in part occurred and in part must occur, he characterizes it in addition as a process which develops according to a definite dialectical law" (*op. cit.*, p. 136). In other words, the process of proof need not be dialectical. At best, the dialectic is *one* of a number of modes of proof even when the subject matter under investigation is historical. It cannot be true, then, that all thinking—even all valid thinking—is dialectical any more than the fact that I can translate all languages into English establishes the latter as *the* universal language. Nor can it be argued that the universal, constitutive character of dialectic is demonstrated by the fact that knowledge of anything can be acquired only by employing the dialectic method, for there are at least some things which can be known non-dialectically. The question remains whether, and to what extent, the dialectic as a method of proof and as a method of discovery is different from non-dialectical methods, and in what situations its application leads to greater truth than other available methods.

II. DIALECTIC AS THE LOGIC OF TRANSITION

The most relevant suggestion bearing on this question to be found in Engels' writings is that the dialectic method applies to situations where no hard and fast lines can be drawn, where areas of indetermination, critical phases and twilight zones are present. He contrasts the dialectic here with what he calls metaphysical thinking which postulates the unconditional validity of the principle of excluded middle. But metaphysical thinking, according to Engels, cannot give an accurate analysis of even the simplest forms of motion and is conspicuously incompatible with the evolutionary hypothesis. Two of many passages express this meaning of dialectic with forthright clarity. In *Dialektik und Natur*, speaking of transitions in nature, he writes:

"For those stages in natural science, where all oppositions are bridged by intermediate steps, the old metaphysical method of thought no longer suffices. The dialectic which recognizes no hard and fast lines, no unconditionally valid either-or!, which transforms fixed metaphysical differences into each other, mediates opposites and puts at the correct place besides the either-or! the this-as-well-as-that!, (*Sowohl dies—wie jenes!*), is the only method of thought eminently suited to such situations. For daily use, for scientific retail, the metaphysical categories retain their validity." (*Op. cit.*, p. 189.)

In the *Anti-Dühring*, Engels generalizes his criticism and calls the whole of modern science to the bar of dialectic to hear an indictment of its metaphysical character:

"It is, however, precisely the polar oppositions that are set forth as irreconcilable and insoluble, the arbitrarily imposed fixed lines of distinction and differences between classes which have given modern theoretical natural science its limited metaphysical character. The knowledge that these oppositions and differences are indeed present in nature but only with relative validity and that their conceived rigidity and absolute validity is introduced into nature only by our reflective activity—this knowledge is the kernel of the dialectical conception of nature." (p. xix.)

Here again certain crucial difficulties emerge. Either the whole of nature and experience is in a fluid state or the dialectic is not universal. If nothing that exists is *in any respect* sharply demarcated from something else, then the abstractions employed in scientific analysis, which presuppose some such demarcation, must be regarded merely as convenient fictions. In that case, the fruitfulness of one set of fictions rather than another would be a mystery. But if all thought, as Engels continually asserts, is a mirror or image of reality, the recognition of the existence and operative efficacy of fictions necessitates a modification of his theory of knowledge.

More important still, the ontological assumption behind the claim that every *entweder-oder* must be modified by a *sowohl dies—wie jenes* entails the belief that in any situation where a disjunction is employed, a third real or grounded possibility is *always* to be found. Empirically there is no warrant for such a sweeping generalization, and in fact it is flatly inconsistent with the Marxist theory of history according to which at certain historic periods society is confronted by only two possible alternatives. Time and again Engels denied that there was a genuine third alternative in modern times to socialism and capitalism. Those of his followers for whom the slogans socialism or barbarism, democracy or fascism, are not mere rhetoric, cannot square a reasoned defense of the antitheses drawn with an acceptance of the *universal relevance* of the logic of *sowohl dies—wie jenes*.[2] But of course all things are possible by a systematic abuse of definitions.

III. DIALECTIC AS THE LOGIC OF DISJUNCTION

Interestingly enough, Engels' own political experience, combined with his stress upon the facts of polarity, leads him on occasion to speak of dialectical situations as if they were preeminently characterized by the logic of exclusive and exhaustive disjunction. (The identification of polar opposition and dialectic we shall discuss below.) In a passage which begins by stating that "the so-called objective dialectic" obtains for the whole of nature, and that "the so-called subjective dialectic" is merely the reflection of the "movement of opposites" everywhere valid in nature, Engels writes:

[2] *Cf. Lenin.* "Auf der historischen Stufenleiter zwischen dieser Stufe [monopoly capitalism—S. H.] und derjenigen, die man Sozialismus nennt keine *Zwischenstufen* gibt." ("Die drohende Katastrophe und wie soll man sie bekämpfen," *Sämtliche Werke*, Bd. XXI, p. 235.)

"It is in history that the movement of opposites really comes to the fore in all the critical epochs of the leading nations. At such moments a nation has a choice only between two horns of a dilemma: either—or. And indeed the question is always posed quite differently from the way in which the political philistindom of all times wishes to pose it. Even the liberal German philistines of 1848 found themselves in 1849 suddenly and unexpectedly and against their own will faced by the question: either a return to the old reaction in intensified form or progress of the revolution to a republic. . . . Likewise the French bourgeoisie stood before the certainly unexpected dilemma: either caricature of imperial rule, Praetorianism and the expoitation of France by a pack of scoundrels (*Lumpenbande*) or a social-democratic republic." (*Dialektik und Natur, loc. cit.,* p. 190.)

It is clear that it is precisely in such situations that the liberals, of whose undialectical approach Engels speaks so scornfully, seek for third alternatives, intermediate paths, and formulae which attempt to reconcile the irreconcilable. Such a quest, according to the present sense of dialectic, is branded undialectical, even though it invokes the logic of continuity and inveighs against hard and fast lines. But what, now, shall we say of nature in which Engels has assured us no hard and fast lines occur? It is certainly not dialectical in the present sense. In an attempt to escape this obvious difficulty it is sometimes held that the dialectic expresses *both* the logic of continuity (*sowohl dies—wie jenes*) and that of discontinuity (*entweder—oder*). Nature and history provide situations in which the two approaches are legitimate. Granted. But even so, they are not both applicable at the same time, in the same respect, and from the same point of view. Since both cannot be universally applicable, when is the *either-or* aspect of the dialectic to be employed and when *the-this-as-well-as-that?*

No matter what answer is made, it will entail the recognition that recourse must be had to other methodological considerations in order to determine when it is legitimate to apply the narrow form of the principle of excluded middle and when it is not. These considerations, of course, are derived from the logic of scientific inquiry whose task it is to determine whether the material under investigation is such that various formal rules may be significantly applied. Later on we shall see that there is a sense of dialectic which makes it equivalent to scientific method but we shall also see that it is highly dubious whether any science can achieve significant results by denying the principle of excluded middle.

Some dialectical materialists are under the strange delusion that a trichotomy such as "either *a* or *b* or *both*" represents a violation of the law of excluded middle. This would be the case only if *b* were the formal contradictory of *a*, in which case it is simply nonsense to say that they are both true. Sometimes we find ourselves in a position in which we seem to be saying that neither *a* nor its contradictory is true, as e.g., "the soul weighs more than a gram" and "the soul does not weigh more than a gram," but all such statements are pseudo-propositions. They involve a confusion of categories and are meaningless.

IV. DIALECTIC AS POLAR OPPOSITION

Another sense of the term dialectic gives it the meaning of *polarity* and *polar opposition*. For Engels the sources of this conception are to be found in Hegel's doctrine of Essence. Physical phenomena are cited as the most striking illustration of polarity and provide the basic analogy in this respect for all other fields. "Just as electricity and magnetism polarize themselves, move in opposites, so do thoughts." (*Ibid.*, p. 156.) In other passages, he traces its presence in chemistry, biology, and psychology. Nowhere is an analysis given of the logical structure of polarity, so that it is difficult to tell whether Engels is using the concept of polarity metaphorically or whether he actually believes that thoughts, for example, polarize themselves like magnets, which is comparable to saying that the concept of weight itself has weight.

The clearest meaning that can be given to the statement that polarity is universal in nature and history derives from some linguistic principle of significant assertion. Every term which enters significantly into discourse must have an intelligible opposite. This is not an arbitrary rule of language but flows from the fact, recognized both by Hegel and Engels, that everything can be surveyed from at least two different aspects and that the existence of anything involves the existence of at least some one *other* thing. But even so, this by no means justifies the deduction that the other, from which an aspect or thing is distinguished, is *polar* in character, that it necessitates, and is necessitated by, the existence of its opposite. The "poles" of a magnet are such not because the two ends are merely *different* from each other. The two ends still remain different even when demagnetization has taken place. But the polarity is gone. Materially interpreted, either polar opposition means no more than that there are differences in nature, which is true but trivial since it is the kind, quality and degree of difference that are scientifically important; or polar opposition is not at all a universal phenomenon but must be empirically established, once its structure is clearly defined, in various fields and situations.

It must be further indicated that the structure of the polar opposition in magnetism is quite different from the structure of the polar opposition between male and female, arithmetical plus and minus, heredity and environment (the illustrations are Engels'), and bourgeoisie and proletariat. The expression is systematically ambiguous and is of no help in any concrete inquiry which seeks to discover how various elements within a situation are functionally related to each other.

v. "subjective" dialectic

A more special sense of the term dialectic in Engels makes it relevant primarily to the development of concepts. This converts the dialectic into a constitutive principle not of everything but of a determinate realm of existence—the realm of mind. The growth of knowledge, individual and social, is often cited as an illustration of the dialectic process in this sense. Sometimes such statements are accompanied by the remark that the growth of knowledge actually reflects or mirrors the changes and evolution in the subject matter known, from which it would follow that the order of the development of knowledge is the same as the order of the objective development of things. The latter proposition, already explicitly drawn by Hegel, is palpably false and is compatible only with some form of philosophical idealism.

When Engels refers to dialectic as the structure of the thought process, it is to contrast it with other modes of thinking. Man shares with the animals, he tells us, all the activities of the understanding—induction, deduction, abstraction, analysis, synthesis, and experimentation.[3] In these respects, there is no essential difference between man and the animals except in degree. "On the other hand dialectical thinking is possible only for man just because it has as its presupposition the investigation of the nature of concepts themselves" (*op. cit.*, p. 187). It seems, then, that the nature of concepts is the privileged subject matter of dialectic, and further, that all the activities of the understanding enumerated above, which constitute far and away the larger portion of thought, can be carried on without an "investigation of the nature of concepts"—an interesting doctrine if true.

This clearly seems to restrict dialectic to a method of analyzing concepts, although previously it had been characterized as a method of proof and a method of discovery—activities which, according to Engels, man shares with animals incapable of dialectic thought. And even as a method of analysis, Engels does not hesitate to contrast it with mathematical thought. He prefaces some remarks on work as the measure of motion with the observation that "perhaps it will be seen that when it is a question of handling ideas, dialectical thinking at the very least carries one just as far as mathematical calculation" (*op. cit.*, p. 307). The "perhaps," of course, turns out to be purely rhetorical.

Now conceptual thought may be "analyzed" from at least three different points of view. (i) Inquiry may be made into the natural history of ideas, the structure and function of the thought processes out of which they arise—all of which is roughly classified under psychology. Or (ii) the formal relationships between ideas may be investigated so as to disclose whether the systematic pattern of meanings (propositions, statements) involved is consistent—formal and symbolic logic. Or (iii) the relationships between things, symbols, and human behavior may be analyzed in order to show how normative principles of thought arise and operate in inquiry. It is difficult to determine whether Engels' statement that formal logic and

---

[3] "Alle Verstandstätigkeit: *Induzieren, Deduzieren,* also auch *Abstrahieren* ... Analysieren unbekannter Gegenstände (schon das Zerbrechen einer Nuss ist Anfang der Analyse), *Synthesieren* (bei tierischen Schlauheitsstückchen) und als Vereinigung beider *Experimentieren* (bei neuen Hindernissen und in fremden Lagen) haben wir mit dem Tier gemein." *Dialektik und Natur, op. cit.*, p. 187.

dialectic is "the science of thought and its laws" refers to any one of these aspects of thought or to all three.[4] If the dialectic is a description of the ways in which human beings actually think, then all thinking, good, bad, or indifferent, is dialectical, and as pure descriptive psychology, it has little bearing upon the laws of *valid* proof or discovery. If dialectic is not concerned with psychology and sets itself up as a theory of consistent and valid thinking in all fields, then since it has been granted that some people think undialectically and yet not always incorrectly, then the dialectic is universal neither as fact nor norm. The third possible approach to thinking, so far as I know, has not been identified with the dialectic by any canonic interpreter nor has any theory of the nature of signs and symbols been developed.

VI. DIALECTIC AS ORGANIC INTERRELATION

Another meaning attached to the term dialectic in the writings of Engels is asserted to have great heuristic value. The dialectic approach to nature and history recognizes that all things are organically interrelated in one great totality. No object, therefore, can be exhaustively explained in its own specific categories. The totality is such that all of its elements are in continuous interaction with each other so that cause and effect are abstracted, partial phases of an interlocking, developing whole. What is often called "dialectical" interrelation between part and part, and whole and part, is universal and necessary. Many passages can be cited from Engels' writings which imply this view:

"We also find upon closer examination that the both poles of an opposition, like positive and negative, are as inseparable from each other as they are opposed, and that despite their opposition interpenetrate each other. In the same way, cause and effect are ideas that have validity only when applied to the particular case as such, but just as soon as we consider the individual event in its universal connection with the world as a whole are dissolved in the conception of a universal, reciprocal interaction (*Wechselwirkung*) in which causes

4 "Was von der ganzen bisherigen Philosophie dann noch selbständig bestehen bleibt ist die Lehre vom Denken und seinen Gesetzen—die formelle Logik und die Dialektik." *Anti-Dühring*, p. 11.

and effects continually change places, and what now or here is effect becomes there or then cause and *vice versa.*" (*Anti-Dühring,* pp. 7-8.) [5]

Now the statement "all things are interrelated" is, as such, ambiguous, unless it is indicated *how* they are interrelated, or at the very least, what *kind* of interrelation is meant. To say that things are "dialectically" interrelated introduces the conceptions of necessity and systematic connection but still leaves open the question whether they are physically interrelated or logically interrelated. On Engels' view, however, since logical relations are reflections of relations which exist in the natural world, there is no essential difference between causal determination and logical determination. As in Hegel, where a distinction is recognized, it turns out to be merely epistemic.

This conception of universal dialectical interrelation is the fountainhead of Engels' monism and is defended by a number of logical and empirical considerations scattered throughout Engels' writings. The logical arguments are all variants of the Hegelian theory of internal relations. The ascription of any property or relation to a term presupposes the existence of another term. Every term is a congeries of an infinite set of relations all of which are necessary to its nature. Strictly speaking, then, it is impossible to deny that a term has any of its determinate properties without lapsing into self-contradiction. As a matter of fact, however, it is possible meaningfully to deny that a term is characterized by any of its properties or relations except when the latter are part of the *definition* of the term. But if all the relationships into which a thing can possibly enter are already involved in its definition, it would follow that all propositions of fact are analytic, which is clearly false. The influence of the notion of universal, "dialectical interrelation" is also revealed in the curious reluctance on the part of orthodox Hegelians and dialectical materialists to admit that "hypotheticals contrary to fact," i.e., judgments which take the form "*if* a thing or event had been different from what it was," are meaningful assumptions in science or history.

The empirical argument for the dialectical interrelatedness of everything is buttressed by the citation of many instances in which the growth of knowledge has led to the modification

[5] *Cf.* also, *Dialektik und Natur,* p. 219; *Ludwig Feuerbach,* Duncker Ausgabe, p. 54; letters to Bloch, Starkenberg, and Mehring *passim* reprinted in appendix to *Towards the Understanding of Karl Marx,* New York, 1933.

of earlier views held, to the redefinition of concepts, and to the discovery of unifying principles between apparently disparate fields. But it is or should be obvious that the empirical evidence in the nature of the case has to be piecemeal and cannot serve as the premise for a deduction that any new piece of knowldge must *necessarily* lead to the abandonment or modification of the old.

VII. DIALECTIC AS SCIENTIFIC METHOD

There remains, finally, the conception of dialectic which makes it equivalent to scientific method. Although there is little direct statement of this interpretation, suggestions and intimations abound in Engels' discussions. On occasions the critical role of hypotheses is recognized, admission is made of the existence of relatively isolated systems, and the methodological inadequacy of physical and biological "reductionism" is very forcibly stated. In many passages stress is placed upon the relative (and relational), historical and contextual character of judgment, including scientific propositions, and some of Engels' formulations, despite his crude theory of abstraction, would give comfort even to contemporary positivism.[6] When Engels criticizes the excesses of empiricists, it is in order to call attention either to their neglect of hypotheses or their failure to introduce the proper controls in experiment without which observations have no evidential value.[7] A typical passage of this strain in Engels' thought is the following:

"The form of development of natural science insofar as it is reflective is the *hypothesis*. A new fact is observed which makes the customary mode of explanation for facts of the same class impossible. From this moment on, there is a need for new modes of explanation which at first rest upon a limited number of facts and observations. Further observation purifies these hypotheses, eliminates some, corrects others until the law is established in pure form. Were one to wait until the materials out of which the law is derived appear in *pure* form, that would mean to suspend reflective inquiry indefinitely, and already for that reason alone the law would never be established." (*Dialektik und Natur, op. cit.,* p. 155.)

[6] *Cf.* especially *Dialektik und Natur, op. cit.,* p. 237.
[7] (*E.g.,* in his remarks on Wallace and Crookes in his "Natural Science in the Spirit World," *Marx-Engels Archiv,* Bd., 2 pp. 207-216, translated into English in *Marxist Quarterly,* Vol. I, No. 1, pp. 68-76.

Engels very properly adds that the fact that hypotheses succeed each other, so that none can claim to be absolutely true, does not justify the belief that the essence of things is unknowable or that a legitimate scientific distinction can be drawn between appearance and reality.

We are all the more warranted in emphasizing this interpretation in virtue of Engels' claims that the dialectic is a method by which new truths are discovered, for whatever else scientific method may be disclosed to be, it is primarily the organized procedure of inference, prediction, and control by which man extends the boundaries of knowledge.

In this section we have distinguished in the major works of Engels seven distinct meanings of the term dialectic insofar as it bears upon natural phenomena. They are: (1) dialectic as a constitutive principle of all things—a universal form of behavior to which there are no actual or conceivable exceptions; (2) dialectic as the logical pattern of transition and continuity; (3) dialectic as the logic of disjunction in situations where two alternatives are exclusive and exhaustive; (4) dialectic as the principle of polar opposition; (5) dialectic as a special constitutive principle whose existential locus is the development of *concepts;* (6) dialectic as the constitutive and heuristic principle that all things are systematically interrelated, and (7) dialectic as a groping, first approximation to the logic of scientific method. Other meanings may be found but with the exception of conceptions of dialectic that apply only to history and sociology (which are not included in the scope of this chapter) none will be discovered to play a significant role in the corpus of Engels' writings.

It remains to ask now: to what extent are these seven conceptions compatible with each other? And if they are incompatible, which conception(s) of dialectic does Engels regard as most basic to his own thinking?

2. The Ambiguities and Inconsistencies of Dialectic

A first glance at the seven different meanings of dialectic in Engels will show that they fall within three groups: (a) dialectic as a universal constitutive principle, justifying the logic of organic totality (1 and 6 of the enumeration above); (b) in which the constitutive reference of the dialectic is limited to a restricted field, or to a particular aspect of all fields (2, 3, 4 and 5); (c) in which it is synonymous with scientific method.

Are (a) and (b) compatible with each other? Yes, if (b) were subject to *special* laws of dialectic applicable to special fields without impugning the validity of the laws of (a). But there are no dialectical laws asserted to hold for (b) which are not restatements of, or deductions from, the dialectical laws asserted to hold for (a). However, we have seen that the point of the enumeration of special fields of (b) in which dialectic structure is found is to distinguish them from other fields of existence *not* characterized by dialectical structure. Or in other words, what (b) asserts is not "some, perhaps all, fields of existence are characterized by dialectic," but "some fields are so characterized and some are not." It follows therefore that (a) and (b) are related to each other as A and O propositions in the traditional logic, i.e., they are formal contradictories.

Are (a) and (c) compatible with each other? This depends on what we understand by scientific method. Now there is at least one proposition which every theory of scientific method must accept in some form or other if it desires to do justice to the actual procedures of scientific inquiry, viz., that it is possible to discover the functional relationships between a limited number of variables without taking into account the rest of the universe. Without this presupposition—whose fruitfulness proves that it is not arbitrary—scientific experimentation would be impossible. In fact, to say that all things are interrelated is to utter a formula devoid even of heuristic value. When it is invoked as an *obiter dictum*, it will be found that what is meant is that *some* things are related in certain *specific* ways to some other things. It is simply not the case that each additional piece of knowledge leads to a modification of every other piece of knowledge. Nothing can be discovered except on the assumption that the particular situation investigated is determined by a finite number of *relevant* factors. The infinity of universes and the possible infinity of their interrelations, if they have any significance for science at all, mean not that knowledge *must* be inaccurate but merely that there is always something more to be known. At times Engels himself recognizes this, as when he writes: "The extremest limit of our natural science is until now *our* universe and we do not need the infinite number of universes which exist out there in order to have knowledge of nature" (*op. cit.*, p. 159).

Another characteristic property of scientific method is that its techniques involve a transformation of materials, an intervention into natural processes, an introduction of *redirective activities* upon what is given to hand in order to achieve the tested knowledge necessary for prediction and control. Were everything in the world interrelated in one complex network of objective dialectic, then science as a human and cultural phenomenon would be *theoretically* inferrible from the existence of that which is to be known. The world would have to be declared such that it could not *both* be true that (i) it has the structure it is actually discovered to have an (ii) science itself not have emerged. This is to assert, for example, that a star cluster in the heavens or the adrenal glands in man could not possibly exist unless they were discovered. Or, more generally, that it is theoretically possible by an organic logic to prove that a *necessary* connection exists between what is and what is known. This is the open gateway to idealism. Berkeley and Hegel stand on either side of the tortuous path beckoning unwary dialectical materialists who believe this to come closer.

A still more important implication is involved in the view that the historic development of science is subject to the immanent necessities of the one dialectical whole of which it is a part. For science as a phase of human culture is controlled by values, interests and needs which are revealed most clearly in the direction of scientific research and the variety of its applications. Human values, then, on the above view of organic determinism, must have not only a cosmic support but must be constitutively involved in the very nature of things. Like all other things, nature and society must be "dialectically" and, therefore, necessarily interrelated. But for Marxism, as for every other non-Platonic philosophy, there are no values where there is no consciousness, or at least some form of sentience. To make values constitutive elements in the dialectic totality, therefore, is to make consciousness an integral element of all existence, is to endow the scheme of things with some pervasive purpose or system of purposes which is gradually being fulfilled. What this leads to was pointed out by Engels himself when he taxed Dühring with surreptitiously introducing conscious activity into natural processes and relapsing into theology.[8]

A final root incompatibility between (a) and (c) is to be discovered in their respective notions of necessity as applied to existence. In (a) necessity is logical, systematic, and circular. In (c) necessity is conditional and justifies only probability judgments. From the point of view of a philosophy which regards the world as a dialectic totality, the "necessities" expressed by scientific laws are abstract and contingent. Abstract, because they are asserted to hold for all situations which conform to certain initial definitions irrespective of what *other* properties may be present; contingent, because the relationships discovered to hold between the various elements of a situation are not derived from the "systematic dynamic nature" (Hegel) or "the self-moving nature" (Engels) of the objects investigated. For the ordinary scientist, however, there is no such thing as *the* nature of anything with inherent qualities of self-movement which constitute its so-called set of essential attributes. All attributes, properties, and relations possess the same degree of essentiality or inherence except where, in the course of inquiry, he isolates certain characteristics for purposes of identification and uses them as defining traits in subsequent investigation. His mode of analysis is thoroughly relational and when he speaks of the *normal* or *natural* properties of anything he is employing these terms in a statistical sense.

The difference between the concepts of necessity in (a) and (c) may be illustrated by an example from Engels which is all the more to the point because it indicates what meaning the term "dialectic" normally has for Engels himself. In critically discussing "mathematical materialism" which explains the phases of a developed mental process step by step in terms of the functional relationships existing between the elements in any given region of space and time, Engels quotes with approval Hegel's doctrine of *der innere Zweck* (internal purpose). According to this doctrine, the nature of an organism

[8] "...Herr Dühring genöthigt ist, der Natur mehr als einmal bewusste Handlungsweise unterzuschieben, also das was man auf deutsch Gott nennt." *Anti-Dühring*, p. 23.

(and for Hegel, as for Whitehead, all things may be characterized as organisms) determines the specific type of relationship which exists at any time between its constituent elements. It is denied that the nature of anything can be explained as the resultant structure of cumulative, empirically observable relationships between its elements and the complex of environmental conditions. At most, the absence of environmental conditions may prevent the nature of a thing from realizing itself, but once the conditions are present (and something guarantees that sooner or later they will be), then the essential properties of a thing can be explained only in terms of its antecedently defined self-moving nature.

"The point is," writes Engels, "that mechanism (also the materialism of the eighteenth century) never frees itself from abstract necessity and therefore from contingency. That matter has developed out of itself a thinking human brain is for it a purely contingent fact, although every step in its occurrence is necessarily conditioned. In truth, however, it is the nature of matter to progress to the development of thinking creatures and this occurs, therefore, always of necessity when the conditions for it (not necessarily everywhere and always the same) are present." (*Dialektik und Natur, loc. cit.,* p. 292.)

This asserts two things which can never be established by scientific methods. One, that somewhere and sometimes the conditions *must* appear which are necessary for the nature of matter to realize itself in the form of a thinking brain, for if the conditions of emergence *never* appeared, wherein would the *necessity* of the emergence lie except in an arbitrary definition of matter? Second, that the emergence of a thinking brain is not univocally determined by a definite set of conditions, so that the necessity of the emergence of the brain cannot be attributed to the interacting complex of determinate conditions at a given time but to the nature of matter as such—a matter which, Engels tells us elsewhere, is "a pure creation of thought, an abstraction." [9]

That Engels is in earnest with his contention that the nature of matter is such that it must *necessarily* develop into a thinking brain, a striking passage from the same work testifies. "We have the certainty," he says, "that matter in all its transforma-

---

[9] "Die Materie als solche ist eine reine Gedankenschöpfung und Abstraktion," *op. cit.,* p. 234.

tions remains eternally the same, that none of its attributes can ever be lost, and that therefore with the same iron necessity with which, on earth, it exterminates its highest product, the thinking spirit, it must some day somewhere else create it again" (p. 255).

This is a certainty that dialectic (I had almost said religion) may give—science never.

In the light of the foregoing, I think we are justified in maintaining that the class of meanings of dialectic in group (a) is incompatible with dialectic conceived as scientific method, group (c).

Are (b) and (c) compatible with each other? Here we must briefly compare the members of class (b) and (c).

(b)2 and (c). (b)2 is the logic of transition and continuity. It is obvious that scientific method takes note of continuities. In fact it is only in virtue of the application of scientific method that continuities have been uncovered and adequately described. But Engels interprets (b)2 as if it entailed the denial of the laws of identity and contradiction. "Abstract identity, $a = a$, and negatively, a cannot be equal and unequal to a at the same time—are also inapplicable to organic nature" (*ibid.*, p. 157). Were this so, the work of science would come to a dead stop. As we shall see below, where science seems to violate the law of contradiction, it is in virtue of incompatible descriptions and statements, an incompatibility which is a spur either to further qualification of the descriptions or to redefinition—both designed to eliminate contradiction. Engels' interpretation of (b)2 must be declared incompatible with (c).

(b)3 and (c). (b)3 is the logic of disjunction where alternatives are mutually exclusive and exhaustive. This is compatible with (c). In fact, it is a special case of the method of residues. Scientific method, however, never *guarantees* that all the known alternatives are exhaustive unless we are dealing with a proposition and its logical contradictory. And even here it may rule out both on the ground that their meaning content is irrelevant to the specific inquiry. Scientific conclusions, therefore, even when the purely deductive form of the method of residues is employed, cannot give us more than probabilities.

(b)4 and (c). (b)4 is the principle of polar opposition. If

the metaphor of polarity is taken seriously, it is the purest mythology to extend it to everything. In this form, (b)4 is a vestige of the Romantic *Natur-philosophie* and is inconsistent with any non-mystical conception of scientific method. If the principle of polarity states that every scientific category must have an intelligible opposite, then it is "true" and enjoys the status of a syntactical rule of significant assertion. The successful application of this rule in the construction of a scientific system justifies the inference that no situation in nature can be found which is resolvable into one element or possesses only one aspect. Attempts have sometimes been made to interpret the principle of polarity as if it meant that in every situation forces will be found which are moving in opposite directions. But Engels scorns this interpretation as the sheerest commonplace devoid of any possibility of application (*Anti-Dühring*, p. 122).

(b)5 and (c). (b)5 is dialectic conceived as the structural form of the natural history of concepts. If concepts do have this form, (c) is the only valid method by which that fact can be discovered. (c) and (b)5, therefore, are compatible, and related to each other as method and specific conclusion.

There remains the question of the relationships which the different conceptions of dialectic in class (b) bear to each other. To save space we shall state only the conclusions of the analysis.

(b)2 and (b)3, strictly interpreted, are incompatible, especially if both are regarded as having universal import.

(b)2 and (b)4 are incompatible.

(b)2 and (b)3 are related as (b)2 and (c), depending upon how (b)2 is taken.

(b)3 and (b)4 are compatible.

(b)3 and (b)5 are compatible.

(b)4 and (b)5 are related as (b)4 and (c).

We have already answered the first question we set ourselves in Section II. The various meanings of dialectic in Engels are incompatible with each other. The second question is: which meaning does Engels regard as primary in his own thought? Sufficient documentation has been given to indicate that the answer is (1)—dialectic as a universal constitutive principle operating everywhere and in everything. That Engels regards this as the primary meaning of dialectic is apparent also in the fact that the major part of his discussion of dialectic in the *Anti-Dühring* consists of an attempt to state the objective and universal *laws* of dialectic. In short, the laws of dialectic are laws of *ontology*. In Section III we shall critically examine these laws from the point of view of logic and scientific method.

3. The "Laws" of Dialectic

We have already seen that according to Engels dialectic is the science of extremely general, comprehensive, and, therefore, important laws of development in nature, history, and thought. The basic laws of dialectic are three in number. Running reference is made to them throughout all of Engels' writings. The formulation of these laws varies and the only extended discussion of them in the *Anti-Dühring* concerns itself in the main with the citation of illustrations.

The chief laws of dialectic are:

(I) "The identity of contradictories." Sometimes alternate phrasings are found, such as "the identity of opposites." On occasions the term "unity" is substituted for "identity." All four of the following expressions are used interchangeably in the works of most dialectical materialists: (a) the identity of contradictions, (b) the unity of contradictions, (c) the identity of opposites, (d) the unity of opposites.

(II) The law of "the negation of the negation." Sometimes this is called "the law of the transformation of contradictions (opposites) into each other."

(III) "The transition of quantity to quality and vice versa."

I. CONTRADICTION

The fundamental presupposition of all the laws of dialectic is the belief that contradiction "is objectively present in things and processes." To say the very least, this is a strange use of the term "contradiction," for since the time of Aristotle it has been a commonplace of logical theory that *propositions* or *judgments* or *statements* are contradictory, not things or events. Engels is perfectly aware of the traditional usage but argues against Dühring that the refusal to make the concept of contradiction applicable to things is precisely what reveals the limitations of commonsense and formal logic. Indeed, not only does Engels maintain that contradiction is objectively present in nature, he insists that it is "an actual force as well." [10] Literally construed, this would make a physical relation out of a logical category, so that the whole of mathematics and logic would be nothing more than a branch of physics. The difficulties in such a view are enormous. In addition to being flatly irreconcilable with basic principles of scientific inquiry, it cannot even be consistently stated.

If all existence is self-contradictory and, as Engels holds, all correct thinking is an image or reflection of things, then consistency would be an unfailing sign of falsity. The sciences, which regard consistency as at least a necessary condition of truth, could not take a step. If all existence is self-contradictory, then Engels is hardly entitled to say that thought which is a product of nature must "correspond" with it instead of contradicting it.[11] If logic is part of physics, then logical propositions could not possess the qualities of universality and necessity which Engels attributes to them also. And further, if propositions of logic have the same existential character as propositions of physics, then Engels is owing an explanation of why it is that denials of propositions of the first class always lead to statements that are self-contradictory while denials of propositions of the second class never do.

Engels does not concern himself with an answer to these difficulties. Instead, he offers illustrations of the alleged fact that contradiction is objectively present in things and processes. The illustrations are: 1. The existence of motion. 2. The nature of life. 3. The form of the knowledge process. 4. The basic notions of mathematics.

1. *Motion.* The only argument which Engels advances for his contention that motion is contradictory is a variant of one of the general considerations adduced as long ago as Zeno. But whereas Zeno employed it to prove the unreality of motion,

---

[10] *Anti-Dühring*, 12th ed., Berlin, 1923, p. 121.
[11] "... es sich dann von selbst versteht, dass die Erzeugnisse des menschlichen Hirns, die in letzter Instanz ja auch Naturprodukte sind, dem übrigen Naturzusammenhang nicht widersprechen sondern entsprechen." *Ibid.*, p. 22.

Engels uses it to establish the objective existence of contradiction:

> "Motion is itself a contradiction: even simple mechanical change of place (*Ortsbewegung*) can only occur by a body at one and the same moment of time being both in one place and in another place, in one and the same place and not in it. And the continuous occurrence (*Setzung*) and the simultaneous solution of this contradiction is just what motion is." (*Anti-Dühring*, p. 120.)

Now there is an important leap in this argument. For all that Engels could have established by considerations like the above is that certain *descriptions* or *statements* of motion violate the law of contradiction. Before he can conclude that motion itself is contradictory, he must first show that it is impossible to find, and operate with, any other *description* or statement of motion without falling into inconsistency. Not only does he fail to do this; it was already clear in 1894 when Engels wrote the preface to the third edition of *Anti-Dühring* that motion could be described in perfectly consistent fashion. The motion of any particle can be described by an expression indicating that its position in space at any moment is a continuous function of time. And the concept of a continuous function has been made clear without assuming the existence of infinitesimal intervals of space and time which Engels believes to be involved in motion and fundamental to the theory of the differential and integral calculus.

Further, it might be pointed out that, strictly interpreted, Engels' *description* of motion reveals no formal contradiction at all. To say that a body occupies two different places at one and the same time is perfectly legitimate if we recognize that the body has different parts; and there is no difficulty in admitting that a body can be and not be in the same place if we distinguish between different times. And still more, since in *rerum nátura* there are no points without extension or moments without duration, Engels' formulation applies just as much to bodies at rest as to bodies in motion. He would thus be proving too much, for not only would motion be contradictory but its opposite, rest, would also be contradictory. And since everything in the world to which we may significantly apply spatio-temporal co-ordinates is either in motion or at rest, and this not absolutely but always relatively to something else, the term contradiction has no differential meaning. When not actually obfuscating, it is useless. The confusion is confounded when Engels speaks of contradiction as being the driving force of all movement and development, transforming logical notions into *demiurgoi* in a fashion which even the logical idealism of Hegel does not justify.

2. *Life*. In citing organic phenomena as illustrations of the objectivity of contradiction, Engels equates contradiction to *struggle*,[12] and seems to suggest that wherever two terms are so related that they may be characterized as contradictory there is an actual struggle, conscious or unconscious, going-on between them. There is no doubt that *struggle* is an appropriate term to apply to the relationship which exists between social classes, and in the Darwinian sense, to the relationship between biological species, and to a lesser degree even to some of the relationships between individuals within the same species. But since struggles are only found where *living* creatures are found, Engels must have been speaking metaphorically when he suggests that it is a universal and objective trait of existence. Unless, of course, he is to be classified with the Romantic *Natur-philosophen* for whom all nature is animate and who were wont to speak of *things* struggling with each other. We are probably closest to Engels' meaning if we take him to mean that life is contradictory for the same general reason that motion is, *viz.*, that it violates the law of contradiction. In fact, Engels sometimes employs the same formulation in both cases:

"We saw above that life consists before all just in this that a living creature is at each moment itself and yet something else. Life is therefore also a contradiction present in things and processes, continually occurring and solving itself; and as soon as the contradiction ceases life also ceases and death steps in." (*Op. cit.*, p. 121.)

Of course Engels should have added that as soon as the contradiction ceases a new one steps in, for on his own premises only the forms of contradiction change. But there is nothing contradictory about this description of life; it merely suffers from vagueness. Once we introduce the proper distinctions and

[12] "...dass man keine Malthus-Brille braucht, um den Kampf ums Dasein in der Natur wahrzunehmen—den Widerspruch zwischen der Zahllosen Menge von Keimen, die die Natur verschwenderisch erzeugt, und der geringen Anzahl von ihnen, die überhapt zur Reife kommen können." (*Op. cit.*, p. 60.) A strange kind of contradiction that!

qualifications, we can get a consistent enough account of the phenomenon of life. Life is distinguished from non-living things in that it is a self-conserving process, with a physico-chemical structure which regulates the ingestion, digestion, and excretion of food and makes possible selective activity, growth and reproduction. At any definite time, its behavior is a function of a complex of environmental stimuli, and of its own physico-chemical state in relation to which only certain phases of the environment can serve as stimuli. That an organism can keep going only in virtue of the dissolution and assimilation of certain organic compounds from without—"living is a process of dying"—is not a contradiction; nor is it a fact which compels us to utter contradictory statements in describing it except where we are licensed by poetic usage. An animal, for example, can keep on living only if plants (or *other* animals) keep on dying. An animal can keep on living only if it keeps on eliminating its dead cells. But the fact that we distinguish between living and dead cells in any body makes it impossible to say that *in the same respect* and *at the same time* any cell of the body (as well as the body as a whole) is both living and dead. Nor is there any mystery in the fact that we speak of the *same* body although the materials of the body are completely renewed every seven years or so, if we bear in mind that identity, when it is employed as an explanatory category, depends upon some defining perspective. Identity of personality, for example, depends more upon social, legal and psychological considerations than upon physical or biological states.

3. *Knowledge.* One of the most interesting passages in *Anti-Dühring* consists of an attempt to trace the way in which any doctrine that affirms the existence of final, ultimate and eternal truths slips by degrees into ethical and social apologetics. For Engels, eternal truths are either tautologies or trivialities. Absolute Truth is conceived as the limit of the knowledge process carried on by an endless number of generations. As far as the individual thinker is concerned, the knowledge he acquires always contains more elements that can be improved upon than elements that cannot (p. 80). Here undoubtedly Engels has justification in the history of science and the nature of scientific procedure for his stress upon the ap-

proximate character of knowledge. But he professes to find in the self-corrective processes of knowledge a contradiction— a contradiction between thought which is sovereign and absolute considered from the point of view of its ideal *possibility* and *aim*, and thought which is limited and relative in its actual exemplifications. Science strives for absolute knowledge but at any definite moment of time falls short of it; but the contradiction is solved, says Engels, by the infinite progression of the knowledge-getting activities of man:

"We likewise saw how even in the domain of thought we cannot escape contradictions, and how, e.g., the contradiction between man's intrinsically unlimited faculty of thought and its actual existence in men so completely limited by their external conditions as well as in their knowledge, is solved, in what is, at least for us, practically an endless succession of generations, in infinite progress." (*Anti-Dühring*, p. 121.)

Strictly speaking, only problems, puzzles and difficulties are solved, not contradictions. And solutions always involve the elimination of contradictions, not from things, but from our analysis of them. Even, however, if we grant that Engels has described the aim and procedure of scientific knowledge correctly, there is no contradiction involved in positing an ideal, and failing to realize it, any more than there is a contradiction in aspiring towards perfect health and failing to achieve it in some respect. There are two questionable assumptions, however, concealed in Engels' account of the alleged "contradiction" in the knowledge process. The first is that the ideal of scientific knowledge is absolutely valid knowledge, and second that, assuming this is the ideal of scientific knowledge, there must be absolutely certain truths which enable us to order series of truths which are not absolutely certain. For Engels, these absolute truths are limits of unending series of relative truths which approach closer and closer to their limits with the passage of time and the accumulation of knowledge. Modern science, however, is primarily interested in knowledge which is *sufficiently fruitful* and *reliable* to enable us to solve problems of inquiry. Where it employs the term "truth," the reference is to the degree to which a proposition coheres with a set of other propositions and ultimately to its relative adequacy in enabling us to make verifiable predictions. At no point in his procedure is the scientist compelled to assume that there are absolutely certain truths about matters of fact.[13]

Secondly, insofar as science operates with a definition of truth, the definition serves as a *rule* to guide scientific procedure in ordering the reliability of a series of propositions: it does not serve as a warrant for inferring that absolute truth exists as a limit of an infinite series of relative truths. In this it functions analagously to other definitions. A definition of hardness, for example, enables us to order various substances in a series of increasing or decreasing hardness, but it does not at all follow that therefore an absolutely hard substance exists which is the limit of an infinite series of substances of varying hardnesses. Engels' remarks exhibit a confusion between an ordering principle according to which a series is organized and a limit towards which a series converges.

4. $\sqrt{-1}$. Although, as we have seen in Part I, Engels often refers to mathematics as the realm in which undialectical yet valid thinking proceeds on the basis of the abstract laws of identity and non-contradiction, he just as often couples this assertion with the claim that many fields of mathematics are still subject to the higher laws of dialectic where contradiction is king. The chief illustration is drawn from the calculus but is unfortunately vitiated by the antiquated theory of infinitesimals already abandoned by mathematicians in Engels' own day. But even elementary mathematics, according to Engels, teems (*wimmelt*) with contradictions. And the most striking of these is

"The contradiction that a negative quantity should be the square of anything, for every negative magnitude multiplied by itself gives a positive square. The square root of minus one, therefore, is not only a contradiction but even an absurd contradiction, actual nonsense (*wirklicher Widersinn*). And yet the $\sqrt{-1}$ is in many cases a necessary result of correct mathematical operations. (*Op. cit.,* pp. 121-122.)

It would follow that since all thought, particularly when applied successfully to nature, is a "reflection" of natural processes, nature must not only be contradictory but "in many

---

[13] In one of his genial insights which for all their inconsistencies make Engels' writings instructive even to critical readers, Engels recognizes this. "Wirklich wissenschaftliche Arbeiten vermeiden daher regelmässig solche dogmatische-moralische Ausdrücke wie Irrthum und Wahrheit." (*Op. cit.,* p. 87.)

cases" positively absurd. And were Engels to qualify the fidelity and universality of the "reflex" character of thought, it would still remain hard to understand how, by operating with absurd contradictions and actual nonsense, we could so successfully predict, construct and explain things. The absurdity, however, must not be laid to the door of the $\sqrt{-1}$ but to Engels' own characterization of it. The rule that the square of a negative number must be positive holds only for the integers, rational, and irrational numbers, but not for the imaginaries, and this only in virtue of our definitions. It is true that according to some historic definitions of number the $\sqrt{-1}$ could not be regarded as a number, just as, according to a still earlier conception of number, the $\sqrt{2}$ was an illegitimate notion. But all this only led to a *redefinition* of number in which every shadow of contradiction disappeared. Engels' failure to appreciate the logic by which the structure of mathematics has developed is so profound that it leads him to assert that there is a contradiction even in the fact that a root of a ($\sqrt{a}$) should be a power of a ($a^{\frac{1}{2}}$) whereas both symbolic expressions are merely different ways of stating the same relation.

In none of the illustrations considered has Engels demonstrated the presence of contradiction. In all of them, the appearance of contradiction is due to inaccuracy of phrasing or disregard of context.

We are now in a position to look at the first law of dialectic in its variant forms.

a. *The identity of contradictories.* This is neither a law of things nor a law of thought and falls much more properly in the class of real absurdities than does the $\sqrt{-1}$. Taken literally it is a denial of the law of non-contradiction and hence is compatible with any other proposition true or false.

b. *The unity of contradictories.* "Unity" may mean that a proposition and its contradictory furnish a formally exhaustive description of the possibilities of a situation, which follows, of course, from the definition of what contradictories are. Or "unity" may mean, as some of Engels' illustrations suggest, a physical relation. In which case we are dealing with another real absurdity—a logical relation hypostasized into a thing.

c. *The identity of opposites.* Opposition is a term nowhere defined in Engels and is used sometimes in a physical sense and sometimes in a logical sense. In any sense, however, it is hard to determine what is meant by opposites being identical. It seems to mean (i) sometimes nothing more than the principle of significant assertion, (ii) sometimes the universality of polar opposition, and (iii) sometimes the fact that two different aspects of a situation, or two different situations, have, under certain circumstances, identical *effects.* This first meaning is not a law of nature, the second is not universally true of nature, and the third would justify our calling many different things identical irrespective of whether they were opposites of each other or not.

The peculiar meaning which Engels gives to the law of the identity of opposites is revealed in a triumphant comment, in *Dialektik und Natur,* on a sentence from Maxwell's *Theory of Heat.* Maxwell had written: "These rays [of radiant heat] have all the physical properties of rays of light and are capable of reflexion, etc. . . . some of the heat rays are identical with the rays of light while other kinds of heat rays make no impression on our eyes."

"So," adds Engels, "there are *dark* rays of light and the famous opposition between light and darkness disappears as an absolute opposition from natural science. In passing, let us note that the obscurest darkness as well as the brightest light produces the same *blinding* effect upon our eyes and therefore are *for us* identical." (p. 192.)

Other things besides light and darkness can produce a blinding effect upon the eyes e.g., a blow, submersion in water, or coming across an extraordinary howler. They may all be identical for us without being identical in structure or *opposite in character.* It did not require the discovery of electro-magnetic vibrations, whose wave lengths were such that they did not register on the human retina, to establish the fact that no situation in nature is absolutely dark or absolutely light. Nor does the recognition that in nature no regions are absolutely dark or absolutely light justify confusing the *meanings* of light and dark by asserting that an identity or unity relates them. That Engels can speak of *dark* rays of light when he himself admits that "what is light or not light depends upon the structure of the eyes" may seem to be an innocent solecism; but it also serves as a good illustration of how linguistic errors give rise to bad metaphysics.

d. *The unity of opposites.* The most plausible interpretation of this is that all things and situations have a polar structure. But as we have already seen in Section I, polar opposition may mean either that no description of any state of affairs can be understood unless the terms employed have meaningful opposites, or that every state of affairs is capable of *differentiation* in respect to its own parts, elements or neighboring regions. The first view makes of the law a significant rule of syntax; the second merely expresses the fact that differences are observable everywhere, a proposition which, like the proposition that the world exists, is too general to have any heuristic value.

II. THE NEGATION OF THE NEGATION

We shall now examine the second fundamental law of dialectic, "the negation of the negation." This has been often referred to as the soul of the dialectic.

Like the other laws of dialectic, the "negation of the negation" is nowhere strictly defined. It obviously involves a relationship which holds between three terms or phrases in a temporal series. The relationship between any two successive terms in a triad is alleged to be one of logical contradiction or opposition. Before the "negation of the negation" can be completed there takes place "a transformation of opposites (contradictories, extremes) into each other" which, if it means anything at all, asserts that things change in time, that every *distinction* within a temporary process may be regarded as an *opposition,* and that every opposition in time loses its defining character and assumes the traits of its converse. Here again we have no recourse but to examine the illustrations Engels offers of the law of the negation of the negation. And we may be heartened by his assurance that the process it describes is really very simple, "occurring everywhere and every day" and once freed of idealistic fripperies "intelligible to any child." (*Anti-Dühring,* pp. 137-8.)

Of the many illustrations cited by Engels, we shall examine, in the interests of space and the readers' patience, only two—one from nature and the other from mathematics. They are selected because they serve as the stock illustrations in the literature of orthodox dialectical materialism (significantly enough, they are to be found in Hegel's *Logic*).

1. *Growth:* "Let us take a grain of barley-corn. Billions of such grains are ground, boiled and brewed, and then consumed. But should such a grain of barley-corn find conditions which are normal for it, should it fall on favorable soil, then under the influence of heat and moisture there takes place a characteristic change, it sprouts: the grain as such disappears, is negated, and out of it arises the plant, the negation of the grain. But what is the normal life-course (*Lebenslauf*) of this plant? It grows, blossoms, is fertilized and finally produces grains of barley-corn again, and as soon as these are ripe the stalk dies, is in its turn negated. As a result of this negation of the negation, we have the original grain of barley-corn again but not single fold but ten, twenty or thirty fold." (*Ibid.*, p. 138.)

In this cycle of seed, flower and fruit, neither logical contradictories nor contraries enter, for when these are doubly negated we get the original term or proposition $[-(-P) = P]$, and the point of the law is that we never simply come back to our starting point. Phases of the process of growth can be distinguished, of course, but the *number* of such phases depends upon the purpose of our inquiry. Nor is one phase the cause of the subsequent phase, for whether a phase is realized or not depends not merely on the structure of the antecedent phase but on a complex of existing conditions whose presence does not follow in any way from the structure of the seed-flower-fruit cycle.

That the negation of the negation completes itself is a statistical fact which Engels admits when he speaks of the *normal* conditions that must supervene before the barley-corn develops. But if this proves the *objectivity* of the law of the negation of the negation, the admission that sometimes the conditions do not supervene, disproves the *universality* of the law. And what of the grains of barley-corn that are "ground, boiled, brewed and consumed"? The process is scientifically just as normal and natural as when they are used for seed. Ah! says

Engels, this is not playing according to rules. The seed must be so negated that it does not make the subsequent negation impossible. "If I grind a grain of barley-corn or crush an insect, I have indeed completed the first act [of negation—S. H.] but have made the second impossible. Every kind of thing has, therefore, its characteristic way of being negated, so that a development takes place" (p. 154). But scientifically the grinding of a grain of barley-corn or its consumption is just as much a part of its nature, under determinate conditions, as its sprouting. Here, as elsewhere, Engels relapses into the Aristotelian doctrine of essential natures—a conception which is incompatible with the dictum he accepts from Hegel, that the nature of a thing is equivalent to the sum total of all of its appearances and is not a structure existing behind, separate from, or in opposition to them. If anything can be "negated" undialectically this is just as much a part of its nature, and may be just as important for purposes of scientific inquiry and human welfare, as the fact that it can be "negated" dialectically.

A possible answer to this objection may claim that no matter what happens to the grain of barley-corn, it enters into a new situation in which the law of the negation of the negation holds. Thus if the grain is used as feed for cattle, we have a seed-feed-food cycle; if it is ground into powder for *materia medica*, we have a seed-medicine-health cycle; if a wind blows it onto poor soil or into water, we have a seed-decomposition cycle, etc. But from Engels' point of view, such an answer is false, since these cycles do not necessarily—or even usually— lead to the *recreation* of seeds; and from a scientific point of view, it is the barest tautology, for it amounts to saying that anything that happens constitutes a *development*, thus making development synonymous with change: and by definition, anything that happens involves change.

Wherever the principle of the negation of the negation is significantly used, as in history, it presupposes human activity which realizes a possibility grounded in the structure of the situation. Concrete practice (*Praxis*) is the synthesis; the plan which is counterposed to and suggested by the situation is the antithesis; and the original situation with all its difficulties and problems serves as thesis or starting point. This may be rewritten in such a way as to make the presence and guiding influence of human *needs* more explicit. But however expressed, there is always reference to a plan, purpose, or interest, itself always accessible to scientific analysis, and which accounts for the specific way a situation is negated, as distinct from all other possible ways. Even aside from the confusion between logical and physical categories, Engels' characterization of *natural* processes as subject to dialectical negation introduces an element of consciousness as a pervasive trait of all things, and is, therefore, incompatible with the materialistic and scientific assumptions of Marxism.

2. *Mathematics.* Engels' treatment of mathematics leaves something to be desired from the standpoint of clarity and consistency. His theory of knowledge requires that *all* thought be a reflection of existence. By a reflection is meant sometimes a copy, or image, sometimes merely an effect, and sometimes an abstraction. Mathematical relationships, therefore, are in no way to be explained as free creations or conventions. "In no way does the mind concern itself in pure mathematics only with its own creations and imaginative products. . . . Pure mathematics has as its object the space forms and quantitative relations of the real world, consequently, a very real stuff" (*Anti-Dühring*, p. 25). Mathematics abstracts from the specific content of things and concerns itself with their general forms. But at this point Engels adds the strange doctrine that only at the very end of the process of abstraction do we reach the domain of free creations ". . . only at the very end [of these processes of abstraction—S. H.] do we first come to the free creations and imaginations of the mind, *i.e.*, to imaginary magnitudes.[14] The apparent derivation of mathematical magnitudes from each other proves not their a priori origin but only their rational interconnection" (p. 25).

But it is precisely this rational interconnection between mathematical concepts which shows the absurdity of regarding some mathematical relations as "real" and others as "imaginary." Mathematically, they are all in the same boat—either they are all free creations or none of them is. When Engels asserts in his *Dialektik und Natur* that whoever attributes to

[14] ". . . und kommt dann ganz zuletzt erst auf die eigenen freien Schöpfungen und Imaginationen des Verstandes, nämlich die imaginaren Grossen."

the $\sqrt{-1}$ any kind of reality outside of our own heads might just as well believe in spooks,[15] the same applies to all other numbers, including $\sqrt{2}$, —1, and 1. The source of Engels' confusion is to be found in an inadequate conception of abstraction and a faulty definition of mathematics. His theory of abstraction fails to distinguish between physical abstractions —like perfectly elastic bodies and frictionless engines—and mathematical "abstractions" which are really not abstractions at all, except in a vague psychological sense, but logical definitions. And the definition of mathematics, as the science of quantity and space, central to Engels' discussion, simply overlooks the fact, which was well-known even in his day, that many branches of mathematics do not concern themselves in the least either with quantity or space.

Since, for Engels, all thought including mathematical thought is a "reflection" of nature, then if the law of the "negation of the negation" holds for the latter, it must hold for the former. Nothing could better demonstrate the fantastic consequences of such a notion than Engels' own key illustration and the admissions he is compelled to make in defending it:

"The same is true in mathematics. Let us take any algebraic magnitude whatever, say, a. If we negate it, we have $-a$ (minus a). If we negate this negation, by multiplying $-a$ with $-a$, we have $+a^2$, i.e., the original positive magnitude, but at a higher level (Stufe), namely, the second power." (Anti-Dühring, p. 139.)

Engels anticipates the objections which are on the lips of his readers. If we negate $-a$, we do not get $+a^2$, but $-(-a)$ or a, the original term. Or if we want to get a^2, we need merely multiply a by itself without resorting to the first negation, etc. To all of these objections, Engels replies with a sentence which gives the whole show away. "I must so construct (einrichten) the first negation, that the second remains or becomes possible" (p. 145). And the second negation must be constructed in such a way that the Aufhebung of the first gives the original entity on a "higher" plane. What could be more explicit than the recognition that in pure mathematics, at any rate, the operations employed depend upon our definitions, *our* constructions, *our* choice of one set of rules rather than another, and not at all upon the objective structure of a dialectic which is found in nature? And how could Engels overlook the implications of his concession that at least some mathematical operations, like ordinary double negation $[-(-a) = a]$, which is basic in elementary algebra, do not conform to the precious law of the negation of the negation, alleged to be universal in validity?

Disregarding the implications of his own statements, Engels presses on to deliver a final thrust against those who like the unfortunate Dühring have protested that Hegel's principle of the negation of the negation, even when it appears in the writings of avowed materialists as a literal law instead of a poetically justified metaphor, is nothing else but a vestige of theological mysticism. "If he desires to banish it [the law] from thought, will he please be so kind first to banish it from nature and history and invent a mathematics in which $-a \times -a$ is not $+a^2$" (*ibid.*, p. 146).

Alas! Dühring could easily have obliged him, for it is perfectly easy to invent a mathematical system in which $-a \times -a$ does not equal a^2. The operation of multiplication can be defined in such a way as to make the product of $-a$ and $-a$ not a^2 but $-a$ or even 0. In fact, we do not have to invent a mathematical system. We need only point to the Boole-Schroeder algebra in which $a \times a = a$ and $-a \times -a = -a$.[16]

III. QUANTITY AND QUALITY

Of all the so-called laws of dialectic, the law of the transition of quantity into quality comes nearest to suggesting a valid scientific principle. But even it is burdened with a cluster of misleading associations and inaccurate formulations. Sometimes this law is considered to be a special case of the law of "the identity (unity, interpenetration) of opposites (contradictories)" on the mistaken assumption that quantity and quality are *logical* contraries. In his discussion of the law in

[16] *Cf.* Lewis and Langford, *Symbolic Logic*, New York and London, 1932, p. 29.

Anti-Dühring Engels speaks of the "transformation" [17] (*Umschlagen*) of quantity into quality and vice versa, which adds confusion to vagueness, for although quantities may vary and qualities may vary and the relationship between the variations of both may be described, as the case may be, by continuous or discontinuous functions, it is absurd to say that quantity ever *becomes* quality or quality quantity. Further, sometimes this law is so formulated as to suggest that quality first comes into existence as a result of variations in quantity, as if every quantity were not already a quantity *of* something already possessing quality. And when this is recognized as an error, it is often incorrectly held that quantity and quality are strict correlatives. It is overlooked that quality is logically prior to quantity. We cannot speak of quantities without presupposing the existence of qualities, but it is possible to speak of qualities in situations where it is *problematic* whether or not quantities, as a matter of *fact*, can be reliably ascribed to qualities, and in other situations where as a matter of *syntax* it is impermissible to predicate quantity of quality. For example, it is still an open question as to whether we can predicate quantity of intelligence; and no one, strictly speaking, can quantify qualities like innocence or perfection.

The illustrations which Engels uses from chemistry, economics and cavalry tactics indicate that the law expresses nothing more than the simple principle that gradual variations in quantity, at a certain point, result in the sudden appearance of a *new* quality. Since in science and daily life the appearance (or disappearance) of these new qualities can only be controlled by changing the quantitative relations with which qualities are correlated (measured), it is permissible to say that sometimes gradual variations in quantity *cause* new qualities to emerge. From the time of Galileo, the methodological principle of science has been that all qualitative differences are expressible in terms of quantitative differences—a principle which, of course, does not justify an *identification* of quality with quantity.

That gradual differences in quantity or degree lead, at certain critical points, to sudden differences in quality or kind is a proposition which must be qualified in several important

[17] Pp. 33, 127, 129.

respects before it can be regarded as a valid generalization. First of all, this is a principle which cannot be asserted to be *universally* true, for there are many qualities which permit of indefinite variation without making way for other qualities. Weight, for example, does not disappear to make way for a new quality when more and more stones are added to a heap; nor, to take a quite different quality, is learnedness succeeded by a new quality when one learns more and more things. Secondly, if the new quality which suddenly arises is a genuine emergent, then the principle has little scientific value because it can only testify *after the fact*, so to speak, that a new quality has suddenly appeared, whose presence could not be inferred from the presence of the qualities and quantitative relations of the component elements of its antecedent states. This would make *new* qualities essentially unpredictable. The difficulty is that some of Engels' illustrations suggest he is speaking of these qualities as genuine emergents and therefore completely novel, and yet at the same time he refers to them as if they were quite predictable. Thirdly, the *attribution* of *suddenness* and *novelty* to a quality does not depend merely upon the effects of the gradual variation in the quantity with which the quality is correlated (measured) but is relative to some perspective of interest, need, or attention. For example, to a *musician*, the qualitative difference between *any* two successive notes on a scale may be every whit as absolute, sudden and novel as the qualitative differences the physicist observes when the sound waves vary from just below the point of minimal audition to just above the point of maximal audition.

This last point may be made clearer if we examine Engels' stock illustration of the third law of dialectic.[18] Under normal atmospheric pressure, water changes from a liquid to a solid at 0°C. and from a liquid to a gas at 100°C. Ice and steam suddenly appear at these critical points. But for certain purposes the qualitative difference between water at 10°C. and water at 99°C. may be even more relevant than the difference between liquid and steam. To the tenant waiting for his radiator to get warm, it makes little difference whether water at 99° or steam circulates in the pipes. But the differ-

18 For Hegel's discussion of this illustration, *cf. Science of Logic*, Eng. trans., Vol. I, pp. 389-390.

ences in the temperature of water may make all the difference between feeling chilled or comfortable. The qualities which we name when we describe what water feels like to the hand are no less real than the qualities which describe what it looks like to the eye. There is always more than one series of variations in quality which can be correlated with any given series of variations in quantity. And the characterization of any change in a quality series as sudden always *follows* a discrimination of the one quality series, as against the others, which is relevant to our purposes in a concrete situation. The tea-drinker notes with dismay that his water has gone up in steam; the physician can sterilize his instruments just as well in steam as in boiling water. The cook may wring his hands because the water mixed with other ingredients is not at the right temperature; the porter may be completely insensitive to any differences. The quality variations are all equally objective; and they *may* all depend upon one fundamental series of quantity variations. But we cannot assume that the *suddenness* with which a quality appears in one series of variation, will always enable us to make legitimate inferences about what will be experienced as sudden by those whose interests and attention are concerned with *other* series of quality variations.

One final word about quality. Insofar as we are considering concrete qualities which have a definite existence in space and time, like green, hard, glassy, it is meaningful to speak of variations in, and succession of, qualities; but insofar as qualities refer not to concrete traits of experienced things but to *definitions* which enable us to order and classify these traits, *e.g.*, greenness, hardness, glassiness, it is impermissible to say that is subject to spatio-temporal variation and succession. Two different shades of green have not more or less of the quality (definition) of greenness in them any more than an object which is twice as hard as another exemplifies the quality (definition) of hardness twice as strongly. To overlook this distinction, which corresponds to the traditional distinction between particulars and universals, is to be committed to the belief that the quality of greenness is itself green and the quality of hardness hard.[19] The law of the transition (trans-

---

[19] For an elaboration of this distinction, see Dewey, "Characteristics and Characters: Kinds and Classes," *Journal of Philosophy*, No. 10, May 7, 1936.

formation) of quantity into quality, as formulated by Engels, in its claims to be valid for all qualities, sins against this distinction. It ignores the fact that there is a class of qualities of which we can only say either that objects exemplify them or do not exemplify them, and not that objects have them in some degree or other.

We must conclude that the so-called universal laws of dialectic are neither laws of nature nor of mind nor of logic.

4. Dialectic as Mythology

If we have established anything so far, we have shown that the only sense in which the dialectic is applicable to nature is the sense in which it is an abbreviated synonym for scientific method. And as a confirmation of this conclusion we need only ask of those who deny it, to point to a single case of knowledge discovered by, or explicable in terms of, the dialectic method which cannot be more simply certified by the canons of scientific method. As an additional task, we might challenge them to translate the findings of modern science into the language of dialectic, and to compare the structure of propositions so derived with those of science in respect to verifiability, simplicity, systematic connection, and fruitfulness for the acquisition of new knowledge. If the fundamental laws of dialectic, analyzed in the preceding section, are held to be integral to the conception of dialectic, then it is doubtful whether any translation can be made, for we have seen that these laws violate the fundamental principles of logic, scientific method, and, in places, of coherent syntax.

If it is asserted that dialectic is a *theory* of scientific method, then its "laws" would not be "laws" of nature but rules of valid scientific procedure. But the very language of these rules is such that *any* kind of procedure, scientific or not, valid or not, is equally well or equally ill described by them. Nor is it the business of any theory of scientific method to pretend to be in the first instance a method of discovery and a method of proof, as believers in dialectic claim it to be.

Those who interpret the dialectic method as scientific method brought to critical self-consciousness must be wary of accepting the historical paternity which Engels has invented for the doctrine. By this is not meant his reference to the embryonic dialectic method of the Greek philosophers, although even here the obvious unscientific character of their philosophy and the absence of experimental science, as we understand it, in their time, makes the existence of the ancestral line somewhat dubious. What is meant is Engels' specific attempt to draw a straight line of derivation from Kepler to the Romantic *Natur-philosophen* (Goethe, Oken, Treviranus, and others), through them to Hegel, and from Hegel to modern dialectical materialism instead of from Galileo, to Newton, to modern natural science. Engels cites with approval Hegel's contention that Kepler, not Newton, was the real founder of celestial mechanics, refers to Newton as an *Induktionsesel*,[20] claims that modern scientists can with profit still go to school to Hegel, and quite explicitly invokes the mystic romantic seers whose work was an amalgam of theology and science as the inspired precursors of dialectical materialism. *They*, and not Galileo, Newton, Laplace, were the great "Utopians." "The *Natur-philosophen* are related to consciously dialectical natural science as the Utopians to modern communism" (*Anti-Dühring*, p. xvi).

It need not be denied that the Romantic natural philosophers hit upon some notions concerning evolution and magnetism which were later developed in more scientific form, but these were in the nature of lucky hunches and had no logical connection with their intuitive method and their philosophy of magical idealism.

If the dialectic method is another name for scientific method, then the question of its universality must read: Is scientific method universally *applicable?* To which the answer is that all events can be approached scientifically, although it does not therefore follow that whatever can be scientifically approached results in a science. That depends upon the complexity of the subject matter involved, the degree of regularity in the phenomena observed, and the practical resources at the command of the scientific community. That Marx believed that scientific method is the only valid method of acquiring and certifying new knowledge and that there is no inherent obstacle in the structure of things or the human mind to prevent their

[20] *Dialektik und Natur, op. cit.*, p. 152.

scientific study is indisputable. But his acceptance of scientific method as the only valid method of extending and certifying knowledge does not justify in the slightest degree the absurd claim that Marx (or Engels) anticipated the subsequent results of applying scientific method. Like the religious fundamentalists who see in every new scientific discovery a confirmation of some Biblical text, some orthodox dialectical materialists see in the progress of modern science a progressive vindication of the doctrines of the founding fathers. Thus, for example, J. D. Bernal asserts, "From the dynamics of relativity motion and mass become equivalent. This conclusion, which required all the refinement of mathematical technique of Michaelson and the mathematical genius of Einstein to demonstrate in the 20th century, was grasped in principle by Marx and Engels before the middle of the 19th century." [21] Surprisingly enough for this view, Einstein's own comment on Engels' *Dialektik und Natur*, when the manuscript was submitted to him by Bernstein, reads, "Its content is not of any special interest either from the standpoint of contemporary physics or of the history of physics." [22] [23]

Mr. John Strachey, whose ignorance of scientific method and philosophy is equaled only by his presumption in dogmatizing about matters he does not understand, contends that Engels anticipated in a striking way the discoveries of Freud. He then goes on to say that the findings of psychoanalysis "provide the most striking confirmation yet obtained of the validity of dialectical materialism," as if dialectical materialism were a specific, psychological hypothesis. [24] The most extravagant claims of all are made by J. B. S. Haldane in recent writings, particularly his introduction to the English translation of *Dialectics and Nature*.

If the dialectic method, properly understood, is nothing but

[21] *Aspects of Dialectical Materialism*, London, 1934, p. 101.

[22] Quoted by D. Riazanov, *Marx-Engels Archiv*, Bd. 2, p. 141.

[23] It should be observed that on the fundamental question of the nature of space and time Dühring anticipated developments much more accurately than Engels, who subscribed in an obscure way to Newton's theory of absolute space and time. Einstein's great indebtedness is not to Mach's theory of science but to his relational conception of space and time. Mach, in turn, pays Dühring quite handsome acknowledgments in his *Science of Mechanics*, particularly with reference to Dühring's critical work (Eng. trans. p. xi).

[24] *Cf.* his introduction to Osborn's *Freud and Marx*, A Dialectical Study, London & New York, 1937.

scientific method, then the dialectic, as it applies to the realm of history and sociology, is a name for the operation of scientific method in that specific field. It was in the name of scientific method that Engels protested against the attempt to reduce history and psychology to physics. "We are certain some day experimentally to reduce thinking to molecular and chemical movements in the brain; but is the essence of thinking therewith exhausted?" (*Ibid.*, p. 167.) Not that thinking is possible without the presence of molecular motion of some sort, but this motion it shares with non-thinking organisms as well as inorganic things. Consequently it cannot serve as a clue to its distinctive quality or nature. Again, it was in the name of scientific method that Engels protested against reducing history to biology. The "struggle for existence," made an all-inclusive explanatory principle after Darwin, is dubious enough, even as a purely biological category, for there is more in nature than struggles, but when applied to history, Engels maintains, it overlooks the fact that men are distinguished from other animals in that they produce, and do not merely collect, the means of life. The differences are subject to other laws and descriptions. "The carrying over of biological laws of animal societies to human societies without further qualification is therewith made impossible" (p. 191).

It is sometimes maintained that the dialectic method is the method which corrects the errors scientists fall into when they wander into fields outside their special interests. But it is obvious that the errors so made result from a violation of scientific method and can be corrected without invoking any other method. The errors of those who believe that the dialectic method is something different from scientific method are no less egregious than are those of spiritualistic minded scientists, and less entertaining.

We conclude, then, that the dialectic method can claim to have meaning and validity only when it is understood to be synonymous with scientific method; that since in its traditional formulation it is burdened with many misleading and mistaken conceptions, it would be more conducive to clear thinking if the phrase were dropped; that its retention engenders a mythical philosophy of nature, prepares the way for a doctrine of "two truths," one ordinary, scientific and profane, the other, esoteric, "dialectical" and "higher"; and, finally, that it encourages an attitude which easily leads to censorship, dictation, and persecution of scientists.[25]

In identifying the only intelligent meaning that can be given to the dialectic method with scientific method, it is not implied that the nature of scientific method is so clearly defined that universal agreement exists concerning all of its principles. On certain problems, especially those involving induction and probability, not to speak of meaning and verification, there is considerable divergence of opinion. It may even be that every systematic theory of scientific method is committed to some "metaphysical" presuppositions, whatever these are. But scientific philosophy as distinct from traditional dialectics not only arises out of reflection upon the procedures of the sciences, it receives its test in the fruitfulness of its bearings upon those procedures. In order to justify its claims that it adds to knowledge and understanding, it must offer a coherent account of these procedures, or call attention to and eliminate inconsistences in the statements made in the communication of scientific findings, and interpret science as a human enterprise in relation to other aspects of social life and experience. Short of this, the very least it can do is to avoid infecting scientific minds with the errors that have been permanently embalmed in spiritualistic metaphysics. Historically and analytically, the belief in a *Naturdialektik* has been a central doctrine of every system of metaphysical idealism from Plotinus to Hegel. Almost every variety of dialectical materialism current today is a bastard offspring, fathered by a politically-motivated metaphysical idealism upon the body of modern science.

5. *Appendix: Einstein on Engels*

We have quoted Einstein's judgment to Bernstein on Engels' scientific manuscripts, not to settle any questions by authority, but to indicate how they impress a great scientist

---

25 For an account of the mischievous role which the notion of dialectic has played in contemporary Russian science and philosophy, see J. Rosenthal, "On the Soviet Philosophical Front" in *The Modern Monthly*, Dec. 1936, and subsequent issues.

who is not without sympathy for the more democratic aspects of Engels' social views. Even if Einstein's judgment were different, the validity of our critique of Engels' ideas would remain unaffected. But apparently, dialectical materialists set great store by Einstein's judgment. One of them, D. J. Struik, has even gone so far as to quote Einstein in such a way as to suggest that he regards Engels' *Dialectics and Nature* as of great significance, flagrantly suppressing Einstein's judgment of its scientific worthlessness. (*Philosophy of Science*, Vol. 1, p. 123.)

Other Stalinists, when they have not resorted to such crude distortions, have circulated the legend that Bernstein showed Einstein, not the entire manuscript, but only the section on electricity which is admittedly worthless. The latest Stalinist who has repeated this story is J. B. S. Haldane in his introduction to the recent English translation of *Dialectics and Nature*. Haldane, who even in the tragic days of war, created merriment on two continents by soberly confessing that he had cured himself of gastritis by reading Lenin, admits that Engels made some serious mistakes. He argues, however, that Engels would have corrected all of these mistakes if he had ever been able to complete and publish the manuscript; and that even if he had not corrected them, some of these mistakes would have been extremely fruitful for science. He adds: "When all such criticisms have been made, it is astonishing how Engels anticipated the progress of science in the sixty years which have elapsed since he wrote. . . . Had Engels' method of thinking been more familiar the transformation of our ideas on physics which have occurred during the last thirty years [Einstein, Planck, etc.] would have been smoothed."

It is therefore not without interest to learn that Edward Bernstein's statement, made to the present writer in Berlin in 1929, that Einstein had seen and judged the whole of the manuscript is true. This is confirmed by a letter from Professor Einstein himself, a translation of which is herewith reproduced with his permission.

Dear Professor Hook;
Edward Bernstein placed the entire manuscript at my disposal. My expression of judgment referred to the whole of it.

I am firmly convinced that Engels himself would have found it ridiculous, if he could have seen how great an importance, after such length of time, is being attributed to his modest attempt.

Sincerely yours,

(signed) A. Einstein.[26]

Princeton, New Jersey

den 17 Juni 1940

[26] Sehr geherter Professor Hook:

Eduard Bernstein hat mir das ganze Manuskript zür Verfügung gestellt und meine Meinungsäusserung bezog sich auf das ganze Manuskript. Ich bin fest davon überzeugt, das Engels selbst es lacherlich finden würde wenn er sehen könnte, das seinem bescheidener Versuch nach so langer Zeit so grosse Wichtigkeit beigelegt wird.

Mit ausgezeichneter Hochachtung,

A. Einstein

CHAPTER TEN

SCIENCE AND THE NEW OBSCURANTISM

1. Science and Social Consciousness

ONE OF THE interesting cultural phenomena of the last few years is the awakening of men of science in Anglo-American countries to the crucial social issues of the day. More and more they are beginning to realize that their scientific careers and, to some extent, the direction of scientific research, depend upon how events, outside of their laboratories, turn out. More and more the ideals of co-operative freedom and applied intelligence, integral to the procedures of science, are being set up as criteria of a desirable social order. The most important cause for this reorientation of interest is the rise of Fascism abroad and its threat at home. Not without influence have been the writings of men like Dewey in America and Russell and Hogben in England.

As was to be expected, political groups have not been slow to move in and organize the social consciousness of scientists. The most vociferous of these groups in England and America has been the Communist Party and its open and secret fellow-travelers. In England, and to a lesser extent in France, it has succeeded in attracting to its colors some notable names, among whom may be mentioned Needham, J. B. S. Haldane, Bernal, and H. Levy. With intense and laudable enthusiasm, they have undertaken to make the scientific specialist aware of his social responsibilities. In this they should be supported even by those who do not share their specific political commitments. But unfortunately this is not their only activity; nor is it the task which receives the most emphasis. Coupled with a call to scientists to correct their social myopia are two other things: (1) a glorification of the scientific life in the Soviet Union, and (2) an attempt to win scientists to a philosophical outlook upon the universe, the metaphysics of orthodox dialectical materialism, which allegedly validates the ideals of socialism.

My primary concern in this chapter is with the peculiar metaphysical views this group believes to be entailed by an acceptance of socialism—views which have led to the expression of some of the choicest bits of high nonsense in contemporary philosophy. They are offered in the name of Marxism and socialism with the result that they tend to prejudice critical minds, already aware of their social responsibilities, against the entire socialist movement, and to confuse others.

Before considering the new "scientific philosophy," I wish to say a word or two about the first point—the glorification of the scientific life in the Soviet Union. If there is anything which gives an air of cynical disingenuousness to this movement, it is its eloquence about the repression of the scientific spirit in Germany, Italy, England—indeed, anywhere in the world—and its utter silence about the ruthless extermination of politically non-conforming scientists, or scientists who run foul of the Communist Party line, in Soviet Russia.

With the Soviet-Nazi Pact, criticism of the intellectual repressions even in Fascist countries has ceased. The whole weight of denunciation has been directed against infractions of scientific freedom in the democratic countries. As deplorable as these are, compared to the absolute cultural terror imposed upon politically unorthodox scientists in Germany and the U.S.S.R., they seem to be minor.

Since the October Revolution, the Communist Party line in Russia on the cultural and scientific front has changed several times. The decisive causes of the change have always been political considerations, domestic and foreign, for according to the orthodox Communist faith, scientific theories are not politically neutral. With every major change in the political line, the sciences are overhauled in order to determine what is safe and what is dangerous. In the early years, the Einstein theory was sharply criticized for its alleged philosophical idealism. A few years later, it was possible to accept it without being denounced as a bourgeois idealist. Today, Einstein's denial of the infinity of space and time is once more assailed as "counter-revolutionary bourgeois ideology." [1]

Whenever the Party line changes, a purge of those who do

---

[1] *Astronomical Journal of the Soviet Union*, Dec., 1938. *Cf. also* Prof. A. V. Hill on the state of Russian science in *New Statesman & Nation*, Jan. 27, 1940.

not follow the change takes place in all educational institutions. Whether it be the alternate acceptance and rejection of the views of T. H. Morgan in biology, or stress upon one or another factor in the interpretation of history, the consequence has been that hundreds have been deprived of their posts and livelihood, often of their freedom, and in stubborn cases, even of their lives. The political leaders of Russia are keen about applied science. So are the political leaders of Italy and Germany. But the scientific temper is both distinct from, and more fundamental than, applied science. And since the state philosophy of the Soviet Union, according to its own spokesmen, extends to *all* fields of culture, to speak of freedom of scientific inquiry in Russia is a brazen-faced imposture. It is the counterpart of the claim that Russia is a democracy.

How brazen this contention can be may be illustrated in the following: The Summer 1938 issue of *Science and Society* leads off with an article by H. E. Sigerist on "Science and Democracy," an extremely superficial analysis, in which great encomiums are paid to the Soviet Union because of the role which science plays in Russian life and the alleged pervasiveness of the spirit of scientific inquiry. This is followed by another article, "Revolt Against Formalism in the Soviet Union," by Georges Friedmann, a French Stalinist, in which in the most casual way, as if it were a matter of course, it is admitted that the representatives of the Communist Party impose their line on every phase of culture from philosophy to architecture. In other countries, *freedom of scientific inquiry means that workers in the field are to be permitted to reach their own conclusions through the free play of critical method, without let or hindrance by ecclesiastical or political authorities.* In Russia, this freedom is allowed only insofar as the conclusions reached are agreeable to the ruling party. For example, some time ago, the Russian historians were ordered to make the customary revision of textbooks to fit the needs of the time as interpreted by the leaders of the Communist Party. When it was finished, there appeared a severe criticism of it in *Pravda*, objecting to this, prescribing that, and adding the words, as if to leave no doubt that orders are orders, "such must be the line throughout the textbook on modern history." The

criticism was signed by Stalin [2] and two of his political subordinates. Whenever we hear people protesting against such
practices in other countries but remaining silent about similar
and even worse things in Russia, or attempting to gloss them
over, we have every right to question their sincerity. Whatever
else they may be interested in, they are not interested in freedom of scientific inquiry.

2. *The New Dispensation*

The new dispensation which the scientific neophytes of Stalinism bring to their fellow scientists is neither clear, nor uniform, nor consistent with itself. All of them make great play
with the dialectic or the dialectic method, yet none of them
makes clear what the dialectic method is and how it differs
from scientific method. The dialectic method is not merely an
interpretation of the nature of scientific method because to
the dialectic method there corresponds an *objective* dialectic
which is universal. But the objective reference of scientific
method, on this view, is also the dialectic in nature, society and
mind. How, then, does the dialectic method differ from scientific method in its approach to the objective reference of both?
Every answer to this question in the writings of orthodox
dialectical materialists leads either to the innocuous position
that the dialectic method is the scientific method of studying
the history of science in relation to society, or to the statement
that scientific method and dialectic method are the same and
yet not the same, although the respects in which they are one
or the other are not specified. This last characterization is
admitted to be contradictory but so is nature!

There is no hope of getting a formally clear statement of
the nature of dialectic or dialectic method where contradiction
is regarded not as an embarrassment but as a virtue. Perhaps,
then, it will be instructive to examine what the philosophy of
dialectic materialism is supposed to accomplish. There are
always two claims made for it. It is asserted that (a) not only
is it compatible with the facts of science but that it inspires
fresh advances in science. Thus Prenant, a French biologist,
in his *Biology and Marxism*, asserts that as distinct from all

[2] Reprinted in *International Literature* (Moscow), No. 9, 1937, pp. 53-54.

other kinds of philosophy which are also compatible with science, the Marxist philosophy is capable of "providing sound and fruitful working hypotheses likely to lead to fresh advances in biology." [3] Needham, a biochemist, affirms in the preface to the same book that this is also true in his own field. J. B. S. Haldane, in a feeble reply to a critic, maintains that a good deal of his recent work in genetics "has been inspired by my gradually increasing knowledge of dialectical materialism." [4] Bernal, a crystallographer, admits that "it is extremely difficult to give examples . . . but from my own experience I found Marxist methods invaluable for arriving at new conceptions." [5]

The second claim (b) is that by the application of the dialectic method to nature and society, we win the insight that socialism is inevitable. Two of many possible citations will suffice us. Needham writes: "The higher stages of organization towards which we look and for which we work have all the authority of evolution behind them. The devil, as Hippolytus said long ago, may resist the cosmic process. But the last victory will not be his." [6] And H. Levy, who is less given to theological language, after laying down a qualitative law which, he claims, is both universal and objective, insists: "What our qualitative law apparently predicts is simply the inevitability and nature of the change, and that we human beings will inevitably make the change." [7]

Let us examine these two claims.

3. *The Proof of the Pudding*

(a) Were it true that scientific discoveries result from the conversion of scientists to dialectical materialism, it would be incumbent upon all who are interested in the growth of new knowledge to press it upon the attention of practicing scientists. The fact that several scientists have testified to the fruitfulness of a dialectic principle, which they cannot even adequately define, is no more evidence of its being so than the

[3] Eng. trans. p. xix.
[4] *Science and Society*, Vol. 2, p. 239.
[5] *Ibid.*, Vol. 2, p. 64.
[6] *Modern Quarterly*, London (1938), I, 1, p. 50.
[7] *A Philosophy for a Modern Man*, London, 1938, p. 215.

testimony of even greater scientists from Kepler to Pasteur that certain metaphysical and religious beliefs have led them to fruitful hypotheses and discoveries. Indeed, it is not even clear that even those who claim to be inspired by this philosophy believe that there is a necessary connection between their philosophy and their discoveries. "I do not claim," Haldane writes, "that these results could not have been obtained without a study of Engels. I merely state that they were not reached without such a study . . ." It may very well be that here we have only a *post hoc propter hoc.* Certainly, all the above mentioned scientists have made discoveries *antecedent* to holding this philosophy. And presumably they would grant that there are many scientific problems which they have failed to solve even *after* their philosophical conversion. At best, then, there is very slender evidence of any positive correlation, not to speak of significant connection, between the acceptance of dialetical materialism and the discovery of new scientific truths.

It is a matter of record that many, if not most, of the leading figures in the history of science who have been inspired by extra-scientific philosophies have professed a quite different set of metaphysical principles from those of Haldane *et al.*

What would Haldane do in their case? He would not deny that their consciousness of a significant connection was a fact, but he would demand other evidence of the alleged heuristic value of their metaphysical, religious, or psychological assumptions. We propose to proceed in precisely the same way with Haldane. If we ask for the evidence that his philosophy of dialectical materialism has a logically relevant bearing upon his scientific work, what do we find?

We find that the work to which he refers us, and which follows his conversion to dialectical materialism, does not differ *in principle* from the work which preceded his conversion, that conclusions opposite to those enunciated in his recent work are perfectly compatible with the tenets of dialectical materialism as he states them, and that *if* different conclusions from those reached by Haldane are untenable, it is because they violate familiar principles of scientific method and not the dialectic law of "the negation of the negation." And, oddly enough, some of his social pronouncements are as ill-founded as excursions of other "idealistic" scientists in this field, and are hard to square with the theory of historical materialism which he also accepts.

The work to which Haldane refers us is a study of haemophilia in the royal families of Europe.[8] He follows the conventional treatment and data of other investigators, which he admits is correct as far as it goes. "But it is undialectical." Why? Because *assuming* that the frequency of haemophilia is not diminishing, it does not explain how the supply is kept up. Haldane's explanation is that the supply is kept up by the process of mutation. By extrapolating the relative frequency of haemophilic cases in England, he asserts that in each generation one out of every 50,000 genes which are normal for blood clotting becomes a gene for haemophilia. Natural selection prevents its dispersion. "Thus the actual frequency of haemophilia represents a balance between the opposing processes of mutation and natural selection."

Where in all this does dialectical materialism come in? Assuming certain data, and an interest in the problem of the origin and recurrence of haemophilia, Haldane has invoked a well-recognized principle in modern biology. This is not to detract in the slightest from Haldane's scientific achievements any more than to criticize the philosophical *gaucheries* of Eddington and Jeans is to dispute their scientific eminence. Further, it should be pointed out that Haldane, far from solving the problem, has set up an hypothesis on the basis of very limited data, with no indication of what further experimental findings to expect. And what he seems to stress the most, viz., his having published "the first serious estimate of the rate of mutation of a human gene," is a simple but extremely hazardous induction from a rather arbitrary initial estimate of its present frequency. But my interest is not to raise these and many other questions which suggest themselves to me as difficulties in the way of Haldane's conclusions. It is quite possible that all of these objections will turn out to be completely unfounded. What is clear, however, is that Haldane's conclusions will be accepted or rejected to the extent to which they fulfill the requirements of established scientific

[8] *Modern Quarterly*, London, 1, 2, pp. 129-138.

theory and practice in genetics. At no place do his dialectical formulae enter relevantly into his analysis.

Nor does his philosophy safeguard him from certain confusions which permeate some of his recent work. Thus, he seems to think that to say "we do not understand the nature of the process of mutation" is equivalent to saying that a mutation "is an uncontrollable event." There are many things whose natures we do not "understand" but which we can easily control. Haldane himself in another connection asserts "it is even now not in the least clear why ice melts at 0° C.";[9] but this is certainly subject to control. And when he writes: "If the uncertainty principle is correct, it [mutation] is by its very nature incapable of control by man,"[10] it is hard to see what the uncertainty principle has to do with it, particularly in view of the fact that Haldane in another of his recent works[11] refers to the new species which men have produced. To say that we cannot control, at present, mutations in the genes of human beings is justified by scientific evidence. To say that by their very nature such mutations are *uncontrollable* may be dialectical but it goes beyond the evidence.

The social and historical consequences which Haldane draws from his studies have even less to recommend them. He writes as if the affliction of haemophilia were a "sterilizable" trait and is positively indignant that the crowned heads of Europe did not take better care in choosing the mothers of future royalty. He is bitter about the strait-laced Victorian era which hushed up unpleasant facts of heredity; about a royalty which sold the people out by not correcting the consequences of a mutation "in a nucleus of a cell in one of the testicles of Edward, Duke of Kent, in the year 1818"—the original source of haemophilia in the royal families of Europe. Even if compulsory sterilization for the carriers of haemophilia had been in force, he is frankly skeptical of the willingness of the Medical Officer of Health for Westminster to enforce them on Queen Victoria and her daughters—the future Empress of Germany, the future Princesses of Hesse, Schleswig-Holstein, and Battenberg, and the future Duchess of Argyll. These views of

[9] *Science and Society*, 2, p. 240.
[10] *Modern Quarterly*, London, 2, p. 482.
[11] *Science and Society*, I, p. 482.

Haldane are more congenial to a rambunctious eugenic tory than to a scientific socialist. I don't propose to discuss them but to set them down as mutations of dialectical materialism or of popular-frontism.

But Haldane's argument that haemophilia has played a dramatic part in recent European history, and that Queen Victoria, the daughter of the above-mentioned Edward, has played "a minor but *not insignificant part* in bringing about the Russian and Spanish revolution," [12] and that "a rather more materialistic outlook on the part of kings and their advisers might have altered the course of history"—demands discussion. For it reveals a fantastic misconception of the dominant social forces which have molded Western European history, and a type of causal inference incompatible with the scientific quest for proximate causes. By the same logic, one could prove that since Queen Victoria's existence depended upon a long line of ancestors down to the furry cousins of the ape, all of them had a not insignificant part in bringing about the Russian and Spanish revolutions.

To give even a semblance of plausibility to this "scientific" pendant to the theory of historical materialism, Haldane is compelled to invent his facts as he goes along. After March 1917, he says, "the fact that Alexis was a haemophilic must have militated against the proposal that he should succeed his father when the latter abdicated," as if the accession of Alexis would have stemmed in the slightest the Russian Revolution. In Spain in 1931, since the son of the dethroned Alfonso XIII was a haemophilic, this "unquestionably made it harder for moderate monarchists to propose the replacement of the reigning sovereign by the heir-apparent." There is no evidence that considerations of this sort significantly influenced the march of events either in Russia or Spain. Haldane's extension of his biological principles to history is on all fours with the attempt of the Social-Darwinians to extend biological principles of society. If dialectical materialism has led Haldane to such rash and demonstrably false notions of the historical process, scientists would be well advised to steer clear of it and similar mystical doctrines. It is unnecessary to discuss his remark that "at the present moment we have some slight evidence

[12] Italics mine.—S.H.

for the inheritance of a make-up leading to industrial economic success under capitalism." [13] If there is such a gene, and I think American studies have long since exploded this view, then we must admit that its discovery was inspired by the reactionary philosophy of some eugenists. Would Haldane allow them to claim for this philosophy the same heuristic significance that he claims for dialectical materialism?

4. Inevitability

(b) Dialectical materialists have been much exercised by the "idealism" of modern physicists. Following Lenin's confusion between subjectivism and idealism, they have been unable to indicate in just what this idealism consists. When Prenant says that "Marxist philosophy is materialist: by this is simply meant that it declares the existence of the world outside ourselves to be without question," [14] his definition would make many idealists, as well as theologians, materialists. The idealism of modern physicists, the least common denominator, so to speak, of all their philosophical constructions, is the belief that the universe is meaningful, i.e., that the processes of nature not merely support or condition human ideals but in the very warp and woof of things there is some spiritual thread which is continuous, if not altogether one, with the spirit of man. The doctrines of the scientific knights of dialectical materialism, as we shall see, amount to precisely the same thing except that nature and the *Natur-Dialektik* guarantee different ideals—socialist ideals.

Consider, for example, the implications of the sentence cited previously from Needham, as well as of the following: "If we look through the whole of evolutionary history ... we cannot but see a progressive rise in the level of organization, exceedingly slow but also very certain." "Fascist philosophy runs counter to the entire trend of evolution and if we may judge from the past it will perish like everything else which resists this trend." Values, consequently, are *objective in nature*. Natural processes slowly but inevitably insure the emergence of **progressive organization and doom social philosophies like**

[13] *Science and Society*, I, p. 486.
[14] *Op. cit.*, p. 18.

Fascism to defeat. It is not surprising that both Prenant and Needham laud L. Henderson's *The Fitness of the Environment*, which undertakes to prove that "life, exactly as we know it, is implicit in cosmic evolution," [15] and that it is impossible for the physical conditions of life to be what they are without life necessarily existing.

Now it is a long step from the view that *without* nature there would be no life, to the view that given nature (i.e., the inorganic world) life and human life *must* emerge. It is a still longer step from the view that the existence of society is conditioned by natural processes to the notion that the triumph of certain social ideals (*ours*) is involved in them while certain others, the enemy's, must be frustrated. Views of this sort can only be held by a form of absolute idealism which maintains that since everything is logically involved in everything else, it is impossible for any particular thing not to be and other things to remain the same. Theoretically we should be able to logically deduce social ideas from scientific facts; the good from the existent, and the existent from the good. In one breath dialectical materialists of this stripe deny that they are mechanists who assert that all qualities and levels are reducible to variations in quantity; in another they read back into nature, by the fallacy of division, all the qualities which appear at any level of experience.

5. *Dialectical Extravaganza*

The logic of the lie demands that it be supported by another lie. Similarly for an absurdity. There is no absurdity to which a dialectical materialist will not resort to defend another absurdity. It is extremely painful to observe this in the writings of H. Levy, who at one time was critical of the doctrine, but who subsequently, for political reasons, hurled himself into its embraces without stopping even to answer the objections he had previously urged against it.

Levy's belief in the "inevitability" of socialism is purchased at the cost of his own theory of isolates developed in his earlier book, *The Universe of Science*. An isolate is any situation or aspect which is examined independently of its contexts, his-

[15] Prenant, p. 81.

tory, or possible interactions, just as we might examine the structure of a gasoline engine without taking note of the uses to which it will be put. No isolate will be found *completely* isolated from everything. For many purposes we will have to consider its context. Any prediction which we make about its behavior as an isolate is subject to the corrections that arise from contextual influence and from interaction between it and other natural processes and events. If we consider the social system as a whole, as an isolate in respect to the rest of nature, Levy believes it can be shown (and we shall have more to say about his specific social views later) that its laws drive human beings to socialism. Curiously enough, although the inevitability of the final outcome is assured, Levy asserts that there are two alternative routes by which it may be reached—the democratic route, shorter and less costly, and the fascist route, longer and more costly. But by any route, socialism, sooner or later! Everything about it may be conditional, its time, place, and leadership—but not its inevitability.

Let us grant for the moment that Levy has demonstrated that the structure and dynamic of the social isolate are such that they inevitably generate not only the technological possibility of socialism, but the human consciousness of its desirability, the courage to fight for it, and the wisdom to win the battle. By his own principle, however, the social system is not unaffected by natural and cosmic processes which in the main run their course independently of social activity. How does he know that none of a thousand and one natural contingencies like plague, flood, earthquake will not wipe out civilization? By what kindly dispensation will nature "stay her hand" until socialism has been reached? In some passages he intimates that even social processes may lead to the destruction of our civilization just as past civilizations have been wiped out. Men may march right up to the goal of the classless society and yet fail to achieve it. On Levy's view, however, no matter how far back they are thrown and no matter how often, the immanent dialectic of technological processes will carry them to socialism. Even if nature has to develop another species of man, in the event that the present species becomes extinct, socialism will come. Engels and some of his Russian disciples (Rudas) suggest it may be on another planet. This is not a novel view—in theology. What is novel is that this religious conception of "inevitability"—nothing can occur in nature which will blast man's highest hopes—is presented under the aegis of an antireligious scientific philosophy.

This mode of thought carries Levy to an extravaganza whose analogue can only be found in the writings of the romantic *Natur-philosophen* of the early 19th century. He is discussing artificial delay in the inevitable phase change by which qualities are transformed. The law in question, like all the laws of dialectic, is universal and objective—applicable to nature as well as to society. "This conception," he writes, "is very important indeed when we come to consider the nature of the resistance that is offered to social and political change, but we can illustrate it more directly in the first instance from some of the scientific examples we have already given." [16] And he considers these examples in a section entitled, "Artificial Delay in Phase Change—Mechanical Fascism." (*sic!*)

Take the case of a body moving in a liquid. If the body is moved very quickly, whirlpools are formed in its wake. Suppose we want to prevent whirlpools from appearing. We take a hollow body and punch holes in it in a certain way and we find that we can increase the speed of the body without producing whirlpools. But if the speed is increased too much, "finally, in spite of this artifice, turbulence is set up by those fluid layers further removed from the boundary of the body. The artifice merely postpones an inevitable process."

Fascism is sooner or later defeated in nature just as it is in society!

But notice. Turbulence is set up only *after* a certain speed has been exceeded and at a point *beyond* the boundary of the body. Is it also inevitable that we *must* exceed this speed, and that the turbulence set up beyond the boundary of the body must inevitably affect the usefulness of this process in its industrial application? Obviously not. And besides, what is artificial about these restraints? When they occur in nature, as they sometimes do, they are just as natural as that which they restrain; and when they occur in society, they are just as natural as other social processes. Mechanical fascism, indeed! It would seem as if the whole of applied science consists in im-

[16] *Op. cit.*, p. 125.

posing "artificial" restraints upon natural processes. It would also appear on Levy's view that there is such a thing as biological fascism, the use of artificial preservatives "to delay the transformation of food-stuffs and fruits from the nutritional to the poisonous stage." In fact, I gravely suspect that all the practitioners of the healing arts, all physicians, nurses, and medical research workers everywhere must, on this analysis, be regarded as a pack of biological fascists. For do they not apply "artificial" restraints upon the progress of disease and the onset of death, artifices that "merely postpone an inevitable process"? A genuine fascist can use this kind of mythology much more effectively for his purposes than can a socialist.

Sufficient has been said to indicate the absurdities into which dialectical materialists are led by their quest for ontological laws which presumably justify the program of a political party. But before concluding the discussion, I wish to cast a closer glance at two books which have been hailed as presenting full-bodied authoritative treatments of science and society from the standpoint of dialectical materialism. They are the already mentioned Prenant's *Biology and Marxism* and Levy's *A Philosophy for a Modern Man*.

6. *Dialectics and Biology*

(1) Prenant's book is an attempt to consider an entire field from the standpoint of dialectical materialism in order to show that the latter is "of the nature of science itself, the experimental method continued without a break but now not afraid to face its own implications." Very good. How then does it differ from any other competent survey of biology? What problems does it solve that are not solved elsewhere, what confusions current in experimental biology does it eliminate, what scientific advance of any kind does it make? So far as I can see, aside from some frankly speculative notions about the origin of life, and related problems of evolution, which are far from meeting the critical questions they provoke in the reader, the book is not distinguished from other ordinary books on biology except in being interlarded with quotations from Marx, Engels and Lenin, and in its espousal of a crude and irrelevant metaphysics. Prenant thinks he is committed to a

critical experimental method, while Needham interprets his thesis in such a way as to suggest that Prenant is almost a logical empiricist. Dialectical materialism "as the quintessence of the scientific method itself" not only aids the biologist in showing what the best hypotheses are but also "by indicating which questions are meaningless and which are answerable."

And yet at the very outset Prenant shows a very queer conception of what scientific method is. "If the book is good," he writes, "it is because it is a Marxist book and not in spite of it. If it is bad, that is not because it is Marxist, but because it is not Marxist enough." Good or bad, then, this book must be a tribute to Marxism. If every Marxist author on biology were to write this way, no matter if all their books were bad, the evidence would still pile up in favor of Marxism. But what has Marxism to do with biology anyway? Prenant says that his book attempts "to take from modern biology the essential facts on which Marxism in part reposes." What part of Marxism reposes on modern biology? The theory of the class struggle? Historical materialism? The doctrine of surplus value? By 1849 Marx and Engels had enunciated *all* of their fundamental doctrines—even the principles of their philosophy were on paper. Modern biological developments begin with Darwin, more than a decade later. On what biological facts did (or does) Marxism repose so that if they were questioned Marxism would crash to the ground? Marx and Engels, to be sure, like most scientific-minded men of their times, accepted the Darwinian and post-Darwinian findings. *But so did many of their opponents.* In fact, there is not a single law of biology which is not perfectly compatible with the *advocacy* of mutually opposed social philosophies and political programs. The evidence for Marx's historical statements is to be found in his historical analysis, and not in physics, biology, or any other natural science. Prenant believes that Marx's social and historical analyses are valid. Does he believe that they would lack validity if the subsequent epoch-making discoveries of Mendel and DeVries, upon which modern genetics rests, had not been made?

To applaud the vague guesses which Engels made when he discussed biology is pitiful, and sometimes takes the form of imposture. Engels may have made some happy guesses (the unhappy ones are barely mentioned); so have many others who are not Marxists or dialectical materialists. But the truth is that even after Darwin's work, Engels clung to some key Lamarckian notions. He believed, for example, that *need* sometimes influenced the appearance of organs, and that acquired variations of this kind were hereditary. Not a single member of the new school of biological-dialectical-materialists so much as mentions this, though they exploit every recondite suggestion Engels made to show how fruitful his metaphysics is. Nor do they mention the fact that these views of Engels have been used as rationalizations for the periodic persecutions of Russian geneticists who have followed T. H. Morgan.

One is bewildered by the naïveté, downright contradiction, and ignorance of the meaning of Marx's ideas which pervade Prenant's book. I give an illustration of each.

(i) Straining with might and main to find something which would justify distinguishing "Marxist biology" from any other kind, Prenant delivers himself of this. "Without losing sight of the unity of all matter, Marxist biology still insists that the phenomena of life have their own characteristics, which must not be *forced* to conform to known physico-chemical formulae." [17] Has there ever been a single biologist anywhere who insisted, nay, who even so much as suggested, that the characteristics of life must be *forced* to conform to physico-chemical law? There is not a single biologist in the world who would not subscribe to Prenant's statement. The question is: Which aspects of living behavior are subject to physico-chemical laws and which are not? And this question cannot be settled by Marxism any more than by Henry Georgism or Thomism, but only by the experimental activity of scientists.

(ii) Dialectical thought is "of the very nature—the quintessence of scientific method." So Needham. So Prenant. But lo! We find that there is such a thing as *logical* thought which is not dialectical, and which scientists often use validly. The physicist occasionally may be logical and scientific: not so the biologist. Why? Because the physicist "has to deal from time to time with objects which are only relatively unstable." But "the insufficiency of purely logical thought in biology" is due to the fact that "by its nature this form of thought always

[17] P. 62; italics in original.

leaves out of account the very thing which is the essence of life—motion." [18] The physicist studies matter but not life whose essence is motion. Consequently, he can be logical without being dialectical and still be a good scientist. And matter— what is its essence? Prenant answers with a citation from Engels: "Motion is the mode of existence of matter."

Everything is now clear. Logical thought, which is guided by the law of non-contradiction, cannot do justice to motion. Physicists study matter whose mode of existence is motion. Physicists, however, can validly use logical thought. *Any two of the foregoing three sentences entail the contradictory of the third.* Could inconsistency be more flagrant? The trouble apparently is not with M. Prenant's thought processes, for its root lies, as we have been taught to believe by his fellow dialectical materialists, in the fact that the universe is contradictory. The universe not only guarantees man's highest ideals but his logical mistakes.

(iii) Where principles of logic and scientific method are violated with such carefree abandon, it is not surprising to find that the leading tenets of Marx's thought are treated in no less cavalier fashion. Prenant concludes a chapter on the origins of human society with a rapid sketch of pre-history from "the primitive communism of the savage horde" through clan society and "its inevitable disintegration on the appearance of classes." He admits that this is in part hypothetical and that the development may not have been everywhere uniform. He adds: "But what is essential is that from the beginning to the present day human society has evolved under the permanent and *fundamental* influence of its *material* relationship with Nature. This is the *basic* principle of historical materialism." [19] What a comedown from Marx's insight to the simplism of the geographical interpretation of history! So, the transition from slavery to feudalism, from feudalism to capitalism, from capitalism to Hitlerism in Germany and Stalinism in Russia—has been fundamentally determined by man's material relationship with *nature*. Shades of Buckle, Taine and Ellsworth Huntington!

[18] Pp. 58-59.
[19] P. 43; italics mine.—S.H.

7. *Dialectic and Physics*

2. Levy's *A Philosophy for a Modern Man* is the most ambitious of the recent productions of this school. In fact, it is nothing short of an ontology, since his aim is to find "a generalized law of Movement" whose validity can be illustrated in all fields from physics and mathematics to politics. The book is marked by a strenuous effort to save every dictum of orthodox dialectical materialism, of which Levy has been critical in the past, and to work into the exposition materials from modern science. The result is, apart from the exposition of commonly known scientific matters, the most tortured kind of interpretation and glaring inconsistency. Nothing is established except what is begged to begin with. In his social theory it turns out that Levy is wedded to a demonstrably false technocratic conception of history.

To spare the reader, I shall not discuss typical inconsistencies like the belief that ideas are true when they "reflect actual parts or aspects of the universe," and superposed on it the notion that men can make ideas come true. Nor his abuse of elementary logical distinctions in order to force the Brownian movements into the pattern of "the unity of opposites." ("At one and the same time there is united in it, like an ant-heap, the two opposite qualities *rest* and movement, statistical rest, atomic movement." As if the opposite of statistical rest were not statistical movement, and of atomic movement, atomic rest!) Nor his scandalous misinterpretation of the history of philosophy according to which all contemplative philosophies have necessarily been idealistic, English empirical philosophy divorced from life, and dialectical materialism the only doctrine that has stressed the continuity of theory and practice. I shall restrict myself to his fundamental ontological principle and his fundamental social theory.

Here is the way in which Levy states the universal and objective law of dialectic stripped of its Hegelian terminology.

"Consider a given state or situation S, in which there resides a certain quality Q which is undergoing intensification. S has an internal structure or composition, of such a nature that the intensification of Q arouses in it or intensifies in it a structural change q. The quality q is recognized by the fact that its intensification is inimical to the continued existence of the given state S. Accordingly at a critical stage of q, the state S is transformed by it into a new qualitative state T." (p. 112.)

Throughout the book T is invariably referred to as "higher" than S.

Of what significance is this dialectical law?

To begin with, in every situation, S, there are some qualities (q's) which do not undergo intensification. The intensification of Q may give rise to an intensification of some internal structural change which is *not* inimical to the continued existence of S. Levy says that q is recognized by the fact that its intensification is inimical to S. What this means is that he has *defined* q in this way, that is not a prediction to be verified, but the isolation *after* a process has run to completion, of some internal structural change whose intensification is a function of Q. Any other internal structural change whose intensification is not inimical to S *is ruled out* as a q. And when Levy adds that at a critical stage of q, S is transformed into a T, this is merely a consequence of the *definition* of a Q. This is what it *means* to say that the intensification of q is inimical to S. The whole account is a backdoor admission that whether we are to characterize a situation as dialectical or not depends upon *our* purposes or interests. There is nothing objective about it until we make our selection of the qualities we are interested in. There is nothing universal about it unless the sole existence of our interests and their fulfillment are guaranteed. There is nothing higher about the outcome, T, except in relation to *our* values. It has neither explanatory nor heuristic significance. After scientific discoveries have been made and tested by the ordinary procedures and canons of scientific method, it is possible to fit some of the results into this verbal scheme. But they can also be fitted into other verbal schemes. There is no demonstrable advantage in using Levy's language in describing the methods, procedures and results of science. And as we have shown, there are many disadvantages.

Dialectical materialism is sometimes recommended to "bourgeois" scientists in order to prevent them from adopting an unscientific view on the social sciences. But alas! the social doctrines of dialectical materialistic scientists are no more scientific than those of their idealistic colleagues. This may be illustrated by an examination of the main conclusion which emerges from Levy's "scientific study of social development." This conclusion allegedly illustrates the principle of dialectic as stated above. According to him, *"the drive of technique is ultimately the main causal agency which, as it rises, accentuates and enriches also the quality of communal life. It corresponds to the causal agent Q of our chapter on the transformation of qualities."* (p. 194.) Technique, then (which Levy mistakenly identifies with the mode of economic production—i.e., property relations), is the main causal factor of social development. It accounts not only for the development of society but for the quality of social organization, "the technical level of a community sets also the level of its social life." The higher the technique, the higher the level.

All we need do is to ask what are the main causal agencies of the drive of technique to see that far from being an ultimate cause (as if science were interested in ultimate causes), technique itself is influenced by the very social relations which here appear as its effect! Since the discovery of techniques is the direct result of the application of scientific ideas, Levy's own view opens the door to the idealistic interpretation of history which he repudiates. But there are much greater difficulties that lie directly on the doorstep of this simple theory. If the level of technique determines the level of culture, then since the technique of modern Germany is considerably "higher" than the technique of, say, pre-war Germany, Levy should regard modern German culture as "higher" than the comparatively golden days of the free trade-union and socialist movement. And since the technical level of the U.S. is immeasurably higher than that of the U.S.S.R., it is strange that he should regard the culture of the U.S.S.R. as higher. Even if we were to admit that the technical level of both cultures was the same, Levy, on his own scientific theory of social development, would be completely stumped to account for their vast cultural and political difference. As for technique being the driving force of historical *development*, why, what is that but the much scorned Social-Democratic legend that socialism must arrive in those countries, like England, which have a highly developed technological plant, before it arrives elsewhere? England, Marx wrote, was already technologically ripe for socialism as far back as the last quarter of the nineteenth century. Yet Levy believes that it is in Russia that socialism has already been achieved!

Levy seems to be vaguely conscious of these difficulties. In order to escape them, he is compelled to play fast and loose with his laws of social development. The upshot is the wildest confusion in which you can pay your political money, and take whatever choice the exigencies of a party program demand. We are told that the sequence of stages through which England has passed "from Feudalism to Mercantilism, on to Industrialism, were not peculiar to England alone." Not only are they illustrated in modern Western Europe but even in ancient Greece! Greece went through a Mercantile stage, a form of factory system and an Imperialistic or Colonial stage before it fell into decay—all this while slavery was its dominant mode of production and its level of technique was comparatively constant. It is admitted that what followed Greek imperialism was not socialism but destruction. Presumably this was inevitable; as inevitable as the transition in modern times from imperialism, not to destruction this time, but to triumphant socialism!

Levy qualifies his law of social succession by the statement that "what is invariable is the *order* in which they [the phases] come," not the duration of the time period in which they occur. There is unevenness in development and Russia shows that several phases of social development can be telescoped "by conscious group action." Conscious group action in this case is *not* driven by the level of technique, since Levy admits that the Russians began to develop their technique *after* they did the telescoping. But telescoping can only take a society *through* stages at high speed; it cannot *skip over* stages. "If it [Russia] succeeds, and who can now doubt that untimately it will, it will provide another illustration of how history can be guided *consciously* at high speed through stages that might have taken many generations of unconscious effort." But when did Russia go through even at high speed, the phase of finance capitalism? Not only the facts of nature but the still living record of history must be tortured into a mechanical schema. If the rest of the world had the technique, and Russia had the guiding consciousness which produced those "remarkable" cultural products that the rest of the world still lacks, how can this be squared with the "law" that the level of technique determines the level of culture?

Very simply. By considering both from "a wider perspective, that of the whole of human society." From this perspective, according to Levy, the unevennesses appear as internal stresses and strains. But this change of perspective to "society as a whole" is irrelevant. By adding together his two incompatible accounts, Levy is merely compounding the difficulties. The capitalist world has the technique, and Russia the guiding consciousness. If we consider them together in one perspective, Levy argues, we can see that a socialist culture exists in Russia, that it has been produced by technique, and that it must spread to the rest of the world. Why? Where is the evidence? This is not an argument but a pious wish and does not in the least extricate Levy from the insuperable contradiction into which his technological interpretation of history has landed him. His own premises together with the observable historical facts entail conclusions which he cannot square with his faith.

Just as the slogans of democracy can mask tyranny and oppression, so can an obscurantist philosophy cloak itself in scientific terminology. But in one case as in the other, just as soon as we confront verbal professions with the concrete procedures which accompany them, their true intent is revealed. There is no more justification for a *party* line in philosophy or science than there is for a party dictatorship under genuine democracy or socialism. Just as one can accept the scientific findings of the greatest figures in the history of science without the religious and metaphysical prepossessions with which they often interpreted them, so can we accept the substantial work of the lesser figures we have discussed in this chapter without their political and "dialectical" extravaganzas.

The most distressing feature of this new philosophical faith is not its confusing effect upon the minds of its adherents.[20]

[20] This confusion sometimes takes a highly comical form. In his latest book, *Science and Everyday Life*, J. B. S. Haldane tells us that "I had it [gastritis] for about fifteen years until I read Lenin and other writers, who showed me what was wrong with our society and how to cure it. Since then I have needed no magnesia." What is comical, here, is not the report of the fact—which there is no reason to deny—that Lenin is better than magnesia for settling Mr. Haldane's stomach. Given his temperament that is what we should expect

Rather is it to be found in its corrupting influence on their critical integrity whenever the ideals of free scientific inquiry, which they profess to uphold passionately in England and America, are invoked in criticism of the intellectual terror that grips Russian science. It is bad enough that free-born Englishmen and Americans who are eloquent about violations of academic freedom and of untrammeled scientific inquiry anywhere in the "bourgeois" world, should be silent about the incomparably more ruthless persecution of heterodox and nonconformist thinkers in Russia. But what shall we say when they *openly* extenuate and condone these practices in Russia? On this score, the poison-ivy wreath must be awarded to J. B. S. Haldane, who extenuates the Russian persecutions on the ground that in England and America, too, scientists sometimes suffer because of their views. [21] What he overlooks is the difference between organized, officially sanctioned purges carrying with them sentences of exile and death, in Russia, and episodic violations of an accepted code of freedom in democratic countries. But most important of all, he fails to grasp the significance of the fact that honest minds are just as much opposed to restrictions upon free scientific inquiry in their own countries as they are to the Russian and German practices. Persecution is not less persecution when it is carried out under the aegis of dialectical materialism than when it is justified in the name of Americanism, Catholicism, Hitlerism, or the safety of the British Empire.

That Haldane and his confreres are unable to recognize these distinctions is the most damning testimony of the social effect of their philosophy. If that philosophy were only false, it would constitute only another footnote in the history of human error. But it is worse than false, for it constitutes a powerful threat to freedom of scientific inquiry everywhere.

as a consequence of the perfect "sumptuosity of security," to use the phrase of William James, which rapturous faith in Lenin and Stalin accord. What is comical is that Mr. Haldane should regard this as bearing in any way upon the validity of dialectical materialism. After all, the Church can make older and better substantiated claims for the beneficial effects of religious faith on the human stomach than anyone can for Lenin or magnesia. Reading and believing Hitler and Mussolini have an even more potent effect; they obviate the necessity for many of taking castor oil, an enforced dose of which is often the unhappy consequence of reading and *disbelieving* them. Mr. Haldane's pharmaceutical argument proves too much.

[21] *Cf.* his reply to Prof. A. V. Hill in the *New Statesman & Nation*, Feb. 8, 1940.

CHAPTER ELEVEN

DIALECTIC IN SOCIETY AND HISTORY

THE TERM "dialectic" is almost as old as the practice of philosophy. Like many other labels of great antiquity, it has been used as a tag for concepts, activities, and situations of the most heterogeneous variety. Few philosophers have ever employed the term in the same sense as any of their predecessors. Indeed, rarely is it the case that any philosopher has consistently adhered to any one meaning in his writings. What *the* dialectic is, therefore, can no more be adequately treated short of a history of its definitions in use from Plato to the present than we could straightway say what *the* empirical, *the* reasonable, *the* sensible, *the* romantic, and similar terms mean in the history of philosophy. What is true of Plato, Aristotle, and Plotinus—all of whom employ the term "dialectic" and all in different senses—is the general rule for every other period of philosophy.

None the less, it is possible to indicate the chief classes of meaning within which the various uses of the term fall, and to investigate the kinds of problems and intellectual motivations which have impelled philosophers to distinguish between what is dialectical and what is not. It is also possible to point out certain characteristic errors and dangers which have accompanied the use of the term "dialectic." The only alternative to this procedure is to present one's own theory of dialectic. This I shall not do. Instead I shall argue that it would be best in the interests of clarity to let the term sink into the desuetude of archaisms. Further, I shall try to show that this is the only legitimate moral that can be drawn from any critical investigation of the assumptions and types of procedure most frequently designated as dialectical in the history of thought.

There are two generic conceptions of dialectic under which the various meanings of dialectic may be subsumed. The first is the conception of dialectic as a pattern of existential change either in nature or society or man where the "or" is not exclusive. The second is the view that dialectic is a special method of analyzing such change. Usually, but not always, it is held that the method of dialectical analysis in some sense "reflects" or "corresponds to" the dialectical pattern of change. In any case, there is always a distinction drawn, though with no great regard for consistency, between the dialectical type of change and other kinds. When the dialectic is identified with change as such, it is explicitly contrasted with some other natural or supernatural element which is regarded as undialectical, e.g., unchanging form or pattern. Similarly with the conception of dialectic as method. Whether taken as a method of analysis or discovery or both, it is always distinguished from other methods called undialectical, i.e., metaphysical, scientific, commonsensical, etc. This last distinction is of the first importance. For the alleged justification of the dialectic method consists in its power to lead us to the discovery of new truths or to a deeper and more adequate understanding of old truths not accessible to us by any other method.

1. Dialectic as the Pattern of Existential Change

In a previous chapter I have examined the concept of dialectic in its presumed applications to the world of nature. In the present chapter I wish to discuss it in relation to the historical and cultural disciplines.

What is the dialectic when it is conceived as a constitutive principle in history and culture? Here we must distinguish between three subclasses of conceptions.

I. DIALECTIC AS PENDULAR RHYTHM

The first of these is the view that the pattern of dialectical change in history is found in a pendular rhythm or eternal repetitive seesaw between tendencies, forces, institutions, styles of thought, and morals. On this view, every activity, in virtue of its very pervasiveness and triumph, tends by force of immanent necessity to bring about its own opposite. Convention leads to revolt and revolt to convention, peace to war and war to peace, despotism to democracy and democracy to despotism, empiricism to rationalism and vice versa. So far as I am aware, no one has understood the concept of pendularity as involving a literal return to some previous phase, for this would mean that the initial polarity was the final polarity. The history of culture or of any aspect of culture would then be sufficiently described in one formula and no allowance made for the rich variety of forms that fall outside the arc of the pendular swing. And, in fact, even when it is admitted that oscillations between tendencies never carry the pendulum back to the very same place, the whole notion of periodicity seems inadequate to the *historical* character of cultural phenomena. It is nothing but a mechanical analogy imposed upon a material which in large measure reveals continuities, transitions, cumulative developments. Its inadequacy is expressed by the arbitrary character of the time span it takes for this swing rhythm to fulfill itself. Its use in suggesting points of similarity between anything present and past is blind and irrelevant except in relation to some specific hypothesis that involves references to other factors which do not necessarily have periodic character. And without such an hypothesis, the analogy is likely to distract our attention from what is historically new in any given epoch. The uncritical comparisons between modern totalitarianisms and those of ancient or medieval times is a case in point.

The most serious defect, however, of this view of dialectic is in its conception of immanent necessity. It states some periodic law on the basis of a simple and risky induction from a few cases. It then uses the law to explain and predict other historical events. It thus combines a kind of mystical rationalism with a crude empiricism. It overlooks the fact that in scientific inquiry the observation of a genuine periodicity or fluctuation is rarely taken as a brute fact or ultimate datum. It marks the beginning of a problem, not the close of an inquiry. And the problem usually is to discover how the periodic changes are functionally related to, or determined by, other factors in the environmental medium or background. Here there are no immanent necessities.

II. DIALECTIC AS STRUGGLE

The second conception of existential dialectic in society and history identifies it with the fact and pattern of struggle. On this view, wherever human beings live in association with each other, struggles, conflicts, and oppositions of varying intensity are bound to ensue. The conditions under which, the objects over which, and the occasions on which struggle breaks out— vary from one dialectical theory to another. When it is consistently held, it flatly contradicts the naïve belief that the social harmony and peace, envisaged by all chiliastic doctrines, can ever prevail in the relations between men. But the view is rarely held in a consistent way. In the interests of political mythology, the dialectic of struggle is usually restricted to a certain set of antagonisms assumed to be basic to all others. With the elimination of the conditions which breed these antagonisms, it is predicted that all other antagonisms will disappear. The result is either an *a priori* belief that social war is an inexpugnable feature of all social life or chiliasm in pseudo-scientific dress—a belief in a predestined day when all men will be brothers and no one will re-enact the role of Cain.

The trouble with both of these alternatives is that they deal with "struggle" in the large. Like all vague monisms, despite their suggestive character, they are incapable of scientific verification. Verbally, they are compatible with any known state of affairs. Empirically, we do not know struggle but struggles. And these are neither absolute nor unconditional. That is to say, the same individuals who are members of groups engaged in some specific struggle may also be members of groups engaged in some specific form of co-operation or solidarity. And every specific struggle is contingent upon factors which if not modifiable are at least variable. In the absence of a precisely defined schedule of the kinds of struggle, their degree of pervasiveness, and their interrelationships, significant causal analysis is very difficult. Thought moves on a pre-scientific level contenting itself with some traditional conception of human nature. The traditionalism of social neo-Darwinism, which from propositions about man's biological organism makes inferences about history and society to the end of all time, is matched by the fantasies of millenary Utopianism which, from evidence that *some* socially undesirable traits of historical behavior may be removable, makes inferences about the future which would require that man cease being a biological organism.

III. DIALECTIC AS HISTORICAL INTERACTION

The third and most common objective reference of dialectic is to the pattern of interaction between "objective conditioning features of the environment," and man considered as an active agent in the historical process. The dialectical problem par excellence on this view is how man changes himself, or how men, as a class, change their social status, by reacting upon a changing social environment. Sometimes concern seems to be with the way in which "the will," operating within a causally or finalistically determined system, expresses its own form of determination as a principle of freedom, making a difference to the system and at the same time making itself different. Sometimes the concern seems to be with the way in which qualities of feeling and emotion, whether derived from inner impulses or outer impacts, become transformed by virtue of the ideas and activities in which they are expressed. Most often, the problem is to account for the fact that ideals or resolutions, which are an outgrowth of that which is apparently neither, are capable none the less of modifying their own conditions. The idealistic version of dialectic meets the difficulty by assimilating things to mind; the materialistic version of dialectic interprets mind as a specific form of adaptive behavior. In both types of solution human activity, informed by ideals, introduces changes in the original situation whose difficulties provoke action. The dialectical nub of the process is considered to be the element of creative redetermination produced in the self or the world by human ideals and practice, and the subsequent modification of human nature by the control of things and institutions.

Now strictly considered, all these forms of activity and the problem of interaction associated with them, fall within the realm of individual and social psychology, and testify to the fact that the latter is a comparatively undeveloped discipline whose very key concepts are subject to ambiguity and dispute. Particularly is this true for what may be called the field of personal psychology. Those who regard the problems of individual life in the dramatic form in which they are experienced when momentous decisions, conversions, and actions occur, as the only genuine concern of the philosophical psychologist, seem to me, for all their elaborate verbal constructions, to be expressing in a disguised way only their own concern or preference for certain problems which have autobiographical significance. Their new and arresting vocabulary baptizes the events in question so that we know that they are crisis phenomena not in the life of man, as is alleged, but in the lives of some men. But they do not explain them. At best, they convey a sense of their high importance. So far as I can see, the chief insights of Kierkegaard, Heidegger, Jaspers, *et al.*, are already involved in the dictum of Lichtenberg that the verbs which express personal existence are irregular in all languages, which even on the most *outré* metaphysical theory of language justifies the not very exciting conclusion that the mode of man's existence is in some ways different from that of other things in this world.

The crucial problem suggested by the use of dialectic in this sense is not the existence of the facts of social, personal, and moral experience, nor whether they have a call upon our attention, but whether the *descriptions* of these facts in the *language* of dialectic are valid, and by what objective techniques of inquiry the validity of these descriptions is to be established. The most momentous conclusion which is hung upon the allegedly dialectical character of consciousness, individual or historical, is that its investigation entails an abandonment of the principles of scientific empirical procedure, not to speak of ordinary canons of logic, which are granted a limited validity in other fields, and the adoption of a new dialectic method of thought or apprehension. What this dialectic method is we shall discuss later. But there is nothing in the descriptive account of the phenomena of conscious human action that makes necessary an appeal to non-scientific types of investigation and inference. Suppose it is true that every act of inquiry affects the quality of the state of personality which is being investigated; suppose it is true that in knowing, processes are set up that transform the situation which is being known; suppose, to use another of the stock illustrations of the dialectic situation, it is true that human beings, whose behavior has been predicted, are influenced to some extent in their behavior by that prediction. In all of these cases, the situation becomes more complicated, the observed data and effects are indirectly connected with the quaesitum, and reliable knowledge may be harder to get. But the complexity of a problem is an invitation to extend and refine existing methods of analyses and inquiry, particularly if they have proved adequate to the solution of simpler problems in their respective fields. It does not warrant a jump to a distinction between two kinds of knowledge or to two radically different methods of acquiring knowledge.

2. *Dialectic as a Method of Understanding Change*

We now turn to a consideration of those conceptions of dialectic which identify it with a method of thought—conceived not merely as a mode of analysis which uncovers assumptions and elicits the consequences of asserted meanings, i.e., the familiar method of clarifying ideas—but dialectic as a fruitful method of discovering truths. Those who hold that there is something dialectical in the world of nature or history usually assert that truths about it can be disclosed by the dialectical method alone: there are some, however, who deny that there is an existential dialectic, but affirm that whatever *is* in the world can be understood with the help of the dialectical method. The exercise of the dialectic method is usually attributed to a certain intellectual power or faculty, reason as distinct from the understanding, synoptic insight as distinct from discursive thought.

What is this dialectic method? Here again we can only understand it by examining the intellectual procedures of those who claim they are using it.[1] When we do this we find not one but several basic notions or principles of procedure in the writings of those who identify themselves as dialecticians.

I. DIALECTIC AS INTERRELATEDNESS

One of the most important categories of dialectic method is the principle of *interrelatedness*. Used in social inquiry, this has led, since the time of Hegel, to the perception that certain cultural patterns and ideals are so pervasive that a sharp separation of the fields of law, religion, politics, and

[1] I have omitted specific discussion of Marx in this connection because, whether or not we regard his findings as valid, I believe it can be shown that he made no distinction between the dialectic method, as he understood it, and scientific method as applied to the historical and cultural sciences.

economics from each other makes unintelligible the structure, problems, and indeed the very history of those fields. Used in the analysis of individual acts of behavior, it often uncovers not merely the physical and biological systems in which they appear as elements, but a pattern of social values to which these acts owe their distinctive significance. From this point of view, a culture may not be a seamless web, but it is more than an aggregate of unrelated individual activities in a frame of chance-assorted institutions. No matter what we understand by "understanding" in social inquiry, it always presupposes that a thing is placed in context, connection, or relationship with other things. Now so much, every theory of scientific method would assert, and not merely for social inquiry but *all* inquiry. What is distinctive, however, about the category of interrelatedness in the dialectic method is that it recognizes no limitation upon the principle. For it, *all* things are interrelated in a definite kind of pattern whose nature we shall later indicate; and this is asserted not as a heuristic principle, subject to the *piecemeal* verification of scientific method but as a dogma. It is not enough on this view to say that some cultural wholes are related in some determinate ways to other wholes. What is asserted is that all wholes are related to each other in the same or similar way as the parts of any whole are related to each other. Where this cannot be established for any event or for a whole domain of events, the dogma is not modified, but the event or domain in question is characterized as in so far incomplete, unintelligible, accidental, and an "inferior" order of "reality" is attributed to it.

The excesses to which the dialectic method, conceived as the principle of cultural interrelatedness, can go is best illustrated in Spengler, for whom one style of the soul informs and unites such apparently different things as oil painting perspective, printing, the credit system, long range weapons, contrapuntal music, and differential calculus; while another style of the soul is found organically unifying the nude statue, coin-currency, the city state, Euclidean geometry, and the burning of the dead. Here we have organicism gone mad, buttressed by dubious scholarship, substituting impressionist principles of integration for clearly defined forms of interrelation, and in the end compelled to rule out as atypical, "unreal," or as cultural aberrations whatever does not yield to arbitrary intuition. Spengler is the best but by far not the only representative of this tendency. Many orthodox dialectical materialists proceed in the same fashion, except that instead of the style of the soul they substitute the style (forces) of production which "in the last instance" determines everything significant in art, biology, physics, military warfare, the clothing industry, and the movies.

II. DIALECTIC AND HOLISM

It is clear, then, that the concept of interrelatedness as used by the dialectic method goes hand in hand with the concept of *totality*. In many writers it is this term which receives the chief emphasis. Here, too, in so far as it is a way of asserting that there are no ready-made atomic facts, observation of which is a final validation of an isolated judgment, it states what is recognized by every adequate account of scientific method. Even the most rigorous analysis takes its point of departure from some vaguely apprehended qualitative whole or situation; and every significant observation involves a whole body or system of knowledge. But what distinguishes the scientific from the dialectic use of totality is its attempt to predict, with the greatest exactness possible to the material, the behavior of some particular whole by formulating certain abstract general laws that hold for the elements of all totalities in the same relevant class. According to the customary use of dialectic method, on the other hand, it is *theoretically* impossible to formulate laws that are instrumentally valid for individual totalities without these laws being *necessarily* modified by their organic interrelation with other aspects of totality. That is to say, not merely is it asserted that no set of laws can completely determine all the specific aspects of the behavior of an individual totality— which every student of scientific method would grant—the dialectic method affirms that the very meaning and validity of these laws must of *necessity* be affected by the structure of the concrete totality to which it is applied. This, of course, is involved in the Hegelian theory of the concrete universal and its doctrine that all relations are internal. From them it follows not merely that scientific knowledge is incomplete, but that it necessarily distorts, not merely that abstractions are for certain purposes inadequate, but that they are vicious, and that the laws which state how they are related are unintelligible.

In actual practice those who have used the dialectic method most plausibly in the cultural disciplines have done little more than to show that the totalities of culture and history are more inclusive than those of natural science, and that consequently although the laws of natural science retain their validity in the more inclusive situations, it is possible to formulate social laws to do justice to the distinctive character of cultural and historical totalities. But this does not justify the belief that the rationale or logic of scientific method becomes altered when its subject matter is historical and social rather than physical. Theoretically, there is no reason to deny the possibility that social and historical laws may be reduced to special expressions of more general physical laws (i.e., given certain general physical laws, certain special data of observation, and certain rules governing inferences for the class of phenomena in question, it may be possible to deduce biological or social laws). But on the other hand, there is no reason to assert that they necessarily must be reducible, except in a special technical sense that applies not to laws, but to how concepts are to be introduced, a sense which has nothing to do with traditional "reductionism." The empirical fact is that social life is the most inclusive form of totality that we know, that *some* but not *all* forms of biological and psychological interaction, observed to hold outside of a social context, are modified when they are found within this totality. The investigation of the extent to which, and the specific ways in which, this is accomplished, however, needs no special dialectic logic to reach scientifically valid conclusions.

III. DIALECTIC AND INQUIRY

Historically, the actual technique of the dialectic method from Proclus to Hegel, where it is not synonymous with logical analysis or the art of clarifying a position by question and answer, consists in showing that every concept or category or judgment implicitly involves its contradictory, and that these contradictories together, instead of negating each other, logically involve another concept or category or judgment in which, for the moment, they enjoy a differentiated compatibility. This is the famous *dialektischer Dreitakt* by which logical thinking marches to the One or the Absolute Idea. Logically, of course, the whole process does not survive a second glance. The confusion between the concepts of contraries, contradictories, opposition, and otherness is palpable. Just as Nicholas von Cusa calmly uses the phrase *coincidentia oppositorum*— the identity of opposites—interchangeably with *connexio oppositorum*—the unity of opposites—so Hegel speaks of the *Einheit* and *Identität* of *Widersprüche* and *Gegensätze* as if they meant the same.

Looking away from the fatal difficulties which attend any attempt to take the dialectic method literally, we may ask: What do we discover to be the case when those who claim to be using dialectical procedures reach conclusions or make analyses which on *other* grounds we are prepared to admit as valid? In all such cases, I think that what we find is this. We begin with some vague conceptions and definitions which are set to work to solve some felt difficulty in a situation. We develop therefrom an ordered set of implications which are established as a system in terms of which the structure or behavior of the given and similar situations are so described that the felt difficulty or problem is resolved. We then discover (1) either that certain incompatibile judgments follow from the premises, or (2) that some particular subject matter which is outside of our system and yet seems to be continuous in certain respects to the subject matter within the system, cannot be intelligibly characterized. In the first case, we go back to our premises and clarify ambiguities; in the second, we redefine the terms in our premises or add new premises with a direct eye to the new material. Both are special cases of the logic of redefinition as it functions in inquiry. Illustrations abound on all sides, e.g., changes in the definition of number to include the so-called irrational and imaginary numbers; in the definition of atom from Democritus to the present; in the definition of organism to include unicellular entities; in the definition of property to include copyrights and good will, etc.

Procedures of this kind are familiar in all fields. They are phases of scientific inquiry. Far from affirming, they contradict the claims made for the dialectic method. For what is called the movement of dialectic method is here obviously neither universal, nor necessary, nor immanent, as all versions of the theory contend it must be. The synthetic construction in any situation can never be deduced from the logical character of what the dialectic miscalls contradictories. There is always a number of syntheses or supra-ordinate systems that can be constructed to resolve "oppositions." The particular syntheses made are always oriented to a problem, an interest, a need, i.e., to the exigencies of something outside the conceptual system. *In abstracto* all oppositions may be solved, but *in concreto* what prevents us from admitting that some oppositions may be irreconcilable? What, indeed, save the unverifiable dogma that there must be some underlying harmony in the scheme of things, that all difficulties and problems must have single, determinate solutions? Here again specific answers can be given only to specific problems.

IV. DIALECTIC AND DESTINY

The presupposition of the dialectic method is not merely that whenever it is applied some totality is present. So much, we have seen, any method of inquiry, with certain modifications, grants. What is usually asserted is that the whole which the dialectic method explores is also a value whole. Again not merely in the sense that the quest for an answer involves the recognition of the value of truth, nor, in the sense that values provide, in Rickert's phrase, "an historical center" around which the materials of culture study and history can be organized. What is meant is that each System has a value co-ordinate. Without reference to this value co-ordinate, the direction of the development of the system is unintelligible and all description therefore becomes a correlation of unessentials. This value is at least as objective as any other feature of the system, and is more important because by some hidden telic causality it controls what is ultimately realized and what not. The dialectic method presumably shows that the ground-consequent, cause-effect, and stimulus-response relationships within any system can exist only as part of the means-end relation. Not the means-end relation of ordinary purposive action but Means-End relation in some cosmic sense.

Thus, for Hegel, particular passions and interests may have particular causes and be directed towards particular human ends, but the final result, guaranteed by an inner necessity, is not the accomplishment of these empirical ends but of some Divine End—Self-consciousness or Freedom. Other Hegelians differ from Hegel merely in the character of the End which they spell out of immanent social processes. Whenever, in the field of natural science, a distinction is made between scientific and dialectic method, the latter is supposed to demonstrate that some organisms are higher and better (in an absolute sense) than others, that the processes of nature are such that the appearance of man on this earth or elsewhere is not contingent but necessary, and similar conclusions. In history and politics, whenever the dialectic method is distinguished from the scientific method, it is harnessed to the belief that history has some goal which will inevitably be realized, that temporary setbacks and defeats are necessary to the ultimate triumph of man's highest ideals, meaning one's own. In other words, it is not the patterns of causality which the dialectic method uncovers but the patterns of destiny.

3. *Sense and Nonsense in Dialectic*

In the first class of conceptions of dialectic we have considered, i.e., where dialectic is taken existentially, it is clear that we are confronted by a set of material hypotheses concerning the organization of society and the historical course it will take. The difficulty with all of these hypotheses is that, as formulated, they are so vague that no matter how events turn out, it is possible to claim some validation for them. They then function somewhat like the conceptions that Henri Poincaré calls "neutral hypotheses," i.e., assumptions such that even if we had started with opposite ones, it would not be necessary to change any of the empirical results. These neutral hypotheses are always dangerous if their character is misunderstood, for they may lead us to bring our inquiry to a halt just at the point where it really should begin.

Suppose that we accept for the moment the conception that history develops in periodic or swing rhythm. What, even if taken in conjunction with specific data, can we predict from it? Merely, that no matter how history turns out a time will come when we will be able to construct *some* periodic classificatory scheme which will illustrate the principle. But our primary scientific interest is in predicting as closely as we can the specific form of the institutions of tomorrow. To do this, we must proceed from a whole cluster of assumptions about (1) the relevant factors that may be now observed at work, and these are always many; (2) the relative weight of these factors; and (3) the historical effects of knowledge and ignorance of (1) and (2). The hypothesis of oscillating rhythms in history enables us to make no predictions except that the civilization of the future, in certain, not too carefully defined respects, will be different from the civilization of today—if there is a civilization.

Or let us look for a moment at the dialectic conceived as the principle of class struggle. Here we have an hypothesis according to which class struggles, where a class is defined by reference to the role which a group plays in production, are the key to juridical, political, national, religious, and even philosophical conflicts. Predictions have been made on the basis of it which to some extent have been verified. But I am acquainted with no theory of the class struggle at present which does not use the term "class," not to speak of "struggle," in several different senses, so that it is easy for the uncritical-minded to interpret almost any kind of struggle as a "manifestation" of class struggle. Even on the rare occasions when the writers of this school adhere to a single meaning of the term "class struggle" and recognize the existence of other kinds of struggle, the conclusions are hardly testable. The predictions that (1) the class struggles of tomorrow will take a certain form because of the character, intensity, and conditions of the class struggles of today, and (2) that the national and ideological conflicts of tomorrow will take a certain form because of the character, intensity, and conditions of the class struggles of tomorrow—can receive scientific confirmation only when we develop some commonly-agreed-on measure of the intensity of class struggles, and can evaluate the independent strength of other types of struggle—and their effect upon class struggles.

We may put the point we are making in this way. Every theory in this existential sub-type of dialectics begins with an initial monism which it is compelled to qualify by reference to the reciprocal and interactive effects of many different factors. The monism is then abandoned and it is asserted that Spirit or mode of production, technology, or the great man is the dominant (or most fundamental or most important) cause of historical or social development. But there is no way to "measure" the dominant factor in general unless this means that many more cultural phenomena can be shown to depend upon X than upon any other factor. This is a proposition about comparative frequencies and could only be established as a result of a vast statistical study of cultural dependencies which no one has ever adequately undertaken.

The confusion comes from speaking of the dominant factor in relation to society or history as a whole, when it only makes sense to speak of something as dominant or most important in relation to some problem to be solved or difficulty to be overcome. There is no such thing as the most important factor in the health or functioning of the human organism. But once trouble arises, analysis may indicate that for its elimination, certain functions of the organism may be more important than others, i.e., restoration at some points is more urgent than others. So in social inquiry. What those who speak of dialectic must mean if they are to avoid tautologies or contradictions is that in reference to some problem or felt difficulty, which may vary with the different values of different groups, the use of certain instrumentalities is more valid than others.

This leaves the third type of hypothesis with which the dialectic in society is identified, viz., the interaction between objective conditions and human ideals, volition, need, and knowledge. Strictly speaking, what we have here is not an hypothesis to be developed but a delimitation of a subject matter in terms of a convenient organizing category. That is to say, dialectic in this sense means that we are to regard the differentiating categorical feature of social and historical subject matter to be value-centered human activity; that no matter how values are to be interpreted, once we know how words designating them are introduced into discourse, explanation in value terms is legitimate but not mandatory in historical and social inquiry; that although they do not function independently of those objective features of the environment which lack value, the distinctive characters of *human* life lie precisely in the way physical and biological energies are organized in a value-making way.

4. Dialectic and the Doctrine of Two "Truths"

When we consider the set of conceptions identified with dialectic as a method of analysis and discovery, we notice that they represent a characteristic exaggeration of some features found exhibited in non-dialectical scientific inquiry. The characteristic exaggeration can always be traced to the more or less explicit assumption that there is some all-pervading plan or purpose in history. The intent of the dialectic method is not to investigate the relationships between the specific empirical *valuings* of men in concrete interaction with the world and each other, but to discover how one great objective Value or Good is being realized in the social and historical process. It is a means of getting by faith what cannot be reached by evidence, obscured by the logically vicious illusion that what has been begged by faith can be demonstrated as a scientific conclusion.

Where faith has political power, i.e., where this objective Value or Good is interpreted by a political party or a church, the sciences are expected to reach conclusions that may be used in some way to justify or rationalize a political program. Where scientific conclusions seem to run counter to the necessities of faith, they, together with the scientists, are "corrected" by the allegedly higher methods suggested by the slogan of "the Bolshevization of Science" [2] in one country, and "the Aryanization of Science" in another. I do not mean to suggest that all proponents of the dialectic method are necessarily committed to such harsh faiths. But I do mean that they are committed to some cosmic faith, and that in distinguishing between dialectical methods and the mundane methods of empirical science, they are driven to the theory of two truths. In practice,

---

[2] The indispensability of the dialectic method and its superiority to all other forms of thought is a cardinal tenet of all varieties of Leninism. The three most important schools of Leninism, those headed by Stalin, Trotsky, and the late Bukharin, are in agreement on this point. Criticism of the dialectic method is proof positive in their eyes of "petty-bourgeois opportunism," and consistently followed must lead to counter-revolution. Since in the eyes of each one the other two are counter-revolutionists, it is questionable whether even from their own standpoint rejection of dialectic is either a necessary or sufficient condition of counter-revolution. In actual fact, the epithet "un-dialectical" is used by them as a weapon in political struggle when the political position itself cannot be defended on grounds that seem reasonable to their own erstwhile followers. It functions as a kind of ritualistic abracadabra to bolster authority, and to reinforce belief in scientifically untenable doctrines which the leader finds politically exigent to uphold.

if a clash between them is recognized, one is subordinated to the other, i.e., the truths of science are abridged in the light of the more inclusive "truths" of faith.

One does not have to believe in the existence of a special principle of dialectic in the world to recognize that the life of man in society is one which reveals modes of behavior that are characteristic of man and not of an ant-hill, or carbon chain, or spinning electron; that in addition to breathing and fighting, he works, loves, and prays. We do not have to desert the empirical plane to discover this. Nor does one have to believe that there is a special dialectic method, distinct from scientific method, to describe and understand this. The investigation is difficult because of the complexity of the phenomena and because our emotional interests are so strongly engaged. But whatever difficulties there are must be resolved *not* by abandoning the rationale of scientific method as we know it in the field of our most reliable knowledge—the quest for verifiable hypotheses, the deduction of consequences, experiment under controlled conditions, or where this is not possible, careful use of the comparative method of agreement and difference—but by elaborating specific methods of inquiry within the basic unity of scientific method. True, the work will never be finished. True, there will always be some need for redefinition. And these are the only truths that can be distilled from the pretentious pronouncement of the dialectic method—truths that may be recommended more appropriately to absolutist metaphysicians than to scientists.

Looking back upon the long history of the use of the term "dialectic," it seems to me that a justified moral emerges from our discussion, viz., that the term "dialectic" is so infected with ambiguity, that it is not likely to function as a serviceable designation for any concept or intellectual procedure in any inquiry which aims at the achievement of reliable knowledge about ourselves and the world we live in.

CHAPTER TWELVE

THE MYTHOLOGY OF CLASS SCIENCE

1. *Science and Nationalism*

A RECENT DISPATCH from Germany reports that a group of *gleichgeschalted* mathematicians at the University of Berlin have laid down a program for the Aryanization of mathematics. Previously German philosophers had declared that the germs of National Socialist thought were already to be found in pre-Socratic Ionian philosophy. And since the time of the dispatch, some influential German physicists in solemn conclave have excoriated "Jewish physics" as incompatible with the spirit of "German science." The report went on to state that in mathematical research "German intuition, which was responsible for the concept of infinity, was superior to the logic associated with the French and Italians (*sic!*); that mathematics was an heroic science in that it had reduced chaos to order, which was precisely the mission of national socialism; that German mathematics would remain that of the 'Faustian man' and thus show 'its spiritual connection with the new Germany.' " [1]

It is well to recall, when these and similar episodes occur, that no nation has a monopoly of this kind of nonsense. During the first World War, Pierre Duhem, the great historian of science, published a book, entitled *La Science Allemande*, in which he stressed the great differences between French and German science. In contradistinction, however, to the current claims of German mathematicians, he claimed that the distinctive mark of German mathematics was not "spirit," "common sense" or "intuition" but ponderous deduction. "It is by its persistence in making deductions with the extremest rigor, in following out, without the slightest faltering, the longest and most com-

[1] *New York Times*, Jan. 28, 1934.

plicated chain of reasoning that German algebra distinguishes itself."

The intellectual habits of the scientific historian asserted themselves even in the patriotic broadside, and Pierre Duhem was honest enough to make two admissions—both fatal to his main thesis. The first was that judgments about the intellectual style of a people are not universally true. Depending upon whether one looked at the work of Gauss and Felix Klein, or Weierstrass and Cantor, different characterizations of German mathematics were possible. The second was that true science never bears the mark of a national character. "*It is by its deficiencies, and only by its deficiencies, that science . . . becomes the science of this nation or that.*"

Duhem's foray against German science remained an episode. The Nazi racial myth has spread and hardened into a way of belief. In their pronouncements, those German scientists who have embraced the official mythology, speak of science as if they wished to suspend the necessity of offering rational proof of propositions they call "scientific." Insofar as they succeed in solving problems, however, they must perforce ignore completely their ideological preambles.

The official Russian approach to science is quite scornful of nationalistic interpretations. It substitutes a class interpretation which, even if it be distinguished in intent from the Fascist argument, reproduces its "logic." This it does in the name of a "scientific" socialism, "orthodox" Marxism, and dialectical materialism which before the Russian Revolution were never invoked by authoritative Western socialists for such purposes. With official sanction, and sometimes by official order, those who lay down the party line for Russian culture maintain that it is legitimate—nay, even necessary for correct understanding —to speak of class science. They denounce "bourgeois physics, mathematics and cosmology." They assert that questions of the validity of propositions within any science cannot be dissociated from a class point of view. Since they hold that the class interests of the proletariat are expressed in the philosophy of dialectical materialism (as interpreted by themselves), they project in its name programs for the *reform* of biology, of physics, of mathematics.

What has the reform of society, the reader may wonderingly

inquire, got to do with the reform of biology, physics, or mathematics? The answer is that on the totalitarian view of culture, to which the dialectical materialists subscribe, every existing culture is so highly organic that a change at a certain point must of necessity produce, sooner or later, a change at every point. A profound economic crisis *must* have its effects and parallels on the farthest reaches of theoretical physics; a change in social and political power from one group to another *must* give rise to an advance all along the line of cultural and scientific thought. A typical illustration of this position is found in Professor Colman's article on "The Present Crisis in the Mathematical Sciences and General Outlines for their Reconstruction," in that curious book, *Science at the Crossroads.*

"The position of mathematics," he says, "as that of *any* science, is at bottom determined by the development and the position of the forces of production, of technology and economy. The latter affect mathematics both directly, by presenting it with new problems creating its material basis and supplying its man-power (!), and indirectly through the prevailing outlook upon the world, the philosophy of the ruling class.

"Thus if we wish to deal with the present crisis in the mathematical sciences, we must take into consideration the crisis in the *bourgeois natural sciences,* especially physics. The present paper, however, lays no claim to illumine fully this aspect of the problem presented, *the connection between the crisis in mathematics and the general crisis in bourgeois science as well as its connection with the entire crisis within capitalism as a whole."* (Italics mine.)

We pass over for a moment a whole cluster of errors in this over-simple account of what "at bottom" determines the history of mathematics as well as the quaint piece of, shall we say, proletarian biology, which makes the forces of production the literal father of all mathematicians. Let us first note the argument. The mode of economic production determines the development of science and mathematics; like all the problems of society, the great focal problems of theoretic science—for that is all that "the crisis" in science means—are expressions of fundamental problems of the class struggle; the general standpoint from which the problems of the class struggle are to be settled is dialectical materialism—the philosophy of the proletariat as a ruling class. Consequently, the problems of science and mathematics, too, must be solved from the standpoint of dialectical materialism. And, to be sure, Professor Colman does not disappoint us. He says expressly: "For mathematics there is only one way out; conscious, planned reconstruction on the basis of materialist dialectics."

Without difficulty I could quote similar sentiments from representative Marxists of the various orthodox persuasions about the relationship between theoretic science and politics. Bukharin, Deborin, Wittvogel, Thalheimer, Adoratski, Rudas, Mitin, and others—practically all say the same thing on this question with unimportant variations. They share the fascist assumption that theoretic science is not and cannot be neutral to politics; if and where they differ from the fascists it is over the brand of politics which is to supervise, integrate and reorient the sciences. The assumption they share with the fascists is much more important than their presumed differences. For that assumption is not merely false; it leads in practice to cultural vandalism and intellectual terror.

2. The Meanings of "Class" Science

The conception that a class bias enters constitutively into the natural and mathematical sciences is due to a failure to recognize some fundamental distinctions. These must be drawn if we are to have a clear idea of what we are talking about.

When the class nature of science is spoken of, sometimes all that is meant is the innocuous proposition that certain scientific truths or hypotheses are accepted by some classes and opposed, or not so easily accepted, by others. The Darwinian theory of the origin and evolution of species was strongly opposed in ecclesiastical and conservative quarters but was enthusiastically accepted by the workingclass movement throughout the world. Now the acceptance of the Darwinian theory is not a part of the scientific *structure* of that theory. The acceptance of any theory by a definite class is a sociological fact; so is the *social interpretation* which that class reads or misreads into the theory. Some of the very same social groups which originally opposed Darwinism in England were before long preaching it as part of their gospel of social Darwinism. This was a doctrine which tried to give social content to the biological conception of "variation," "adaptation," "struggle for existence," "survival of the fittest," in order to prove that those who possessed power or property were those who were most worthy of holding it. Of course, it was only by the crudest intellectual violence that they—as well as some present-day Nazis—could force a zoological interpretation of *human* society and history out of the fundamental principles of biology. The social use or abuse to which a scientific theory is put may be a class matter, but it is the veriest nonsense to impute a class character to the theory itself. The theory is either justified by the evidence or not.

Although the acceptance of a scientific theory is a sociological fact it would be a mistake to assume that such an acceptance is *necessarily* a matter of class interest. The dissemination of a scientific theory may be forbidden because it challenges a religious dogma; or because of the political views or racial origins of its creator; but, ultimately, it is the consensus of opinion among scientists themselves which determines the fate of the theory. There are many factors which conspire to prevent a scientific theory, even when the evidence seems to favor it, from becoming accepted intellectual currency in a given culture. When Einstein's theory was proclaimed it had to fight its way against the natural conservatism of habit which rebelled against the paradoxes that followed from the notion of the relativity of simultaneity. In Germany it was opposed by some who regarded it as part of a conspiracy of the Elders of Zion to destroy the Nordic mind. In France it was opposed by some *savants* as another piece of German Kultur. In Russia it was denounced by dialectical materialists as an expression of counter-revolutionary idealism. All this makes an interesting story but it is irrelevant to the question of the nature, structure, and truth of a scientific theory.

3. *Science and Motivations of Scientists*

A more important distinction than that between the structure of science and its acceptance is that between the structure of science and its *motivation*. The failure to observe this distinction is, I believe, the chief source of confusion among those who speak of "class truths" and "class science."

It is well known that many of the great pioneers of science were deeply religious men. This is true even of Galileo whom the Inquisition persecuted not for lack of religious piety but for failing to conform to its totalitarian conception of religious obedience. Newton and Boyle wrote books on miracles and other theological themes. In the *Principia* and in the *Optiks* Newton actually brings God into the cosmic economy. God not only created the world machine, wound it up, and sent it spinning through space, He steps in to prevent the fixed stars from falling into each other and to correct the irregularities in the orbits of planets and comets. Before Newton, Copernicus and Kepler had religious grounds for their belief in the uniformity of planetary motion; if planets did not describe equal paths in equal times they at least swept out equal areas in equal times. Pasteur believed that God would not create a poisonous body without creating a counteracting substance. The list can be continued indefinitely.

It is illustrations of this kind which provide a true premise for a fallacious conclusion. Because religious and philosophical assumptions have indisputably influenced the investigations of many scientists, and because class values are involved in some way in all systematic religions and philosophies, a class nature is fallaciously imputed to the knowledge which is discovered by those who have a class religion and philosophy. Yet it is clear that Newton's God had no more to do with Newton's *science* than Einstein's God with his. Newton's religious notions were *ad hoc* hypotheses which had no organic or *systematic* connection with the body of propositions his work contained. They had no experimental consequences. They pointed to no evidence which could possibly confirm or refute them. They were therefore scientifically fruitless. Nor in fact did any scientist attempt to develop these notions. Laplace was able, later on, to account for the "cosmic irregularities" of Newton's system in terms of Newton's own scientific principles. Laplace said that he had no need of the hypothesis of God. But neither had Newton, for in the nature of the case it cannot function as a scientific hypothesis. He introduced the references to God primarily out of piety but also to gain the right to use "the mathematical approach" to nature which the religious fundamentalists of that day were denouncing as atheism. Marx very aptly remarks in *Die Heilige Familie* that theism for materialists (i.e., scientists) was nothing more than an easy way of getting rid of religion.[2] Personally, in many cases, it was something much more but this was its effect in the history of science.

It may be argued in opposition to the view here defended that it is quite legitimate to regard Newton's religion and philosophy as parts of his science; that the mere fact that they are now regarded as false or antiquated, no more gainsays the right of Newton's total set of beliefs to be regarded as science, than the fact that the Ptolemaic system of astronomy or the phlogiston theory of chemistry are *now* rejected as false, justifies us in refusing to regard them as part of the history of science. The objection misses the essential point. Scientific theories and laws which have been discarded as false or inadequate have in the past helped to increase our store of knowledge in the course of the process of testing them. Or they helped bind together in a systematic way a series of beliefs and observations which otherwise had a miscellaneous character. Newton's religion and philosophy were neither part of the logical structure of his system nor did they entail any experimental consequences. They were scientifically meaningless but socially meaningful.

It may be true, although I have not seen convincing evidence of it, that Newton's *religion and philosophy* were abandoned in consequence of certain changes in the development of English economic class relations which required another type of philosophical justification of the cosmic and social order. Newton's *science*, however, was abandoned not because of the development of class relations but because the weight of scientific evidence turned against it. The distinction involved is quite elementary, but it is upon such elementary truths that the mythology of class science founders.

Pasteur believed that God in His infinite goodness could not have created a scourge for mankind without at the same time creating a remedy. He sought indefatigably for antitoxins and found them. Did that make Pasteur's belief a genuine heuristic principle, a guiding hypothesis, a part of the science of bacteriology? Can it be intelligently used, to paraphrase the dialectical materialists, as a basis for the conscious, planned

---

[2] *Gesamtausgabe*, Abt. 1, Bd. 3, p. 306.

reconstruction of the science of immunology? Certainly not. Only if Pasteur could have predicted in advance *when* and *where* and *to what measurable extent* God's goodness manifests itself, only if Pasteur could have added indices of determination to God's mercy, would his hypothesis be scientific. Religious believers, however, dare not pin their faith in a God whose existence, and therefore whose effects, are subject to scientific determination; if they did, they would not have any. It would not be difficult to show that the entelechies of modern vitalism enjoy the same "scientific" status as the God of Newton and Pasteur.

4. *Revolutionary Mythology and Genetics*

In the exact sciences talk about class truths can easily be exposed either as nonsense or as egregious error. Except when it becomes the faith of totalitarian states, it is a largely harmless intellectual confusion from which no one suffers save those who are the victims of it. In fields such as biology and allied sciences, this kind of nonsense is more widespread, more difficult to expose, and much more dangerous because of the use demagogues can make of it. The Nazi politicalization of the concept of race is the most conspicuous case in point. Although professing opposition to such use, the official spokesmen of dialectical materialism muddy scientific waters in the same way when they contrast a proletarian biology (or interpretation of biology) with a bourgeois biology. As evidence that these two conflicting points of view exist within biology, not merely in the social application of identical biological truths, but in the theoretic structure and development of biological research, writers of this school single out for special emphasis the problem of the inheritance of acquired characters. On the basis of the alleged social consequences of the doctrine, they assert that the view that acquired characters are *not* hereditary is bourgeois; the view that acquired characters *are* hereditary is proletarian. The stuff which has been written in this vein is nothing short of scandalous. It is not new in the literature of this school; nor, unfortunately, is it restricted to writers of one country.

A typical statement may be found in a book by Wittvogel, published during the early years of the German Republic, when the left-wing socialist movement was echoing the slogans of the Russian Proletcult, entitled *Die Wissenschaft der bürgerlichen Gesellschaft*. After describing the two conflicting theories concerning the inheritance of acquired characters, it asks:

"Which tendency is supported by public opinion, i.e., by the capitalistic press, by bourgeois philosophy and the existing private property set-up?

"Naturally, the Constant-theory [*Konstanztheorie*, the view that acquired traits are not hereditary], for from it there follows the senselessness of a general change in the environment, which therewith logically develops into a central argument against the proletarian revolution.

"And in fact: neo-Mendelianism—the most recent form of the Constant-theory—characteristically enough develops most luxuriantly in the United States. Kammerer, on the other hand, 'with his salamanders,' was punished because of the damaging implications of his theory for existing property relations. He was ridiculed and sneered at in a most insidious fashion, and his academic career was blocked."

First as to the facts. Kammerer was not laughed down by his colleagues. He received a respectful hearing in many countries, including the United States, where his book was subsequently published. The trouble was, however, that when his experiments were repeated by others, results quite different from those which Kammerer reported were obtained. And finally when Bateson, the great English authority on variation, took his trip to Vienna to examine Kammerer's latest experiments and discovered that the results had been "framed," Kammerer's work was regarded with great suspicion. This happened, to be sure, after Wittvogel wrote but it is an eloquent object lesson of the dangers run by dialectical materialists, who, because they imagine they are on the "right" side in the class struggle, therefore believe they can tell what theories are "right" or "wrong" in biology or any other science.

The truth of the matter is that there is no *logical* connection at all between the question of the inheritance of acquired traits and the social question. The case for democracy or socialism or Stalinism or Hitlerism no more depends upon biology than it does upon physics.

Suppose, as scientific evidence seems to indicate, that acquired characters are not hereditary. Why does it follow that it is senseless to change the environment so that new and socially desirable characters may be acquired by every fresh generation? Granted that some individuals are naturally better endowed in certain respects than others and that they transmit these traits to their offspring. In what way is this incompatible with a democratic society which seeks to provide an equal opportunity for all to develop their specific talents, with the sole proviso that no one possessing a monopoly of any special talent be permitted to exploit it for his own interest at the expense of the community? And conversely, how does the belief that acquired characters are not hereditary, aid the bourgeoisie? All the intelligent Marxist need do is show that the specific virtues which enabled the bourgeoisie to come to power—the historical combination of thrift, rapacity, secularism, technical rationalism (and, in individual cases, accident)—were precisely the qualities which made for the most rapid accumulation of capital; that latter-day changes in capitalist economy have brought other "virtues" to the fore, such as conspicuous spending instead of saving; and that the needs of our own time and the goals of democratic socialism require the development of new ideals of conduct and character. The *social content* of all values, the specific social expression of all so-called "intuitive or instinctive" tendencies, is acquired. The evidence that it is not passed on in the blood stream is derived in the course of historical and sociological inquiry rather than from biology.

It would be no exaggeration to say that many sociologists as well as almost all dialectical materialists have never grasped the precise point at issue in the biological controversy over acquired characters. They have assumed that if the inheritance of acquired traits were denied, no new biological traits of an hereditary character could be developed in man. But this is a *non sequitur*. The real question in dispute between the neo-Lamarckians and the neo-Mendelians is whether changes in the somaplasm affect the germplasm. No one denies that changes in the germplasm are hereditary or that these changes can be directly induced (for example, among plants and animals by X-rays and chemical injections). Biological science may some day show how the germplasm in man may be directly affected, as distinct from the natural process of mutation, and new traits of a non-lethal kind acquired. Today it simply denies that any somatic traits acquired by the organism set up changes in the germplasm.

The fact that the motivations of scientists, insofar as they are not moved by curiosity and professional interests, are today primarily social and political rather than religious, and that today, as always in the past, their dependence upon those who subsidize their work, may color their philosophical and social interpretations of their findings, does not invalidate any of the distinctions made above. Philosophical interpretations of physics which enstate God, freedom and immortality, or which conclude that love is all, or that only a return to free economic enterprise can save democracy, are part of philosophy not of physics. They constitute a different story altogether. Where philosophical interpretations of physics have *scientific* bearings, as for example, different theories of space and time, no intelligible correlations can be drawn between different philosophical interpretations of a given body of scientific data, and conflicting class interests. In accounting for the evolution of species, Darwin may have emphasized "competition" and "struggle for existence," and Kropotkin "mutual aid." Their social milieu and political sympathies may or may not have been responsible for their stress on one hypothesis rather than another. That is a question for the psychologist or sociologist. If he discovers the answers, they will not be class truths. But insofar as the hypotheses of Darwin or Kropotkin are incorporated into the science of biology, their psychological or social derivation is irrelevant. The entire discussion of the theme of class science by dialectical materialists is vitiated by the failure to realize that without some verifiable concept of *relevance*, one cannot get within hailing distance of scientific method.

5. *Science—Responsible and Free*

There is only one possible approach that an intelligent socialist can take if he is to avoid nonsense or grave error in speaking of the class character of science. He may try to show that present-day class society makes it difficult for scientists to pursue in every respect objective, international and classless truths. He may address his argument to the scientist to establish the ways in which a class society distorts his scientific activity and the ways in which a classless society would liberate it. He may with warrant assert that the liberation of that activity would be accomplished by eliminating the closed doors, the duplications, the economic ambitions, and the artificial restraints which hamper free research today. More than that, he could promise that science and scientists would play a leading, but not a commanding, role in the organization and planning of a socialist society. The direction of much scientific research and many of the types of problems considered would necessarily reflect, as in lesser measure they do even now, human needs.

But—and this is crucial if the scientist, like every other worker, is not to find himself merely a productive arm of a totalitarian state—his scientific theories must not be subject to the dictates of a party, race, or state philosophy. Further, and this is just as important, no matter how intimately science is tied up with the technical needs of a planned society, scientists must be permitted and encouraged, to freely choose their own fields and their own problems. Their association with state planning boards must be *voluntary*. Provision must be made, not grudgingly but gladly, for what may be called socially aimless inquiry into the ways of things and man. That is to say, the same freedom granted to artists to follow their own creative and individual bent must be extended to the scientist, subject, of course, to the severe but essentially non-authoritarian discipline of scientific method. For the experience of discovering things, of finding reasons, of grasping connections and implications, is just as exciting, just as intrinsically desirable as any other aesthetic experience. It cannot be completely hitched to the necessities of what is immediately practical without having an adverse effect, in time, upon these very necessities. Many human blessings have resulted from the play of free intelligence and wayward experiment. But the activity itself is a human blessing even if it is barren of material blessings.

Although the scientific pursuit has its aesthetic aspect, the results of science will always differ from those of art not only in that its statements will be invariant and valid for all classes and all nations but that, if true, they will be true in respect to all individuals.

The origin and results of science, its continued existence, its technical applications are not dependent upon any particular form of society. Nonetheless, it is only in a democratic society that the scientific temper can be brought to bear upon questions of social policy and social values. Why this is so will be apparent when we consider the ideals of the democratic way of life.

CREDO

CHAPTER THIRTEEN

THE DEMOCRATIC WAY OF LIFE

THE GREATEST tribute to democracy as an ideal of social life is unwittingly paid to it in the *apologias* of the dictators of the modern world—Hitler, Stalin and Mussolini. For all of them insist in the shrillest tones that the regimes they control are actually, despite appearances, democracies "in a higher sense." For example, Mussolini in a public address delivered at Berlin in September, 1937, proclaimed that "the greatest and soundest democracies which exist in the world today are Italy and Germany"; while Stalin, after the worst blood purge in history, praises the constitution that bears his name—a constitution that openly provides (in Section 126) for the control of all socio-political institutions by the minority Communist Party—as the most democratic in all history. And here in America, due to the needs of the foreign policy of the various dictatorships, their partisans now wrap up their program of blood and steel in the American flag and make a great verbal play about being defenders of American democracy. Thus, in a letter to the *New York Times* (July 20, 1938) Mr. Fritz Kuhn speaks of Americans who have become members of his German *Bund* (Nazis) "because of their faith in its devotion to the institutions of the United States." With even greater fanfare the American Communist Party has proclaimed its love of democracy to the death on the assumption that Americans neither read nor have memories. Both pronouncements merely reflect the necessities of foreign policy of Germany and Russia respectively.

That the greatest enemies of democracy should feel compelled to render demagogic lip-allegiance to it is an eloquent sign of the inherent plausibility of democratic ideals to the modern mind, and of their universal appeal. But that its enemies, apparently with some success, should have the audacity to flaunt the principles they have so outrageously betrayed in practice, is just as eloquent a sign that these principles are ambiguous. Agreement where there is no clarity merely cloaks differences; it does not settle them. Sooner or later it breeds confusion and confusion breeds distrust. In the end there grows up a venemous rancor which is so intent upon destroying the enemy that it is blind to what the real differences are.

The analysis of the concept of democracy is not merely, then, a theoretical problem for the academician. The ordinary man who says he believes in democracy must clearly understand what he means by it. Otherwise the genuine issues that divide men will be lost in the welter of emotive words which demagogues skillfully evoke to conceal their true intentions. There is such a thing as the ethics of words. And of all the words in our political vocabulary none is in greater need of precise analysis and scrupulous use than "democracy."

Anyone can use a word as a sign for any idea provided he makes adequately clear what he means by it. For example, if a man says, "By democracy I mean a government in which the name of the ruler begins with a D," we can smile at his peculiar definition and pass on. We need not dispute his usage if he always accompanies it with a parenthetical explanation of what he understands by the term. However, if he introduces the term into a political discussion without stating explicitly the special meaning it has for him, we have every scientific and moral right to object. For where words of a certain kind are already in use, to employ them as signs of new meanings without posting, so to speak, a clear public notice, is to be guilty of a form of counterfeit. New verbal signs can always be found for new meanings.

Democracy is a term which has customarily been associated with certain *historical* practices and with certain writings in the history of culture. Instead of beginning with arbitrary nominal definitions, it would be preferable to describe and critically evaluate the growth of democracy in Western Europe from its origins in the Greek city (slave) states to the present. But this could only be essayed in a systematic treatise.

The third alternative—one which we shall here follow—is to begin with a definition which formally is acceptable to most people who distinguish democracy from other forms of political organization, and which is in consonance with at least traditional American usage. We shall then indicate what it implies as far as the structure of other present-day social institutions is concerned, what techniques of settling differences it commits us to, and what fundamental ethical values are presupposed. In this way we shall combine the advantages of `an analytical and "contemporary-historical" treatment.

1. *The Definition Explored*

A democratic society is one where the government rests upon the freely given consent of the governed. Some ambiguity attaches to every term in this preliminary definition. The least ambiguous is the term "governed." By "the governed" is meant those adult participating members of the community, with their dependents, whose way of life is affected by what the government does or leaves undone. By "the government" is primarily intended the law-and-policy-making agencies, legislative, executive, and judicial, whose activities control the life of the community. In the first instance, then, government is a political concept; but in certain circumstances it may refer to social and economic organizations whose policies affect the lives of a large number of individuals. In saying that the government rests upon the "consent" of the governed, it is meant that at certain fixed periods its policies are submitted to the governed for approval or disapproval. By "freely given" consent of the governed is meant that no coercion, direct or indirect, is brought to bear upon the governed to elicit their approval or disapproval. A government that "rests upon" the freely given consent of the governed is one which *in fact* abides by the expression of this approval or disapproval.

A direct consequence of this definition may be that there is no complete democracy anywhere in the world. This no more prevents our employing the term intelligently and making comparative evaluation than the fact that no one is "perfectly healthy" prevents us from making the concept "health" basic to medical theory and practice. There is no absolutely fat man, but we can easily tell whether one man is fatter than another. So long as our definition enables us to order existing communities in a series of greater or less democracy, our definition is adequate.

If a democratic government rests upon the freely given consent of the governed, then it cannot be present where institutional arrangements—whether political or non-political—obviously obstruct the registering or the implementing of the common consent. We do not have to settle any metaphysical questions about the nature of freedom in order to be able to tell when consent is not free. A plebiscite or election which is held at the point of a bayonet, or in which one can only vote "Yes," or in which no opposition candidates are permitted, obviously does not express freely given consent. These are only the crudest violations of the democratic ideal but they are sufficient to make the pretense that the present-day regimes in Italy, Russia and Germany are democratic sound almost obscene.

There are less obvious but no less effective ways of coercively influencing the expression of consent. A threat, for example, to deprive the governed of their jobs or means of livelihood, by a group which has the power to do so, would undermine a democracy even if its name were retained. In fact, every overt form of economic pressure, since it is experienced directly by the individual and since so many other phases of his life are dependent upon economic security, is an overt challenge to democracy. Where the political forms of democracy function within a society in which economic controls are not subject to political control, there is always a standing threat to democracy. For in such a society the possibility exists that economic pressure may strongly influence the expression of consent. Where it cannot influence the expression of consent, it may subvert or prevent its execution. This is particularly true in modern societies in which social instruments of production, necessary for the livelihood of many, are privately owned by the few. A political democracy cannot function properly where differences in economic power are so great that one group can determine the weal or woe of another by non-political means. Genuine political democracy, therefore, entails the right of the governed, through their representatives, to control economic policy. In this sense, it might be said that where there is no

economic democracy—a phrase which will be explained later—
there can be no genuine and widespread political democracy.
The exact degree of economic control necessary to political
democracy will vary with changing conditions. It is clear that
today modern economic organization plays such a dominant
role in social life that political democracy cannot be imple-
mented if it is unable to control economic policy.

A further consequence of "freely given consent" is the absence of a monopoly of education where education includes all
agencies of cultural transmission, especially the press. Important as is the majority principle for a democracy, the
expression of consent by the majority is not free if it is deprived of access to sources of information, if it can read *only*
the official interpretation, if it can hear *only* one voice in class-
room, pulpit and radio—if, in short, all critical opposition is
branded as treason to be extirpated by heresy trials, by re-
education in concentration camps, and by execution squads.
The individual has no more freedom of action when his mind
is deliberately tied by ignorance than when his hands are tied
with rope. The very dependence of modern man upon the
printed word, greater than ever before in history, makes the
public right to critical dissent all the more necessary if common consent is to be free. Not many years ago this would have
been a commonplace. Today apologists have so muddied the
waters of truth that its reaffirmation must be stressed.

2. *Positive Conditions for Democracy*

So far we have been considering conditions in the absence of
which democracy cannot exist. But the effective working of a
democracy demands the presence of a number of other conditions. Among these, the active participation of the governed
in the processes of government is primary.

By active participation is meant not the attempt to do the
specific work of officials but free discussion and consultation on
public policies, and voluntary co-operation in the execution of
mandates reached through the democratic process. Where the
governed feel that they have no stake in the government, indifference results. And political indifference may be called the
dry-rot of democracy. "The food of feeling," as Mill well says,

"is action. . . . Let a person have nothing to do for his country, and he will not care for it."

The country or community, however, is never a homogeneous whole. There may be common interests, but the conceptions of the common interest are never common. Nor in this world can all interests ever in fact be common. If they were, government would be a mere administrative detail. The variety of interests that is always to be found makes necessary that no interest be excluded from voicing its demands, even though these demands may, in the process of democratic deliberation, be compromised or rejected. The only historical alternative to the participation of the masses in the processes of government is the ancient, artful and uncertain technique of "bread and circuses." That the modern bread is smeared with oleomargarine and the modern circuses are cinematic makes no essential difference. Such a technique conceals differences and trouble centers; whereas the methods of participation and consultation uncover them, articulate new social needs, and suggest instrumentalities for handling them. The wisest policy cannot succeed in face of popular indifference or hostility. Even those who believe that the professionally wise men or experts must do the governing exclude at their own peril those whom they would govern from their counsels.

Another requirement for the effective working of democracy is the presence of mechanisms which permit prompt action, through delegated authority, in crucial situations. What constitutes a crucial situation and what specific administrative mechanisms are best adapted to meet it cannot be settled in advance. But it is clear that there is nothing incompatible with democracy in freely delegating specific functions to authority provided that at a certain fixed time an accounting is made to the governed who alone have the prerogative of renewing or abrogating the grant of authority.

Today the very existence of democracy depends upon its ability to act decisively in its own defense. Effective defense against a foreign totalitarian enemy may require extraordinary and exceptional measures of co-ordination and control. Some fear that this is the road to totalitarianism. It *may* be. But the alternative is *certain* totalitarianism. So long as democratic communities are threatened by totalitarian states, they must make provision, openly and after discussion, for delegation of authority to responsible individuals to undertake technical defense in a crisis.

That such grants of authority may be abused goes without saying. It may even be acknowledged that there is no absolute guarantee against the risks of usurpation. But unless these risks are sometimes taken, democratic government may be destroyed by evils whose urgency will not wait until the close of prolonged debate. Common sense recognizes this in case of flood and plague. Flood and plague have their social analogues. *But whatever the crisis may be, the recognition that it is a crisis must come from the governed or their delegated representatives; grants of power must be renewed democratically; and the governed cannot, without destroying their democracy, proclaim that the crisis is permanent.*

The fact that the presevation of democracy sometimes demands the delegation of far-reaching authority, and the fact that the possession of such authority may corrupt those who wield it, reinforces another positive requirement of democracy. To understand this requirement we must take note of the psychological effects of holding power, and the historical evidence which indicates that many democratic organizations, sooner or later, become instruments of a minority group which, identifying its own special interests with the interests of the organization as a whole, keeps power by fraud, myth and force. Taken literally, Lord Acton's maxim, "Power always corrupts and absolute power corrupts absolutely," is an exaggeration. But there is sufficient truth in it to give us pause when we are about to invest individuals or groups with great power, even temporarily. Similarly, Robert Michels's "iron law of oligarchy," according to which democrats may be victorious but democracy never, goes beyond the data he has assembled. But no one can read his powerful case studies and the data presented by other writers like Pareto, Machajaski and Nomad without realizing how plausible Michels's induction is. And when we add to this the degeneration, under our very eyes, of the Russian Revolution—a revolution which began avowedly as a workers' democracy, developed into the dictatorship of the Communist Party *over* the proletariat, and finally took form as the bloody rule of a camarilla that has piled up more corpses in a few years than did the Roman emperors in as many centuries of Christian persecution—the lesson is driven home with sickening force.

This lesson is that a positive requirement of a working democracy is an intelligent distrust of its leadership, a skepticism, stubborn but not blind, of all demands for the enlargement of power, and an emphasis upon critical method in every phase of education and social life. This skepticism, like other forms of vigilance, may often seem irritating to leaders who are convinced of their good intentions. The skepticism, however, is not of their intentions but of the objective consequences of their power. Where skepticism is replaced by uncritical enthusiasm and the many-faceted deifications which our complex society makes possible, a fertile emotional soil for dictatorship has been prepared. The most convincing aspect of Plato's analysis of the cycle of political decay in the eighth Book of his *Republic* is the transition from a hero-worshiping democracy to an absolute tyranny.

Another positive requirement of democracy we have already referred to as economic democracy. By economic democracy is meant the power of the community, organized as producers and consumers, to determine the basic question of the objectives of economic development. Such economic democracy presupposes some form of social ownership and planning; but whether the economy is to be organized in a single unit or several, whether it is to be highly centralized or not, are experimental questions. There are two criteria to decide such questions. One is the extent to which a specific form of economic organization or ownership makes possible an abundance of goods and services for the greatest number, without which formal political democracy is necessarily limited in its functions, if not actually endangered. The other is the extent to which a specific form of economic organization preserves and strengthens the conditions of the democratic process already described.

Certain kinds of economic planning may give the security of a jail—in which, in exchange for freedom, the inmates are given food, clothing and shelter of sorts. But any type of planned society which does not provide for the freest criticism, for diversity, for creative individuality, for catholicity of taste, cannot ever guarantee real security. In such a society the "security" is conditional upon accepting arbitrary bureaucratic decree as the law of life. This is conspicuously true wherever the instruments of promotion are socialized by a non-democratic state. When Stalin tells us that "the dictatorship of the proletariat is *substantially* the dictatorship of the [Communist] Party," he is telling us that the Russian worker can purchase a problematic security only insofar as he accepts this Party dictatorship.[1]

The upshot, then, of our analysis is that just as political democracy is incomplete without some form of economic democracy, so there can be no genuine economic democracy without political democracy. Some may call this socialism. But it is certainly not the "socialism" of either Hitler or Stalin. Nor, despite the fears of frightened tories, of Roosevelt.

3. The Argument against Democracy

Our discussion would be incomplete if we did not consider the chief objections which have been urged against democracy by some of the outstanding thinkers of the past and present. Most of these objections are variants of two fundamental arguments—practical and theoretical.

The practical argument, from the time of Plato down, stresses the imperfections in the actual working of democracy. It draws up a detailed indictment of the blundering inefficiencies of democracies, the influence of demagogy and prejudice in the formulation of their policies, and the operation of certain political mechanisms which place the power of selection of the rulers of the community, actually, in the hands of a minority. And from this largely accurate description of the way in which democracies do in fact work, it is concluded that democracy must be scrapped for another alternative.

---

[1] The quotation is from a speech of Stalin. Compare his *Leninism*, New York, 1928, page 33. That the dictatorship of the Party is *not* a specifically Russian doctrine but an integral part of the Leninist (not Marxist) theory is clear from the "Theses and Resolutions" of the Communist International. Compare also, for the American variant, the following passage from William Z. Foster's *Towards Soviet America:* "Under the [proletarian] dictatorship, all the capitalistic parties—Republican, Democratic, Progressive, Socialist [*sic!*]—will be liquidated, the Communist Party functioning alone as the Party of the toiling masses" (page 275). And yet the Communist Party has such a profound contempt for the intelligence of the American public, and of its own members, that it publicly proclaims itself as the heir of the traditions of Jefferson!

The description may be granted without justifying the conclusion. For unless we know the precise nature of the alternative and how *it* works out in practice, we may legitimately reply that the cure for the evils of democracy is better democracy. This is not a catch phrase. For by better democracy is meant the realization of the conditions and requirements already outlined—or, at the very least, the struggle for them.

And what are the alternatives to democracy with all its imperfections? All alternatives turn out upon analysis to involve some form of benevolent despotism—whether a personal or a class or a party despotism. Now the fatal objection to a benevolent despotism of any sort—aside from the fact that people with different interests have different ideas of what constitutes benevolence—is that no one knows how long the despotism will remain benevolent, not even the despot himself. We may appeal from Philip drunk to Philip sober, but who is to keep Philip sober?

Not a single benevolent act of a despot recorded in history but can be matched with scores of malevolent acts. For every guilty man a dictator spares there are thousands of innocent men he dooms. The *ideal* benevolent despotism is a mere figment of the imagination; and even as an ideal, it is no more promising than *ideal* democracy. Moreover, it is wrong to compare the ideal form of benevolent despotism with the actual practice of democracy. If we intelligently compare the practices of both, whether in antiquity or in the modern world, the lovers of democracy need not fear the outcome.

The second type of argument against democracy, the theoretical, is really presupposed by the first. It holds that, the ultimate end of government being human welfare, only those having the best knowledge and highest intelligence are qualified for the difficult pursuit of discovering the nature of human welfare. Since the problems of government are largely administrative, demanding knowledge and intelligence, and since an effective democracy presupposes the possession of both knowledge and intelligence by the majority of the population, which even the lover of democracy must admit is rarely the case, democracy must be rejected. Plato put the nub of the argument in a metaphor: Who would propose that, setting out on a perilous journey, we should *elect* the pilot of the ship? And yet the pilot of the ship of state has a task infinitely more difficult, and the course of the vessel is beset by many more perils. What rhyme or reason exists, therefore, for electing him? Or as Santayana, a direct lineal descendant of Plato in political philosophy, put it: "It is knowledge and knowledge only that may rule by divine right."

Space permits only a brief indication of the Achilles-heel of this argument. While there may be experts in knowledge of fact, there are no experts in wisdom of policy. Ultimate welfare presupposes that there is an "ultimate good." But a conclave of philosophers gathered together to determine the nature of the ultimate good would resemble nothing so much as the Tower of Babel. Wisdom of policy depends upon knowledge of one's interests. It is true that some men are not clear as to what their own interests are. But it is arrant presumption for other men to pretend to them that they know what their interests "really" are, or what they should be. A parent dealing with children may sometimes be justified in asserting that he knows better than they what their real interests are; but any ruler who justifies his abrogation of democratic control by proclaiming that he knows what the real interests of the governed are better than they do themselves is therewith telling them that they are no more responsible than children. Besides oppressing them, he is insulting them, for he envisages their childhood as perpetual. It is not accidental that we call dictatorial government paternal. In paternal government, however, there is more authority than affection. The paternal ruler often takes his political children for guinea pigs upon whom he can try peculiar experiments. Their peculiarity lies in the fact that, whatever their outcome, the present generation of guinea pigs never recovers.

True, there may be no wisdom in electing a pilot or a cobbler. But in the last analysis, as even Plato was compelled to recognize, it is the user and not the maker who is the best judge of work done. Who wears the shoe knows best where it pinches. On this homely truth every theoretical attack on democracy founders.

4. *The Values and Method of Democracy*

And democracy is more than a pattern of institutional behavior. Democracy is an affirmation of certain attitudes and values which are more important than any particular set of institutions, because those attitudes and values must serve as the sensitive directing controls of institutional change.

Every mechanism of democratic government has a critical point at which it may run wild. It may be formally perfect but actually murderous. For example, the principle of majority rule is a necessary condition of a working democracy. But a majority can oppress a minority. Numbers, even less than knowledge, give divine right, or immunity from folly. A government resting upon the consent of the majority may not therewith be good government—as the tragic history of the oppression of minorities testifies. To the lessons of that history no one can be indifferent; for every member of the community is part of a minority at some point or on some issue. The persecution of the Jews during the last two thousand years is sufficient evidence that political forms by themselves are no safeguards for a minority—even when it is innocent, unarmed and culturally creative.

It is helpful but hardly sufficient to insist that democratic communities must provide for self-government by voluntary organized minorities on all questions which concern the minority rather than the community at large. It is not sufficient because minorities are often in opposition on communal issues, and the very willingness to extend autonomy on "local" issues is contingent upon acceptance of the values of democracy as a way of life.

Now there are three related values which are central to democracy as a way of life.

The first is found in many variant formulations, but common to them all is the belief that every individual should be regarded as possessing intrinsic worth or dignity. The social corollary of this recognition is that equal opportunities of development should be provided for the realization of individual talents and capacities. To believe in the equality of opportunities does not mean to believe in the equality of talents. But it does carry with it a recognition that, under conditions of modern technology, marked inequalities in the distribution of wealth or in standards of living are prejudicial to equal opportunities of development. If it is absurd to ask that identical technical opportunities be accorded the artist and the engineer, the machinist and the administrator, it is not absurd to expect that their living conditions be approximately the same. The ideal of equality is not something to be mechanically applied. But it must function as a regulative principle of distibution. Otherwise endemic conflicts, latent in all human associations, take such acute forms that they imperil the very existence of democracy.

The belief in the equal right of all members of the community to develop their personalities must be complemented by a belief in the value of difference, variety, uniqueness. In a democracy differences of interest and achievements must not be merely suffered, they must be encouraged. The healthy zest arising from the conflict and interchange of ideas and personal tastes in a free society is a much more fruitful source of new and significant experiences than the peace of dull, dead uniformity. Of course there are limits to difference as there are to specialization. For however different people are, they live in a common world, they must communicate in a common language, and accept the common constraints which safeguard the species from extinction. In non-democratic societies this fact that men are always bound in some way by the necessities of living together is used as a premise for constructing vast techniques of repression to choke off differences in almost every way. In democratic societies, however, the same prime fact must serve rather as a condition for enlarging the scope of variation, free play, growth and experiment.

No matter what the values are to which a democracy is committed, situations will arise in which these values conflict or are challenged by still other values. A decision made in one situation does not necessarily stand for all other situations. The ultimate commitment of a democracy, then, must be a faith in some method by which these conflicts are resolved. Since the method must be the test of all values, it would not be inaccurate to call it the basic value in the democratic way of life. This method is the method of intelligence, of critical scientific inquiry. In a democracy it must be directed to all issues, to all conflicts, if democracy is not to succumb to the dangers which threaten it from both within and without. It is not mere chance that the greatest philosopher of experimental empiricism—John Dewey—is also the greatest philosopher of democracy.

To say that the method of intelligence is essential to the democratic process seems like worrying a commonplace. But not when it is realized how revolutionary the impact would be of giving the method of intelligence institutional force in education, economics, law and politics. Policies would be treated as hypotheses, not as dogmas; customary practices as generalizations, not as God-given truths. A generation trained in schools where emphasis was placed upon method, method, and still more method, could hardly be swayed by current high-pressured propaganda. The very liberties granted by free institutions in a democracy provide opportunities for special interests to forge powerful instruments to undermine it. The most insidious of all devices for overthrowing democratic institutions is to acquire protective coloration by hypocritical espousal of democracy, to occupy strategic posts, and to open the gates after the Trojan horse is safely within the city. There is no protection against this save the critically armed mind which is immune to rhetoric and parades, and which does *not* give the fanatic a tolerant kind of credit for being sincere in his belief that the end justifies any means.

Those who believe in democracy must distinguish intelligently and act resolutely. First of all, they must distinguish between honest opposition *within* the framework of the democratic process and the opposition, subsidized and controlled by the totalitarian enemies of democracy, which is a form of treason to everything democrats hold dear. Opposition of the first kind, no matter how mistaken, must be tolerated, if for no other reason than that we cannot be sure that it is not we who are mistaken. Opposition of the second kind, no matter what protective coloration it wears—and it will usually be found wrapped up in counterfeit symbols of patriotism or in recently acquired vestments of the Bill of Rights—must be swiftly dealt with if democracy is to survive.

Minorities know that the majority may be tyrannical. The

tyranny of the mass flows from its insensitiveness to the consequences of means and methods, not only for the minority but for itself. An insistence upon evidence, relevance and deliberation is not incompatible with action; it is incompatible only with blind action. The method of intelligence cuts under the fanaticisms which make a fetish of ends, by stressing the conditions and consequences of their use. It both uncovers and enforces responsibilities in social life. It, and it alone, can distinguish between social conflicts which are negotiable and those which are irreconcilable, and the degree of each. Where conflicts are negotiable, it approaches social problems as difficulties to be solved by experiment and analysis, not as battles to be fought out in the heat of blood lust.

What alternative method can be embraced by a society which permits and encourages plural values and plural associations? The more intelligence is liberated in a democratic community, the greater its control of nature and the sources of wealth; the greater its control of nature, the greater possibility of diversifying interests, values and associations; the greater diversification, the more necessary the function of intelligence to mediate, integrate and harmonize.

ACKNOWLEDGMENTS

It gives me great pleasure to make the following acknowledgments to the periodicals in whose pages the bulk of the foregoing material has appeared.

Chapter II, *The Illinois Law Review*

Chapter III, *The Marxist Quarterly*

Chapter IV, *The University of Chicago Law Review*

Chapters V and VI, *The Partisan Review*

Chapters VII and VIII, *The Southern Review*

Chapter IX, *The Marxist Quarterly*

Chapter X, *The Modern Quarterly*

Chapter XI, *The Journal of Philosophy*

Chapter XII, *The Modern Monthly*

Chapter XIII, *The Southern Review*

Thanks are due to Charles Scribner's Sons and Doubleday, Doran & Co. for permission to quote from Jacques Maritain's *True Humanism* and Leon Trotsky's *The Revolution Betrayed*.

INDEX

ORDER FORM

GREAT BOOKS IN PHILOSOPHY PAPERBACK SERIES

ETHICS

Aristotle—*The Nicomachean Ethics*	$7.95
Jeremy Bentham—*The Principles of Morals and Legislation*	7.95
Immanuel Kant—*The Fundamental Principles of the Metaphysic of Morals*	4.95
John Stuart Mill—*Utilitarianism*	4.95
George Edward Moore—*Principia Ethica*	7.95
Friedrich Nietzsche—*Beyond Good and Evil*	6.95
Bertrand Russell—*On Ethics, Sex, and Marriage* (edited by Al Seckel)	16.95
Benedict de Spinoza—*Ethics* and *The Improvement of the Understanding*	8.95

SOCIAL AND POLITICAL PHILOSOPHY

Aristotle—*The Politics*	6.95
Edmund Burke—*Reflections on the Revolution in France*	6.95
John Dewey—*Freedom and Culture*	9.95
G.W.F. Hegel—*The Philosophy of History*	8.95
Thomas Hobbes—*The Leviathan*	6.95
Sidney Hook—*Paradoxes of Freedom*	8.95
Sidney Hook—*Reason, Social Myths, and Democracy*	10.95
John Locke—*Second Treatise on Civil Government*	4.95
Niccolo Machiavelli—*The Prince*	4.95
Karl Marx/Frederick Engels—*The Economic and Philosophic Manuscripts of 1844* and *The Communist Manifesto*	5.95
John Stuart Mill—*Considerations on Representative Government*	6.95
John Stuart Mill—*On Liberty*	4.95
John Stuart Mill—*On Socialism*	6.95
John Stuart Mill—*The Subjection of Women*	4.95
Thomas Paine—*Rights of Man*	6.95
Plato—*The Republic*	7.95
Plato on Homosexuality: Lysis, Phaedrus, and *Symposium*	5.95
Jean-Jacques Rousseau—*The Social Contract*	5.95
Mary Wollstonecraft—*A Vindication of the Rights of Women*	5.95

METAPHYSICS/EPISTEMOLOGY

Aristotle—*De Anima*	5.95
Aristotle—*The Metaphysics*	8.95
George Berkeley—*Three Dialogues Between Hylas and Philonous*	4.95
René Descartes—*Discourse on Method* and *The Meditations*	5.95
David Hume—*An Enquiry Concerning Human Understanding*	4.95
William James—*Pragmatism*	6.95
Immanuel Kant—*Critique of Pure Reason*	7.95
Plato—*The Euthyphro, Apology, Crito,* and *Phaedo*	4.95
Bertrand Russell—*The Problems of Philosophy*	7.95
Sextus Empiricus—*Outlines of Pyrrhonism*	7.95

PHILOSOPHY OF RELIGION

Ludwig Feuerbach—*The Essence of Christianity*	7.95
David Hume—*Dialogues Concerning Natural Religion*	4.95
John Locke—*A Letter Concerning Toleration*	3.95
Thomas Paine—*The Age of Reason*	12.95
Bertrand Russell—*On God and Religion* (edited by Al Seckel)	16.95

GREAT MINDS PAPERBACK SERIES

Charles Darwin—*The Origin of Species*	9.95
Edward Gibbon—*On Christianity*	8.95

SPECIAL—For your library . . . the entire collection of 42 "Great Books in Philosophy" available at a savings of more than 15%. Only $250.00 (plus $9.00 postage and handling). Please indicate "Great Books—Complete Set" on your order form.

The books listed can be obtained from your book dealer or directly from Prometheus Books. Please indicate the appropriate books. Remittance must accompany all orders from individuals. Please include $3.00 postage and handling for the first book and $1.50 for each additional title (maximum $9.00. NYS residents please add applicable sales tax.) **Prices subject to change without notice.**

Send to _____
Please type or print clearly)

Address _____

City _____ State _____ Zip _____

Amount enclosed _____

Charge my ☐ **VISA** ☐ **MasterCard**

Account # [ ][ ][ ][ ][ ][ ][ ][ ][ ][ ][ ][ ][ ][ ][ ][ ]

Exp. Date _____ / _____ Tel.# _____

Signature _____

Prometheus Books Editorial Offices
700 E. Amherst St., Buffalo, New York 14215

Distribution Facilities
59 John Glenn Drive, Amherst, New York 14228

Phone Orders call toll free: (800) 421-0351
FAX: (716) 691-0137
Please allow 3-6 weeks for delivery